CRITICAL INSIGHTS

Contemporary Canadian Fiction

CRITICAL INSIGHTS

Contemporary Canadian Fiction

Editor
Carol L. Beran
Saint Mary's College of California

SALEM PRESS
A Division of EBSCO Information Services, Inc.
Ipswich, Massachusetts

GREY HOUSE PUBLISHING

Library of Congress Cataloging-in-Publication Data

Contemporary Canadian fiction / editor, Carol L. Beran, Saint Mary's
  College of California. -- [First edition].

  pages ; cm. -- (Critical insights)

  Includes bibliographical references and index.
  ISBN: 978-1-61925-415-2

  1. Canadian fiction--20th century--History and criticism. 2. Canadian fiction--
21st century--History and criticism. 3. Canada--In literature. I. Beran, Carol L.
II. Series: Critical insights.

PR9192.5 .C66 2014
813.009

LCCN: 2014952106

First Print

PRINTED IN THE UNITED STATES OF AMERICA

Contents _____

Resources

About This Volume

The most recent course in Canadian fiction that I offered at Saint Mary's College of California was titled "A Literary Tour of Canada." No, it wasn't a travel course. Rather, the fiction I selected for the reading list took us on a westward journey across Canada from the Maritimes to British Columbia. And although imaginaries of place were often a consideration, we discussed the texts from many perspectives.

I emphasized that I called the course "A" tour because in one semester we could only read a very small subset of available Canadian fiction. The course could have had several totally different reading lists. I called it a "Literary Tour" because we looked at Canada mostly through the lens of literature. Students did, however, present reports about various parts of Canada as we read literature from a particular area. Using Internet resources and the media capabilities of our classroom, we were enticed by tourist ads, heard economic statistics, saw images of the most beautiful (and a few of the most ugly) places in each province, enthused about paintings by Canadian artists, learned about some of each province's most honored citizens, and looked back at the history of various regions and forward to the glorious (or disastrous) future envisioned in these materials.

Imagining a selection principle for a book on contemporary Canadian fiction (other than selecting 1970 as a starting date) was rather like finding a way to organize that course. Again, I chose the approach of a journey from east to west, offering readers one literary tour of Canada, even if, in this book, the writers will not attempt to duplicate the projected images that students brought to the classroom. These stories Canadians tell about themselves, taken in aggregate, offer readers an imaginary of the country—one imaginary among many.

With endless pages, beginning the volume with Annie Proulx's *The Shipping News* and Wayne Johnson's *The Colony of Unrequited Dreams* would have given images of Canada's most eastern areas. Instead, the essays in this volume begin in the Maritimes. Rita Ross compares and contrasts the heroines of two older texts, written well before the starting date of this volume, who have become contemporary Canadian fictions, transcending the works that first introduced them to readers to become part of the current national imaginary. *Evangeline*, a long poem by American author Henry Wadsworth Longfellow, has provided the descendants of early French settlers in the Maritimes with a fiction around which to collect not just their past wrongs, but their present views of themselves: oppressed, yet courageous; separated, yet faithful until death; overcome, yet able to survive adversity to overcome, ultimately, an often marginalized, yet important part of the whole. Evangeline, separated from her love in the historic Deportation imposed by the British, lives on as a myth to symbolize all the terror and joys of being Acadian. Anne, from Lucy Maud Montgomery's novel *Anne of Green Gables,* survives not just as a literary text, but also as a contemporary Canadian fiction, since she has become an icon who—though very specifically attached to a particular time and place on Prince Edward Island—symbolizes for English-speaking Canadians all over the country qualities that unite them. Some feminists take exception to Anne for not being independent enough, for giving up her promising educational opportunities at the end of the novel in order to stay home and care for the ailing, aging woman who has been a mother figure to this orphan. Yet Anne's decision puts her in the mold that some have seen as quintessentially Canadian: privileging the common good above the individual's pursuit of happiness and taking care of those who need care, whether personally, as Anne does, or more generally, through social safety net programs.

Shannon Hengen provides a look at contemporary works of fiction from Nova Scotia, specifically Archibald MacLeod's novel, *No Great Mischief,* and his collected short stories, *Island.* Hengen asserts that these fictions depict the process by which men find their souls. MacLeod's romanticism—perhaps reflecting the influence of British poet John Keats' ideas of the world as a "vale of soul-making" (911), in which humans must learn "negative capability," the ability to live with "uncertainties, Mysteries, doubts" (902) as they "acquire identities, till each one is personally itself" (911)—displays nostalgia for a Nova Scotia of the past as it interfaces with the realities of the modern world.

In A Literary Tour of Canada, I taught (in translation) Anne Hebért's historical novel *Kamouraska*, a compelling exploration of sanity and madness, Church control and human desire, and the position of women, as a way to think about Québec and its place in Canada. In contrast, for this volume, Holly L. Collins has chosen to write on very different texts: two recent works by Haitian immigrants that explore problems of racism in contemporary French-speaking Canada. She sees Dany Laferrière's *How To Make Love to a Negro without Getting Tired* as a book that explodes stereotypes of blackness though hyperbole, and Marie-Célie Agnant's *The Book of Emma* as a novel in which oral history is necessary to make formerly silenced histories of racial oppression known.

"On Contemporary Canadian Fiction" offers a brief look at the work of another fiction writer from Québec, Mavis Gallant. Having lived in Paris for many years, Gallant writes stories that may seem distant from contemporary concerns of French Canada. Yet the four linked stories in *Across the Bridge* about the generations of a Québécois family play with old stereotypes that have been used to avoid looking more carefully at this part of Canada to suggest an imaginary of French Canada in the modern world as it, like all things, slips away in time.

Ontario, Canada's most populous province, is represented in this volume by essays on fictions by Michael Ondaatje, Margaret Atwood, Alice Munro, and Jane Urquhart. Michael Ondaatje, whose fame extends to every place in the world where Hollywood movies are watched, I suggest in "On Contemporary Canadian Fiction," envisions a dark world illuminated by tiny points of light and punctuated now and then by gigantic bursts of light—explosions—whether he writes of a particular historical time and place in Ontario or completely different ones across the Atlantic. The lights that illumine interpersonal relationships among people from disparate ethnic and social groups throughout *In the Skin of a Lion* grow larger and larger in *The English Patient*, culminating in the bombing of Hiroshima and Nagasaki.

Sharon R. Wilson considers Margaret Atwood's newest novel, *MaddAddam,* using a combination of reader-response theory and feminist theory to make sense of this novel in terms of learning how to read a fiction that takes us out of our familiar world. The "Fat Lady Joke" leads Charlotte Templin into questions of how Atwood's comedy points to ways women's bodies are demeaned and what it might mean to women to move beyond such confining images. Templin's focus on the humor in *Lady Oracle* offers a corrective to the criticism looking at serious social concerns in Atwood's work without seeing how its delightful, laughter-evoking aspects support those concerns. As Atwood's Joan in *Lady Oracle* has adventures while escaping Ontario for England and Italy, she encounters obstacles in the traditional comic fashion, humorously presented, although the resolution of the novel does not remove all the obstacles as readers expect in comedy.

Judith McCombs disentangles the layers of Alice Munro's "A Wilderness Station," revealing how the intertwining of stories from such sources as Munro's family history, folktales recounted by the Brothers Grimm, and biblical stories within a complicated narrative of letters and retrospectives creates a complex tale that only tentatively answers the questions it raises. My essay, "On Contemporary Canadian Fiction," engages with two other stories by Munro, "Miles City, Montana" and "White Dump," arguing that theories about Munro's greatness, such as the one that her stories that are like novels, crammed full of relationships, and the one that "Munro's best work is usually about the hidden story of emotion and the secret life, communicated by atmosphere and tone" (May vii) need to be supplemented by another; some of the importance of her work resides in its engagement with questions posed again and again by philosophers, theologians, and artists: Do we have free will or are we controlled by fate? Is individual happiness more important than the common good? Why do bad things happen to good people?

Analogies are the key to Jane Urquhart's recent novels, *Changing Heaven* and *Sanctuary Line,* Patricia Linton argues. Both books assert the influence of art in creating an individual's values, and both center around analogies to natural phenomena—wind and butterflies, respectively—as part of the narrative design.

Carol Shields, having lived in several places in the United States and Canada, writes of both Ontario and Manitoba, among other locales in her various works. In *Larry's Party,* Nora Foster Stovel argues, Shields shows that Larry's mistakes can lead to good results as well as bad ones, in spite of his passivity; Stovel develops these aspects of the novel, along with its imagery of mazes, to show how *Larry's Party* upsets standard definitions of manhood.

Essays on Margaret Laurence, Aritha van Herk, and Robert Kroetsch move this literary tour westward into the Prairie Provinces and northward into the Yukon. My essay on *The Diviners* by Margaret Laurence grafts an older literary theory into recent studies of how literature inculcates empathy in readers to explain the power of this novel. Mary Kirtz reads Aritha van Herk's *Restlessness* through a double lens: feminism plus her own theory of intramodernism, asserting that the book escapes its seeming realism to offer visions of possibilities as yet unexplored. The literary journey across Canada takes a detour north as Aritha Van Herk's unique vision opens new vistas regarding Robert Kroetsch's *The Man from the Creeks* as a fiction in which Kroetsch conjures up historical mythologies and a poet's mythology to explode both extravagantly into a mythology of his own.

Finally, moving into British Colombia, Janice Fiamengo writes that, in the stories set in Vancouver by Asian Canadian Madeleine Thien, rice cooking provides a central image for understanding relationships among the family and tensions between generations, while memory cannot provide the solace and stability characters desire.

Rita Ross' Critical Reception chapter, which follows my opening historical overview, examines several ways that literary critics have looked at Canadian fiction, from Atwood's *Survival: A Thematic Guide to Canadian Literature* in 1972 to Reingard

M. Nischick's 2014 *Handbook of Comparative North American Literature*, a contribution to the emerging field that studies the literature of individual nations in the context of literature from other nations to obtain a global perspective. Ross' timeline of events in Canada and the United States builds on the idea of comparative North American studies. It provides rich contexts in which to set the fictions discussed in this volume. The essay covers topics from literary prizes to presidents and prime ministers, from economic agreements to grass roots movements.

Works Cited

Hebért, Anne. *Kamouraska.* 1970. Trans. Norman Shapiro, 1973. Toronto: Anansi, 2000.

Johnson, Wayne. *The Colony of Unrequited Dreams*. Toronto: Vintage, 1999.

Keats, John. "Letters." *The Longman Anthology of British Literature, Vol 2A, The Romantics and Their Contemporaries*. 2nd ed. Ed. Susan Wolfson & Peter Manning. New York: Longman, 2003. 900–15.

May, Charles E. "About This Volume." *Critical Insights: Alice Munro.* Ed. Charles E. May. Ipswich, MA: Salem Press, 2013. vii–xii.

Proulx, Annie. *The Shipping News*. New York: Simon & Schuster, 1993.

On Contemporary Canadian Fiction

Carol L. Beran

A book entitled *Contemporary Canadian Fiction* obviously focuses on the fictions produced in one nation. Yet nations are not enclosed, isolated entities in the contemporary world; neither are their fictions. In her essay in this volume, Rita Ross writes of a heroine of the nineteenth-century American poem *Evangeline* becoming a contemporary Canadian fiction. Fiction writers as well as characters cross national boundaries both physically and imaginatively. Perhaps the most widely known fact about recent Canadian fiction is that the 2013 Nobel Prize in Literature was awarded to Alice Munro. As she said in her initial statements to the press, this marked an important day for Canadian literature and for the short story:

> "When I began writing, there was a very small community of Canadian writers and little attention was paid by the world," she said. "Now Canadian writers are read, admired and respected around the globe.
>
> She said she was thrilled to be chosen for the prize, adding, "I hope it fosters further interest in all Canadian writers." (Bosman)

The transcript of a recorded interview shown at the Nobel award ceremony reads in part:

> [AS] And the award will bring a great new readership to your work
> . . . .
>
> [AM] Well I would hope so, and I hope this would happen not just for me but for the short story in general. Because it's often sort of brushed off, you know, as something that people do before they write their first novel. And I would like it to come to the fore, without any strings attached, so that there doesn't have to be a novel. (Smith)

Although global imaginaries of Canada and its writing and the short story have, no doubt, changed in the aftermath of the Nobel award to a Canadian writer of short fiction, Canadian fiction and Canadian writers have long been interacting with the world outside Canada, expanding imaginaries of Canada. Mavis Gallant, a Canadian writing from abroad and only occasionally focusing her fiction on Canada, encapsulates the pain brought by time and change to the lives of a Montreal family in the first four stories from *Across the Bridge*. Michael Ondaatje, an immigrant to Canada from Sri Lanka via England, opens up experiences of immigrants to Canada before and during World War II in two interconnected novels, *In the Skin of a Lion* and *The English Patient,* in ways that underscore economic inequalities and racism. Alice Munro, a Canadian writing mostly from within Canada and often about a small region in Canada, not only moves beyond that region in some stories to encompass a larger geographical setting, but also frequently moves beyond the locales in which characters live to explore ideas long debated by Western philosophers and theologians.

Mavis Gallant

Leaving Canada in 1950, Mavis Gallant traveled for some time, and eventually settled in Paris, living there until her death in 2014. Gallant's geographical distance from Canada has led to a large body of work that only occasionally takes place in Canada and often concerns characters with little or no Canadian connection. The four stories of a Canadian family from Montreal in *Across the Bridge*—"1933," "The Chosen Husband," "From Cloud to Cloud," and "Florida"—are told by a narrator who seems detached, distanced from the characters in time and space.

To understand Gallant's outside look at Canada and Canadians, a comparison with Margaret Atwood's inside look is helpful. Atwood, whose extensive Canadian output has been seen as part of the nationalistic movement in Canada, uses words to evoke contemporary life, usually in Canada, often from satiric perspectives. What Atwood calls in a video interview "getting the furniture right" (Lee) is at the heart of bearing witness to the world she perceives.

Like her character Toni in *The Robber Bride*—a professor of history who studies war, but focuses on topics like how the invention of the zipper as a replacement for buttons on men's trousers changed warfare (27–28)—Atwood calls to readers' attention the small, seemingly insignificant, everyday things that affect lives, sometimes in surprisingly major ways.

White Rose gas, consumer surveys, upscale restaurants in the Colonnade on Bloor Street in Toronto, diminishing frog populations, Hurricane Hazel, bowls by Kayo, chocolate truffles from the David Wood Food Shop, "In Flanders' Fields," colored marker pens, salt gardens—these and many more bits of contemporary "furniture" find their way into Atwood's stories. As readers follow the lives of characters in Atwood's fiction, these details help establish realism, define characters, delineate setting, and invoke themes; they also preserve a record of the minutiae that make up everyday life. Taken together, they form an answer to Northrop Frye's question, "Where is here?" (220). In a postcolonial country, where many have looked to England for culture, and where many have feared that the neighbor to the south will overwhelm Canadian culture, Atwood's writing describes what is "here" in ways that make it available not only to Canadians, but to readers worldwide.

On the other hand, getting the furniture right is probably not one of Mavis Gallant's major goals. She writes from Paris in 1981 in "An Introduction" to *Home Truths: Selected Canadian Stories,* "I can vouch for the city: my Montreal is as accurate as memory can make it. I looked nothing up, feeling that if I made a mistake with a street name it had to stand. Memory can spell a name wrong and still convey the truth" (xxii). Gallant quotes Jean Cocteau in French, "*Je suis un mensonge qui dit la vérité*" ("An Introduction" xxii); I am a lie who speaks the truth (trans. Shapiro; Gallant omits *toujours*, meaning 'always,' from the quote). Nevertheless, her use of specific details depicting furniture in her stories brings interior places vividly into view. As the Carettes move from one apartment to another in Montreal, "[a] patched tarpaulin protected the Carettes' wine-red sofa with its border of silk fringe, the children's brass bedstead, their mother's walnut bed with the carved scallop shells, and the round oak table, smaller than the old one, at which they would now eat their meals" (Gallant, *Across the Bridge* 3–4); the details mark the downsizing to smaller, less expensive quarters that prompts this move as well as helping readers visualize the rooms later in the story. However, unlike Atwood, Gallant does not usually name such things as brands to distinguish exactly among times and places. Instead, details of manners present vivid pictures of Montreal expectations of young women: Mme. Carette "trained the girls not to lie, or point, or gobble their food, or show their legs above the knee, or leave fingerprints on windowpanes, or handle the parlor curtains—the slightest touch could crease the lace" (Gallant, *Across the Bridge* 5). Juxtaposing serious advice with trivial prohibitions produces Gallant's typical detached humor in this passage.

The four stories in *Across the Bridge* that focus on Montreal characters (the first three take place in Montreal and the fourth takes place mostly in Florida) rely more on stereotypes of the inhabitants than on individuated portraits of people and relationships—and like any good comedian, Gallant can use words to make type characters walk (even dance) on their own. The Carette women are variants of the virgin, whore, and crone archetypes. When the innocent young girl dreams, "[a]ll that kept the dream from sliding into blasphemy and abomination was Marie's entire unacquaintance, awake or asleep, with what could happen next" (Gallant, *Across the Bridge* 23). In counterpoint, Marie's sister has affairs with a series of married men; Gallant inverts the whore archetype by making Berthe's life sound more exciting than Marie's marriage. The widowed mother, a crone at forty-five ("a long widowhood strictly observed had kept her childish, not youthful" [Gallant, *Across the Bridge* 3]), "recalled what it had been like to have a husband she could consult and admire" but realized she would not be alone during her long, final illness" (Gallant, *Across the Bridge* 22–23). Places float, convenient stages for these stereotypes to walk on, perhaps as they leap "From Cloud to Cloud," to borrow the title of the third story. Being distanced from the characters by the narrator's satiric selection of observations and, therefore, freed from personal hopes and fears about them as individuals, readers instead focus on the absurdities that make the characters amusing and yet, at the same time, heartbreaking, enjoying the mishaps that bring the characters confusion and pain. In "1933," the dog Arno "understood English and French; Mme. Grosjean could only speak English" (Gallant, *Across the Bridge* 6); because the Carettes only speak a few phrases of English, conversations become hilarious, yet sad: "'Berthe asked, in French, 'What is he saying?' Mme. Grosjean answered in English, 'A well-known Irish tenor'" (8).

Word choice keeps readers aware of the characters as characters, increasing the distances between reader and story: "Of course, M. Grosjean did not know that all the female creatures in his house were frightened and lonely, calling and weeping. He was in Parc Lafontaine with Arno, trying to play go-fetch-it in the dark" (Gallant, *Across the Bridge* 9). Terming the women "female creatures" puts them on a par with the dog, diminishing sympathy; the scene juxtaposes their sadness with the dog's playing, while "in the dark" metamorphoses from a literal description into a cliché for the man's lack of awareness. Nevertheless, taken as a whole, the scene may well create empathy for all the characters, caught in an isolation that in these stories seems representative of the human condition, underscored in this quote by "of course." In "The Chosen Husband," Louis chokes: "He was in trouble with a caramel. The Carettes looked away, so that he could strangle unobserved" (Gallant, *Across the Bridge* 19). Even awareness of a potential life-threatening danger cannot cut through the unquestioning etiquette that the women have been trained in since birth. By the end of the fourth story, the narrator's comment that only the fetus understands is less surprising and more amusing than it might have been: "She had gone into French, but it didn't matter. The baby could hear, and knew what she meant" (Gallant, *Across the Bridge* 51). The narrator, distanced throughout from setting and characters, has moved away from the omniscient narrator of so much nineteenth-century fiction, yet, at the same time, she is more omniscient than typical nineteenth-century fictional narrators in knowing what a fetus thinks. Like the dog, the fetus understands both French and English. The effect of the ironies is to increase the distance between readers and characters.

"'Hearts are not broken in Mavis Gallant's stories," Eve Auchincloss wrote in *The New York Review of Books*. "Roots are cut, and [Gallant's] subject is the nature of the life that is left when the roots are not fed'" (Verongos). In the four Montreal stories from *Across the Bridge*, roots are cut not only by deaths of men in the family, or by a Canadian man who reverses the usual pattern of American draft dodgers taking refuge in Canada through his own enlistment in the United States military to fight in the Vietnam War, but also by small seemingly insignificant acts: a man walking the dog without mentioning this, the constant moving from one apartment to another, or Berthe's series of married lovers. Looking back from the vantage point of Paris, Gallant sees enclosed spaces—apartments, rooms, motels—and a constant restless motion from one to the next, motion without purpose: Berthe "enjoyed just walking from room to room" in her large apartment (Gallant, *Across the Bridge* 35). Although the characters are aware of the moon walk, they have a dubious notion of North American geography: "they thought of Vietnam as an American place" (Gallant, *Across the Bridge* 37). Their small world changes so rapidly that the characters often feel bewildered: "Rome was beyond their imagining, though all three Carettes had been to Maine and Old Orchard Beach" (Gallant, *Across the Bridge* 19). Gallant's details suggest an imaginary of French Canada in the modern world based on impermanence; it, like all things, slips away in time.

Michael Ondaatje

Known in the United States as the writer of the book behind the blockbuster Hollywood movie *The English Patient*, Michael Ondaatje has expanded the international imaginary of Canada through his delineation of Canadian and global multiculturalism. "One of the things a novel can do is represent the unofficial story, give a personal, complicated version of things," Ondaatje told an interviewer (Bush 247).

The English Patient won nine Oscars in 1996: Juliette Binoche won Best Supporting Actress for her portrayal of Hana, a Canadian nurse; Anthony Minghella won Best Director; the seven other Oscars included Best Picture. At the time, only two other films, *Gigi* and *The Last Emperor*, had won nine Oscars, and only two films had won more: *Ben Hur* (eleven) and *West Side Story* (ten) (Gray 1). Reviews of the movie based on Ondaatje's World War II novel often focus on the larger-than-life passions in the love story, compellingly acted out by Kristin Scott Thomas and Ralph Fiennes. Detractors complain that the film glorifies illicit love, making it seem incredibly appealing, even when the individual betrayal spawns an international one: the protagonist sells the Allies' maps of Africa to the Germans in order to rescue his beloved. Writing in *Queen's Quarterly*, Thomas Hurka finds fault: "It has a moral perspective on the events it describes, but it is a me-centered and immoral one" (1). He complains that "the movie sympathizes with a choice that is simply morally wrong," that "it sees nothing at all problematic about a choice that, even if not simply wrong, violates an important political duty"; it "casts its moral considerations entirely in the me-centered terms of loyalty and betrayal, never recognizing the impersonal demands that were so central in its setting of the Second World War" (Hurka 4). The name Ondaatje uses for the character of the English Patient, Almásy, is the name of an historic person, a spy who worked for the Nazis and, after the war, for the Soviets in Hungary; Ondaatje answers charges of making light of what people like Almásy did by saying he chose to emphasize Almásy's exploration of the desert for "the emotional, even poetic, view that he was striving for" (Perlez C22). Postmodern fiction frequently appropriates elements from real life; by disregarding factual accuracy, writers create a throb of dissonance among the multiple layers of the text that may subvert the status quo to convey an important point. In *The English Patient,* Ondaatje's appropriation of Almásy's name and some facts of his life juxtaposes the lack of justice in real life with the stricter morality of the novelist's imagined story: the retribution Ondaatje imagines for the English Patient is much more dire—closer to what many might think of as justice—than what happened to the real Almásy. This retribution confronts movie viewers and readers of the novel constantly: Almásy remembers and tells the story of his life, while the image of the English Patient—heavily drugged with morphine,

---

totally bandaged, dying of horribly painful burns—appears on the screen or on the pages of the book; he reveals that his beloved has died alone, injured, in a cave because he could not bring help in time in spite of his political treachery.

These critics also miss the importance of the character of Kip, an Asian. Kip is "a young man of the strangest profession his century had invented, a sapper, a military engineer who detected and disarmed mines" (Ondaatje, *The English Patient* 273). A suspenseful scene in both the book (192–95) and the movie shows him working on a bomb, eventually succeeding in removing its powerful potential to kill. In the book but not the movie, this scene contrasts with the climactic scene: the news that the United States has dropped atomic bombs on Japan. The paired scenes suggest that whereas the Asian uses technological expertise to save lives, the Allies use it to cause death. In the book, Kip specifically blames the British: "When you start bombing the brown races of the world, you're an Englishman . . . You all learned it from the English (Ondaatje, *The English Patient* 286).

The English Patient is a sequel to Ondaatje's 1987 novel, *In the Skin of a Lion*. The earlier book tells the fictionalized story of marginalized people, mostly Greek and Italian immigrants, who built major public works projects in Toronto in the 1920s and 1930s, again using some historical figures re-imagined as characters. Patrick, who has learned from his father the use of explosives to dislodge logjams (hence his name, Pa-trick), continues to use explosives to build a tunnel for Toronto's waterworks and then to help anarchists fight against established powers. In *The English Patient*, we learn that Patrick has died in the war, but his adopted daughter Hana is the nurse tending the burned patient; she has a brief affair with Kip as they wait in a ruined villa in Italy, where they are joined by Caravaggio, an Italian-Canadian thief who, in the earlier novel was nearly killed in Kingston Penitentiary by men yelling racial slurs against Italians. *In the Skin of a Lion* depicts a racist multicultural society warring over the distribution of power and goods; *The English Patient* presents the multicultural world at war over the same things, and yet one Asian knows how to defuse bombs rather than detonate them. The bombs dropped on Japan, however, are beyond the scope of his expertise. If the earlier book makes the divisions between European races visible for readers, the later book expands the divisions to the world as a whole and presents the bombing of Nagasaki and Hiroshima as racist acts: Caravaggio "knows the young soldier [Kip] is right. They would never have dropped such a bomb on a white nation" (Ondaatje, *The English Patient* 286). Hollywood, however, omits this accusation, letting the news that the war has ended serve as the climax of the film, perhaps a tacit assent to the arguments that the Japanese were both racist and brutal during the war and that dropping the bombs saved many lives.[1]

The vision that Kip offers, that explosives can be defused, ultimately does not prevail in the book, whereas it seems to in the movie. These two books by Ondaatje, set in the past, evoke for the present the horror of bombs; if multicultural and interracial conflict leads to explosions of all sizes, including ongoing conflicts in Ondaatje's country of origin, perhaps only the pacific philosophy and actions of individuals, the character Kip or his creator Ondaatje, offer hope for the future—if any hope can co-exist with the fact of nuclear bombs.

The worlds presented in these two books are generally dark, with imagery of night and blindness broken by small points of light from candles, loggers' torches, or car headlights; explosions of bombs show the irony of wishing for light. Ondaatje presents a challenging and disturbing vision, expanding not just the Canadian imaginary or the imaginary the rest of the world has of Canada, but the imaginaries readers hold of their place in the world. By taking his characters to Canada as immigrants in *In the Skin of a Lion* and out of Canada into the midst of World War II in *The English Patient,* he presents Canada in a global context.

Alice Munro

Unlike Mavis Gallant and Michael Ondaatje, Alice Munro has always lived in Canada with the exception of various short visits and visiting writer appointments elsewhere. Her biographer, Robert Thacker, theorizes that a major change took place in Munro's writing and thinking when she returned to London, Ontario, in 1973 and to Clinton, Ontario, in 1975 after living in Vancouver and other parts of Canada since 1951: "Munro returned to Ontario to find it a place she could no longer imagine from far away in distance and time. It was real and immediate, both the place she remembered from her childhood and adolescence and alive in the present moment" (266). The fact that her ancestors had lived there contributed to an "awareness of the web of human interconnection defined by her home place" (Thacker 26). Yet her Nobel Prize suggests she transcends a simply regional or even a national literature. At the Alice Munro Symposium in Ottawa in May 2014, various speakers suggested reasons for Munro's greatness: her ability to cram a novel into a short story, her complexity, and her wide-ranging allusions to the classics were mentioned. I agree with Charles May when he writes, "As Alice Munro well knows, the short story's complexity is due not to how extensively it explores human reality but to how intensively" (4). I would like to suggest a related, but slightly different aspect of her work that contributes to her greatness: she takes the questions that Western theologians and philosophers have debated for centuries and places them in contexts that not only reduce them to daily problems rather than lofty ones, but also suggest myriad answers as complex as any the expert thinkers have suggested, yet simple enough for average readers to understand.

"Miles City, Montana" from *The Progress of Love* includes four stories of potential drowning as it tells of a family driving from Vancouver to southwestern Ontario. The fact that this story begins outside southwestern Ontario, ventures into the United States, and never reaches its destination prepares readers for something beyond a simple focus on southwestern Ontario. In a nursery rhyme, only four of the five little ducks that went away "came swimming back" (Munro 91). Why? Did one drown? Get eaten by a predator? In true nursery rhyme style, the poem does not tell. This rhyme, sung by one of the narrator's children to cheer her quarreling parents, expresses mysteries of life and death. Why is one duck chosen to disappear, while others are permitted to return? The song gives no answers, but adult readers are aware of the principle that says nature preserves the species, not the individual. The narrator tells a story of how she and her father went out to rescue turkeys from drowning in flooding caused by a storm, but "they had managed to crowd to higher ground and avoid drowning" (Munro 94). Instinct? Steve Gauley, an eight year old boy, "drowned, people said, because he was the next thing to an orphan and was let run free" (Munro 104), but the narrator questions this explanation. The narrator's daughter is saved from drowning by a combination of the mother's intuition and the father's quick action, but the father notes that the child was swimming on her own. The narrator questions the reliability of her motherly instinct: "I wanted to warn him—to warn everybody—never to count on it" (Munro 105). Questions about the death of the innocent, the mystery of what causes the end of one life and spares another, are raised by the story, not in the context of a philosophic dialogue or a theological debate, but in the context of everyday happenings that compare the fate of highly vulnerable birds to that of equally if not more vulnerable children. The "trashy . . . imagining" (Munro 103) that the narrator rejects reflects the opposition's argument in a philosophical debate: "But I was compelled to picture the opposite" (Munro 102). Munro's presentation does not attempt definitive answers to the questions it raises; it simply shows various facets of them through their presence in everyday life. The narrator's apparent epiphanies at the end of the story complicate rather than solve the problems raised. Because cause and effect do not pertain with any certainty, what happens in the lives of the characters is as inexplicable as what happens in the nursery rhyme; the outcome of any one potential drowning cannot be used to predict what will happen in the next.

A quotation from *The Poetic Edda,* an Icelandic epic, "It is too late to talk of this now: it has been decided" (Munro 309), suggests in Munro's story "White Dump" from *The Progress of Love* that the question of whether fate or free will determines human life can be asked even in a house on an Ontario Lake—and even in a short story rather than in a national epic. As I explain in an essay on "The Pursuit of Happiness":

. . . in a story like "White Dump," where the word "*Weltschmerz*" announces the contrapuntal theme to the motif of happiness (288), Munro prepares for a specifically pre-Christian philosophy to control the ending by having one character, Sophie, be a professor of Scandinavian languages. The line her daughter-in-law reads at the end of the story from *The Poetic Edda*, a work from a culture that believed strongly in Fate, emphasizes fatedness rather than faith as the controlling factor in life. (Beran, "The Pursuit" 332)

For W. R. Martin, this quotation underscores the irrationality of the emotions (185). However, my research found that

a manuscript draft of "White Dump" shows a different quote from *The Poetic Edda*: "Do you remember what we swore to each other when we lay in bed?" (AMP, third accession, 396/87.3/880812, file 10.8). The change seems to reflect a choice away from simple questions of sexuality and fidelity, of finding happiness through true love, toward complicated philosophical concepts of free will and predestination. (Beran, "The Pursuit" 322)

Sophie's name means "wisdom." Over her lifetime, Sophie has tried to control everything from frogs to poor children, but cannot alter those things or halt her own aging. Awareness that fate trumps free will may be a wise reading of life, yet Sophie does many foolish things as well as wise ones in the story, troubling a simple non-ironic reading (Beran, "The Pursuit" 333).

Sophie is struck, as she flies in a sightseeing plane, not by lightning, but with "a tingle" (Munro 296), an awareness of her own insignificance in a landscape that includes ancient Precambrian rock: "She felt as if it was she, not the things on earth, that had shrunk, was still shrinking—or that they were all shrinking together" (Munro 296). Similarly, Sophie's daughter-in-law, Isabel, imagines that she exchanges glances with the pilot and feels struck by lightning (a bolt thrown by Thor?): "And the promise hit her like lightning, split her like lightning" (Munro 305); it is later that evening that she reads the quotation from the *Edda* at the page Sophie has left open. Munro told John Metcalf, "I'm not a writer who deals in ideas" (56).

Nevertheless, as I noted in "The Pursuit of Happiness," "by dealing with the question of happiness in the lives of characters living in Canada, Munro has presented dramatically a popular, artistic, political, and philosophical concept" (Beran 340). By including happiness and Fate, Munro injects powerful concepts from theology and philosophy into a story of an Ontario family, moving a story that takes place in Canada beyond any one country.[2]

Conclusion

One way scholars have categorized Canadian literature is by saying that it is regional. Texts by Gallant, Ondaatje, and Munro provide both support and opposition to that analysis. Gallant, although she sets some of her stories in Montreal, defies the regionalist credo about the importance of small, precise details depicting the region and its inhabitants. Ondaatje writes as a regionalist in *In the Skin of a Lion*, but globalizes by taking his Ontario characters to Europe and Africa during the Second World War. Munro expands the region she constructs by letting her stories contemplate significant philosophical questions.

Notes

1. Janice Fiamengo pointed out the opposing argument here, one that Hollywood may well have preferred to Kip's point of view.

2. In "Thomas Hardy, Alice Munro, and the Question of Influence," I discuss another example of how Munro explores large philosophical questions with ordinary characters in familiar Ontario settings, comparing her story "Carried Away" with Thomas Hardy's "An Imaginative Woman." Both writers, I argue, "personalize key philosophical questions of their times, letting the insignificant lives of their rural characters manifest significant intellectual patterns of thought" (Beran 248). Fate, in the form of coincidences that seem to pile up against the characters, is foregrounded in both stories (Beran 248–49).

Works Cited

Alice Munro Papers. Special Collections Library, University of Calgary. Manuscripts.

Atwood, Margaret. *The Robber Bride.* Toronto: McClelland, 1993.

Beran, Carol L. "Thomas Hardy, Alice Munro, and the Question of Influence." *The American Review of Canadian Studies.* (Summer 1999): 241–62.

_____. "The Pursuit of Happiness: A Study of Alice Munro's Fiction." *The Social Science Journal* 37.3 (July 2000). 329–45.

Bosman, Julie. "Alice Munro Wins Nobel Prize in Literature." *New York Times.* 10 Oct. 2013. Web. 6 June2014. <http://www.nytimes.com/2013/10/11/books/alice-munro-wins-nobel-prize-in-literature.html?pagewanted=1&_r=0>.

Bush, Catherine. "Michael Ondaatje: An Interview." *Essays on Canadian Writing* 53 (1994): 238–49.

The English Patient. Dir. Anthony Minghella. Perf. Ralph Fiennes, Juliette Binoche, Willem Dafoe, & Kristin Scott Thomas. Miramax, 1996. DVD.

Frye, Northrop. Conclusion to *A Literary History of Canada.* 1965. *The Bush Garden: Essays on the Canadian Imagination.* Toronto: Anansi, 1971. 213–251.

Gallant, Mavis. *Across the Bridge: Stories.* New York: Random House, 1993.

_____. "An Introduction." *Home Truths: Selected Canadian Stories.* Toronto: McClelland, 1981.

Gray, Timothy M. "Oscar speaks highly of 'English.'" *Variety* 31 Mar. 1997: 24+. *Expanded Academic ASAP. InfoTrac.* Web. 31 March 2005.

Hurka, Thomas. "Philosophy, morality, and *The English Patient.*" *Queen's Quarterly* 104 (1997): 46–55. *Expanded Academic ASAP. InfoTrac.* Web. 31 Mar. 2005.

Lee, Hermione. *Writers in Conversation: Margaret Atwood.* ICA/Anthony Roland Collection of Film on Art, 198? [sic]. Video.

Martin, W. R. *Alice Munro: Paradox and Parallel.* Edmonton: U of Alberta P, 1987.

May, Charles E. "On Alice Munro." *Critical Insights: Alice Munro.* Ed. Charles E. May. Ipswich, MA: Salem Press, 2013. 3–18.

Metcalf, John. "A Conversation with Alice Munro." *Journal of Canadian Fiction* 1.4 (1976): 54–62.

Munro, Alice. *The Progress of Love.* Toronto: McClelland, 1986.

Ondaatje, Michael. *The English Patient.* 1992. New York: Vintage, 1993.

_____. *In the Skin of a Lion.* 1987. New York: Viking Penguin, 1988.

Perlez, Jane. "The Real Hungarian Count Was No 'English Patient.'" *New York Times.* 17 Dec. 1996: C17+. *ProQuest Historical Newspapers.* Web. 31 Mar. 2005.

Shapiro, Fred R. *The Yale Book of Quotations.* New Haven: Yale UP, 2006. Web. 27 June 2014. Books.google.com.

Smith, Adam. "Alice Munro—Interview: 'This may change my mind.'" 10 Oct. 2013. Web 6 June 2014. <http://www.nobelprize.org/nobel_prizes/literature/laureates/2013/munro-telephone.html>.

Thacker, Robert. *Alice Munro: Writing Her Lives.* Toronto: McClelland, 2005.

Verongos, Helen T. "Mavis Gallant, 91, Dies; Her Stories Told of Uprooted Lives and Loss." *New York Times.* 18 Feb. 2014. Web. 3 June 2014. <http://www.nytimes.com/2014/02/19/books/mavis-gallant-short-story-writer-dies-at-91.html?_r=0>.

CRITICAL
CONTEXTS

Perceptions of Contemporary Canadian Fiction_____

Carol L. Beran

Many stories can be told about how Canadian fiction has been received; a single essay can only tell one of them. On the publication of new works, critics offer their critiques. Later, these immediate evaluations become affirmed or challenged in critical works, which offer theories that can be used to see works in broader perspectives. One way to think about how the works discussed in this volume have been received, then, is to look at some of these broader perspectives and at some of the ways these changed during the 1970–2013 time period that this volume addresses. The story that this essay will tell surveys several models that tie many works together: these models focus on nationalism, multiculturalism, postmodernism, and globalization as important ways to understand contemporary Canadian literature.

Nationalism: Creating Canons

Margaret Atwood's book *Survival: A Thematic Guide to Canadian Literature,* published in 1972, is a prominent example of both thematic and nationalistic criticism. Atwood posits that nations have distinct literatures that reflect key ideals in their national myths, and that "every country or culture has a single unifying and informing symbol at its core" (*Survival* 31). For England, she says, the Island is the central motif (Atwood, *Survival* 32). Following Frederick Jackson Turner, she identifies the Frontier as the dominating myth for the United States (Atwood, *Survival* 31). For Canada she names Survival (Atwood, *Survival* 32). In Magaret Laurence's *The Diviners*, for example, the motif plays out in the survival of the central figure, Morag, but works out tragically in the lives of her Métis lover and several of his relatives. On the other hand, should Audrey Thomas' *Intertidal Life* or Alistair MacLeod's *Island* be seen as British, given their island settings? Atwood avers these symbols should not be seen as "articles of dogma which allow no exceptions," but as "vantage points from which the literature may be viewed" (Atwood, *Survival* 31).

In a sly reference to a book by her teacher, Northrop Frye, entitled *Anatomy of Criticism,* Atwood writes, "This method will, I hope, articulate the skeleton of Canadian literature. It will let you see how the bones fit together, but it won't put flesh on them" (Atwood, *Survival* 40). Atwood identifies a series of motifs that reflect the Survival idea. Some of these Frye would call archetypes. One example would be what she calls the "Great Canadian Baby" (Atwood, *Survival* 207). The notion that a book ending with the birth of a baby might suggest the birth of a new society makes this a particularly apt motif for relatively new nation—a former colony— trying to assert its individual identity in the shadows of the mother country and the country to the south. However, Atwood describes the child as "the Baby Ex Machina, since it is lowered at the end of the book to solve problems for the characters which they obviously can't solve for themselves" (Atwood, *Survival* 207). Atwood uses a probable pregnancy towards the end of her novel *Life Before Man* as a symbol of a new community coming into being, yet troubles any sense that this baby will provide a happily-ever-after ending for the characters by having the pregnant woman worry about whether she will lose her job because of becoming an unwed mother, and how her partner will react to the news (284).

Victimization becomes a key motif for expressing the concept of Survival. Borrowing from popular self-help books, Atwood identifies four basic Victim Positions. In Position One, the victim denies that he or she is a victim (Atwood, *Survival* 36). Those in Victim Position Two acknowledge victimhood, but feel that whatever victimizes them is too powerful to fight. Victims in Position Three "refuse the assumption that the role is inevitable" (Atwood, *Survival* 37). Victim Position Four encompasses "creative non-victims," those who transcend victimization and are able to tell their own story in original and imaginative ways: "you are able to accept your own experience for what it is, rather than having to distort it to make it correspond with others' versions of it" (Atwood, *Survival* 39).

The Victim Positions, with their natural progression from one to four, work exceptionally well for analyzing characters in Atwood's own fiction. In literature in general, they are most useful as a tool of analysis in stories that show a protagonist progressing to an epiphany. Atwood uses Del Jordan, the protagonist of Alice Munro's *Lives of Girls and Women* as an example of a woman who attains Position Four:

> [Del] has secret ambitions as a writer, again the culture is bent on stunting or destroying them, and the situation is compounded by the fact that the potential artist is a woman. She defies the culture, leaves it, and survives to become an artist; but she transfers her imaginative allegiance from the stylized world of Gothic grotesques she has dreamed up as an adolescent to the small-town "here" she despised when she was actually living in it. She chooses to write from the centre of her own experience, not from the periphery of someone else's, and she sees her act of creation as an act of redemption also. (*Survival* 193)

The heroine of Aritha van Herk's *Restlessness* might be seen as transcending victimization, even victimization by death, since Dorcas chooses her killer and the day of her death, thereby taking control of the uncontrollable. That would place her in the Fourth Victim Position, a creative non-victim, no longer victimized, able to create her own life—and death—story.

Survival as a concept for categorizing large numbers of works has been criticized because looking for a particular subject matter in literary works will automatically select against those works that don't display the given theme, potentially ruling out whole groups of texts, while giving special emphasis to those that reflect the theme. Aritha van Herk's *Restlessness*, for example, might be read not as suggested above, but rather as having an anti-survival theme, challenging survival as a major Canadian paradigm.

Frank Davey has made serious attacks on Atwood's theory and other Canadian thematic criticism. Focus on theme reduces both culture and texts to "catch words such as Atwood's 'victimization' and 'survival'" (Davey 3). He deplores the way Canadian criticism is "reluctant to focus on the literary work—to deal with matters of form, language, style, structure, and consciousness as these arise from the work as a unique construct" (Davey 1); thematic criticism "attends to the explicit meaning of the work and neglects whatever content is implicit in its structure, language, or imagery" (Davey 3). However, it is important to note that readers can do with thematic criticism what Davey says they should do with other kinds: not just show that stories demonstrate the theme, but that they vary, in literary ways, as they do so. The language and other "clothing" an author puts on the theme alters it, too, enlarging any given theme beyond what might seem its limiting boundaries. Or, in the metaphor Frye and Atwood use, readers can put flesh on the bones, and in doing so, reveal both commonalities and differences of literary technique as well as subtle variations on the theme.

Many stories from many nations use Survival as a premise, for example, British writer Daniel Defoe's *Robinson Crusoe* or American author Jack London's "To Build a Fire." Perhaps Davey's strongest criticism of *Survival* is that "Atwood develops her thesis that victimization is a characteristic theme of Canadian literature by ignoring its ubiquity in contemporary world literature" (4–5). Yet Atwood often describes how the Canadian character struggling for survival differs from an American or British character in similar circumstances (see, for example, Atwood 73–75 or 209–10). Davey calls for criticism that studies "that ground from which all writing communicates and all themes spring: the form—style, structure, vocabulary, literary form, syntax—of the writing" (7), rather than simply focusing on meaning.

Canadian nationalism was fostered not only by *Survival* and other works of thematic criticism, but also by literary scholars who met in Calgary and listed one hundred significant Canadian novels, works that express the nation's mythos; the list was published in 1982. "It was composed, virtually in its entirety, of realistic, linear, conventional novels that were the central, defining texts of the new Canadian tradition—one that valued works that affirmed the country and its people," writes Robert Lecker (668). One of the novels discussed in detail in this book, Margaret Laurence's *The Diviners,* made the top ten in that list (see Matthews 151). *The Diviners* offers a particularly interesting example of the Davey/Atwood controversy, as discussed in the chapter on Laurence. On the one hand, I suggest a reading that makes it a highly nationalistic text. On the other, I offer—and prefer—a reading that asks about the literary effects Laurence creates surrounding her characters.

Multiculturalism: Expanding Canons

If one way to define Canada has to do with a unifying symbol— Survival in a harsh world that constantly victimizes its inhabitants— an alternative way has been to think of the nation as a mosaic, a term that *The Canadian Encyclopedia* traces back to John Murray Gibbon's 1938 book, *Canadian Mosaic: The Making of a Northern Nation,* which contrasted Canada's encouragement of immigrant groups to remain distinct with the American melting pot image of assimilation. John Porter used the term "Vertical Mosaic" in his 1965 book, *Vertical Mosaic: An Analysis of Social Class and Power in Canada,* "to convey the concept that Canada is a mosaic of different ethnic, language, regional and religious groupings unequal in status and power" (Vallee).

The mosaic metaphor suggests that Canada is made up of distinct pieces: people of many different ethnic backgrounds, both native and immigrant. Some critics looking at the literary canon believed that it should reflect that diversity by including works by formerly marginalized groups. Other critics, such as Davey, believed that concerns about writing itself and literary genre should be preeminent in selecting Canadian texts. By the 1980s and '90s, exploding canons became an important task that literary critics set for themselves.

Robert Lecker's 1990 article in *Critical Inquiry* "The Canonization of Canadian Literature: An Inquiry into Value," takes the Canadian canon to task for not analyzing the values it perpetuates in its choices. He complains that the canonizers created "an image of themselves and their values" (Lecker 657); he terms this "cultural self-recognition," and goes on to state, "Literature becomes a means through which Canadians can know themselves and verify their national consciousness" (Lecker 662). Values in works selected for the canon include "a preoccupation with history and historical placement; an interest in topicality, mimesis, verisimilitude, and documentary presentation; a bias in favor of the native over the cosmopolitan, a concern with traditional over innovative forms . . ." (Lecker 657). Works that are experimental or show international influence get excluded, Lecker avers, "because they are somehow treasonous in their alignment with things foreign" or "because in being 'experimental' they are antirealistic, anticonservative, anti-Canadian" (669). Thus, many works by women, native Canadians, and people of ethnicities other than the dominant British Isles group would automatically be rejected for canonization. Lecker calls for "the rehistoricization of Canadian literature—not in terms of the vague notion of value embedded in rhetoric and propaganda of our inherited school, but in terms of a new and rewritten conception of history as a narrative that is not received but created, not dictated but free, false, in flux" (671).

In 1982, Canada repatriated its Constitution; this document includes the Charter of Rights and Freedoms, which acknowledges the equal rights of all Canadians. The definition of Canada as a multicultural society fosters embracing differences. Including in any Canadian canon works by members of diverse ethnic groups, religious persuasions, and sexualities becomes essential, if the canon is to give a glimpse of the nation.

In this volume, Holly L. Collins discusses two fictions written in French in Québec by Haitian immigrants, Marie-Célie Agnant's *The Book of Emma* and Dany Laferrière's *How to Make Love to a Negro without Getting Tired.* Similarly, Janice Fiamengo writes about Madeleine Thien's *Simple Recipes,* a book of short stories by an Asian Canadian writer, which is part of the new canon. Because of the movement both in Canada and elsewhere to expand canons, these texts—and more like them, if there were more space—can be included in a volume on contemporary Canadian fiction.

Postmodernism: Exploring one Postmodern Genre

The postmodern period in literature began after World War II; postmodern writers attempted "to break away from the modernist forms, which had, inevitably, become in their turn conventional, as well as to overthrow the elitism of modernist 'high art' by recourse for models to the 'mass culture' in film, television, newspaper cartoons, and popular music" (Abrams & Harpham 227). Robert Kroetsch, for example, as Aritha van Herk talks about in her essay in this volume, offers a revision of a doggerel ballad about the Yukon Gold Rush as a basis of his *A Man from the Creeks*. Similarly, van Herk's novel *Restlessness* deconstructs popular genres: the thriller and the murder mystery.

In *Surviving the Paraphrase,* Davey supplements his critique of thematic criticism by proposing several analytical projects. One of these he terms "Discontinuous Structure in Post-Modern Canadian Writing": it "could directly attempt, on the basis of Canadian literature, an elucidation of the problems and advantages of discontinuous literary structure. Such structure has been at the core of most significant new writing in Canada in the last decade," he wrote in 1983 (Davey 9). He acknowledges that literatures of other countries use this literary technique, but "the opportunity nevertheless exists for a literary problem important to all literatures to be usefully discussed strictly in terms of Canadian writing" (Davey 9).

Linda Hutcheon picks up Davey's challenge in *The Canadian Postmodern: A Study of Contemporary English-Canadian Fiction,* but goes beyond his suggestion of discussing the use of discontinuous structures as she discusses many aspects of one genre of postmodern writing in Canada: fiction. According to Hutcheon, postmodern art "is openly aware of the fact that it is written and read as part of a particular culture" (1); it seeks "to trouble, to question, to make both problematic and provisional any . . . desire for order or truth through the powers of the human imagination" (2); and it "implicitly challenges any notions of centrality in (and centralization of) culture" (3). "It is . . . the place where the centre is paradoxically both acknowledged and challenged," Hutcheon writes, and the border is its preferred space (4). Postmodern irony "refuses resolution of contraries— except in the most provisional of terms" (Hutcheon 5); verbal irony, along with word play "can subvert the authority of language, language seen as having a single and final meaning" (7). Parody, which "both asserts and undercuts that which it contests" (Hutcheon 7), and intertextuality, which "brings about a direct confrontation with the issue of the relation of art to the world outside it" (9), are key techniques in postmodern fiction. Ultimately, Hutcheon notes, postmoderrn fiction problematizes certainties: "Perhaps the loss of the modernist faith in fixed system, order, and wholeness can make room for new models based on things once rejected: contingency, multiplicity, fragmentation, discontinuity" (19). In her definitions of postmodern fiction, Hutcheon implicitly takes up Lecker's challenge to conceive of not just history but also literary form as "not received but created, not dictated but free, false, in flux" (671).

In *The Canadian Postmodern*, Hutcheon discusses many of the writers considered in this volume, including in her book chapters on Margaret Atwood and Robert Kroetsch, whom she calls "Mr [*sic*] Canadian Postmodern" (160), and parts of chapters on several others. For example, she notes that "Kroetsch's novels assert the male myths of the quest journey (that of Odysseus, Orpheus, Conrad's Marlow the knight errant, and so on), in order to show the male (and female) cultural roles as fictions, as constructed by culture rather than as 'natural' in any sense of the word" (Hutcheon 7). *The Man from the Creeks,* the work by Robert Kroetsch that Aritha van Herk discusses in her chapter here, takes for its intertext an older Canadian poem plus an event from history, the Yukon Gold Rush, and revises long-accepted cultural myths. Hutcheon's definition of 'historiographic metafiction" fits well with the discussion of Michael Ondaatje's *In the Skin of a Lion* and *The English Patient* in "Thinking about Contemporary Canadian Fiction" in this volume: "In historiographic metafiction we are lured into a world of imagination only to be confronted with the world of history, and thus asked to rethink the categories by which we normally would distinguish fiction from 'reality.' Reading becomes an act of philosophical puzzling as well as one of co-creation" (17). When Hutcheon talks of how "[b]oth metafiction and reader response theory have worked to make us aware of the active role of the reader in granting meaning to texts," she touches on the process that Sharon R. Wilson describes in her theoretically-based chapter on Margaret Atwood's *MaddAddam.*

Mary Kirtz's essay in this volume has an especially close relationship with Hutcheon's concepts of postmodernism. Kirtz has defined what she calls "intramodernism," the space of tension between realism and postmodernism:

> by using the formal structures of realism—but at the same time hinting at various ways that the nature of the constructed reality within these structures might be questioned—the writers of intramodernist fiction call attention to classical realism's unexamined belief in our own absolute reality (209; see also Kirtz's essay in this volume).

Hutcheon explains how the Canadian interest in regionalism in literature has been metamorphosed by postmodernists into "a concern for the different, the local, the particular—in opposition to the uniform, the universal, the centralized" (19). Atwood's interest in getting the furniture right (Lee; see also "Thinking about Contemporary Canadian Fiction" in this volume), therefore, can both be seen as part of the documentary realism Lecker sees as a hallmark of the old canon (657) and as a postmodern rebellion against "the universal, the centralized" (Hutcheon 19).

Globalization

Recently, literary scholars have considered ways of looking beyond national boundaries to compare works from what have previously been thought of as separate literatures. For example, comparative North American studies places Canadian literature in the context of American and Mexican literature.

Davey writes that:

> it is not unfair to say that the bulk of Canadian literature is regional before it is national—despite whatever claims Ontario or Toronto writers may make to represent a national vision. The regional consciousness may be characterized by specific attitudes to language and form, by specific kinds of imagery, by language and imagery that in some ways correlate with the geographic features of the region. (10)

However, in North America, regions do not stop at the border between the United States and Canada. Both countries have Pacific and Atlantic coasts, the Rocky Mountains extend north/south through both nations, as do the prairies.

The Palgrave Handbook of Comparative North American Literature, edited by Reingard M. Nischik, offers somewhat theoretical essays about different kinds of comparisons that might be made among the literatures of several nations in North America (and possibly including not just Canada, the United States, and Mexico, but also Central America); however, the essays focus mostly on comparing the literatures of the United States and Canada. Nischik notes that, in spite of commonalities, there may be problems in comparing these two literatures when, for example, there is no Canadian Dream parallel to the American Dream ("Comparative North American" 7). The goal is "to combine research paradigms that have long been disconnected" (Ernst 259). Essayists write on topics such as comparing indigenous writings in the two countries; assessing imaginaries of the North in English, Canadian, and Québécois texts; looking at Modernism in both countries; comparing texts from Acadia and Louisiana; letting imaginaries of the city in the literature of the two countries interact; or understanding what regionalism means in a bi-national context.

Florian Freitag's chapter on "Regionalism in American and Canadian Literature" notes the importance of understanding regionalism, long seen as writing centered on a small, marginalized part of a larger whole, in "transnational, hemispheric, or even global contexts" (199). If a region is defined in relationship to what is outside, in Comparative North American Studies, the outside can be not just the nation, but the continent (Freitag 200-201). Emphasis on Canadian literature's regionalism may be an attempt to break away from the centralizing tendencies of thematic criticism and a way to define the special character of Canadian writing (Freitag 204-205).

This book's literary tour of Canada encompasses many of its regions. With its timeline showing important events in Canada and the United States between 1960 and 2013, the book offers ways to begin enlarging the context of Canadian Studies to Comparative North American Studies.

Conclusion

The time period between 1970 and 2013 has encompassed an expansion of Canadian fiction. Its reception by critics saw Canadian fiction as contributing to Canadian nationalism, as part of a canon that needs to be expanded to reflect the many different cultures that comprise Canada, as contributing to a distinctive postmodern genre, and as part of North American culture and global culture.

Works Cited

Abrams, M.H., & Geoffrey Galt Harpham. *A Glossary of Literary Terms.* Boston: Wadsworth, 2012.

Agnant, Marie-Célie. *The Book of Emma.* Trans. Zilpha Ellis. Toronto: Insomniac P, 2006.

Atwood, Margaret. *Life Before Man.* New York: Warner, 1979.

_____. *Survival: A Thematic Guide to Canadian Literature.* Toronto: Anansi, 1972.

Davey, Frank. *Surviving the Paraphrase.* Winnipeg: Turnstone, 1983.

Defoe, Daniel. *Robinson Crusoe.* 1719. New York: Washington Square, 1963.

Ernst, Jutta. "Modernism in the United States and Canada." *The Palgrave Handbook of Comparative North American Literature.* Ed. Reingard M. Nischik. New York: Palgrave Macmillan, 2014.. 257-76.

Freitag, Florian. "Regionalism in American and Canadian Literature." *The Palgrave Handbook of Comparative North American Literature.* Ed. Reingard M. Nischik. New York: Palgrave Macmillan, 2014. 199-218.

Frye, Northrop. *Anatomy of Criticism: Four Essays.* 1957. New York: Atheneum, 1968.

Gibbon, John Murray. *Canadian Mosaic: The Making of a Northern Nation.* Toronto: McClelland, 1938.

Hutcheon, Linda. *The Canadian Postmodern: A Study of Contemporary English-Canadian Fiction.* Toronto: Oxford UP, 1988.

Kirtz, Mary. "Inhabiting the Dangerous Middle of the Space Between: An Intramodernist Reading of Robert Kroetsch's *Gone Indian.*" *The Great Plains Quarterly* 14.3 (1996): 207–217.

Kroetsch, Robert. *The Man from the Creeks.* Toronto: Random House, 1998.

Laferrière, Dany. *How to Make Love to a Negro Without Getting Tired.* Trans. David Homel. Vancouver: Douglas & McIntyre, 2010.

Laurence, Margaret. *The Diviners.* 1974. Toronto: McClelland, 1993.

Lecker, Robert. "The Canonization of Canadian Literature: An Inquiry into Values." *Critical Inquiry* 16.3 (Spring 1990): 656–71.

Lee, Hermione. *Writers in Conversation: Margaret Atwood.* ICA/Anthony Roland Collection of Film on Art, 198? [sic]. Video.

London, Jack. "To Build a Fire." *Literature: An Introduction to Fiction, Poetry, Drama, and Writing.* Ed. X. J. Kennedy & Dana Gioia. 11th ed. New York: Longman, 2010. 114–124.

MacLeod, Alistair. *Island: The Collected Stories.* Toronto: McClelland, 2000.

Matthews, Lawrence. "Calgary, Canonization, and Class: Deciphering List B." *Canadian Canons: Essays in Literary Value.* Ed. Robert Lecker. Toronto: U of Toronto P, 1991.

Munro, Alice. *Lives of Girls and Women.* 1971. Winnipeg: New American Library of Canada, 1974.

Nischik, Reingard M. "Comparative North American Studies and Its Contexts: Introduction." *The Palgrave Handbook of Comparative North American Literature.* Ed. Reingard M. Nischik. New York: Palgrave Macmillan, 2014. 3-31.

Porter, John. *The Vertical Mosaic: An Analysis of Social Class and Power in Canada,* Toronto: U of Toronto P, 1965.

Thien, Madeleine. *Simple Recipes.* Toronto: McClelland, 2001.

Thomas, Audrey. *Intertidal Life.* Toronto: General Publishing, 1984.

Vallee, Frank G. "Vertical Mosaic." *The Canadian Encyclopedia. Historica Canada,* 16 Dec. 2013. Web. 26 June 2014. <http://www.thecanadianencyclopedia.ca/en/article/vertical-mosaic/>.

van Herk, Aritha. *Restlessness.* Red Deer, Alberta: Red Deer College Press, 1998.

A Literary, Sociocultural, and Political Timeline for Canada and the United States, 1960–2013____

Rita Ross

The past five decades have seen momentous and lasting changes in Canada and the United States. This timeline lists the works discussed in this book as well as some other important literary publications of the period. The timeline also presents a brief overview of some of the political and sociocultural events that occurred while the books covered in this volume were being written and read. For the most part, the events listed are self-explanatory, although some are elaborated with additional background in the Notes.

Some important changes occurring over the past decades are not easy to pin down to a particular date, and some occurred over a longer period of time. Here are some of the trends that have most impacted Canada and the United States. Some of these have followed a similar path in Canada and the United States, while other cases underline crucial differences between the two countries.

- **Struggles for rights and empowerment** by groups formerly victimized or excluded. The aims and activism of each of these groups often affected the others.

  - Women's groups became active on a number of fronts, including abortion rights, advocacy for the Equal Rights Amendment (in the United States), and increased participation in the political process and office-seeking.
  - Racial and ethnic minorities saw momentous changes. In the United States, the "Civil Rights" struggle began with African-Americans in the US and spread to other minority groups. The US movement was paralleled by activism in Québec, which has had a profound effect on constitutional debates in Canada.
  - A youth counterculture movement beginning in the 1960s transformed young peoples' perception of

themselves and their relationship with their parents and with the greater society. Young, often college-age, people marched against the Vietnam War and for civil rights and used new modes of dress and musical preference to distance themselves from older generations.

○ Indigenous groups, usually referred to as "Native Americans" or "Indians" in the United States and as "First Nations" in Canada, began legal activism and worked for the beginnings of international solidarity across borders.

○ Homosexual rights, sexual and gender liberation, and the right of personal sex/gender self-identification became increasingly important in both countries. The struggle was broadened to encompass "LGTB" (Lesbian-Gay-Transsexual-Bisexual) and "queer" categories.

• **Environment.** Awareness and activism about the environment and dangers posed to it grew, as citizens and politicians both grappled with deforestation, species loss, air pollution, water shortages, and climate change. Energy and the economy are factors closely intertwined with environmental issues. In Canada and the United States both, these concerns often focus on the Arctic.

• **Energy** issues, such as availability and security, as well as effects on the environment and transition to renewable sources, such as solar and wind energy, have become increasingly complex. The Athabasca "Oil Sands" or "Tar Sands" in Alberta and the proposed Keystone XL Pipeline are sources of tension between Canada and the United States.

• **Globalization.** Increasing economic interdependence and the globalization of capital and labor have led to both the possibility of increased prosperity as well as to worldwide recessions that can threaten international stability. Canada and the US have both seen an increase in income inequality.

- **Health care** is an area of major difference between Canada and the United States. In Canada, the universal, one-payer system is extremely popular; in the United States, fears of "socialism" have resulted in resistance to government-sponsored health care systems.

- **Immigration** and paths to citizenship are perceived and handled differently in the two countries. Canada needs immigration and actively encourages it. The United States has a large illegal immigration problem that has become politically divisive.

- **Wars** and military actions, declared and undeclared, have resulted in cooperation between the two countries in some cases and conflict in others: Canada supported the Gulf War following Iraq's invasion of Kuwait and the war in Afghanistan, but refused to participate in the Iraq invasion of 2003. The "War on Terror," heightened by the September 11, 2001, attacks on the United States, has led to increasing concerns about security and accompanying issues of privacy.

- **Communication technology** has radically changed the way we exchange and receive information. Personal computers, email, the Internet, cable television, and cell (mobile) phones have transformed the world as it was in the 1960s.

The Timeline

Year	Canada	United States
1960	• Prime Minister (PM) John Diefenbaker, Progressive Conservative (1957–1963) • Canadian Bill of Rights (largely superseded by Charter of Rights and Freedoms, 1982) • Jean Lesage elected premier of Québec; "Quiet Revolution" begins[1] • Canada does not participate in Vietnam war; officially "non-belligerent"	• President Dwight Eisenhower, Republican (1953–1961) • Increased involvement by US in Vietnam (war ended in 1975)
1961	• Governor General's Award for Fiction (French language) to Yves Thériault for *Ashini* • The Office québécois de la langue française (Québec Board of the French Language) created to protect the French language in Québec	• President John Kennedy, Democrat (1961–1963) • "Freedom Riders" against racial segregation and oppression in the South

1962		• Nobel Prize in Literature to John Steinbeck • *Silent Spring* by Rachel Carson, an early inspiration for the environmental movement
1963	• PM Lester Pearson, Liberal (1963–1968)	• Betty Friedan, *The Feminine Mystique.* Beginning of "second-wave" feminist movement • March on Washington for Jobs and Freedom; Martin Luther King, Jr.'s "I Have a Dream" speech • President Kennedy assassinated • President Lyndon Johnson, Democrat (1963–1969)
1964	• Beatles' first North American tour includes shows in Vancouver, Montreal, and Toronto	• Beatles' first North American tour • Civil Rights Act • Free Speech Movement at UC Berkeley • New York World's Fair

1965	• Carl F. Klinck, ed., *A Literary History of Canada* • The "Maple Leaf" adopted as the official national flag of Canada • Auto Pact between Canada and the US, tightly integrating automobile manufacturing • Canada increasingly becomes haven for war resisters from the US, including draft evaders and deserters	• Voting Rights Act • Immigration Reform Act creates modern immigration system • Auto Pact between Canada and the US, tightly integrating automobile manufacturing
1966	• Governor General's Award for Fiction to Margaret Laurence for *A Jest of God* • Prix Médicis to Marie-Claire *Blais for Une saison dans la vie d'Emmanuel (A Season in the Life of Emmanuel)* • Medical Care Act: beginning of near-universal health care	• Founding of NOW: National Organization for Women

1967	• Governor General's Award for Fiction (French language) to Jacques Godbout for *Salut Galarneau!* (translated into English as *Hail Galarneau!*) • Canadian Centennial celebrations • Expo 67, World's Fair in Montreal • Commercial oil production begins in the Athabasca Oil Sands (aka "Tar Sands")[2]	• "Summer of Love," youth counterculture gathering centered in San Francisco, but also happening elsewhere (including Canada)
1968	• Governor General's Award for Fiction to Alice Munro for Dance of the Happy Shades • Governor General's Award for Fiction (French language) to Marie-Claire *Blais* for *Manuscrits de Pauline Archange* and Hubert Aquin for *Trou de mémoire* Michel Tremblay, *Les Belles-Sœurs* (English "The Sisters In-Law"), play	• American Indian Movement (AIM) founded • Democratic National Convention riot • Assassinations of Robert F. Kennedy and Martin Luther King, Jr.

1969	• Governor General's Award for Fiction to Robert Kroetsch for *The Studhorse* Man • Final report of the Royal Commission on Bilingualism and Biculturalism[3] • Official Languages Act, following on Royal Commission report, gave equal status to French and English in Canada	• Kate Millett, *Sexual Politics*, landmark work of feminist literary criticism • President Richard Nixon, Republican (1969–1974) • American Indian Movement activists occupy Alcatraz Island in San Francisco Bay
1970	• PM Pierre Trudeau, Liberal (1968–1979) • October Crisis[4]	• National Book Award for Fiction to Joyce Carol Oates, *them* • Shootings of Vietnam War protesters at Kent State University, Ohio, by National Guard • First Earth Day, often considered beginning of modern environmental movement
1971	• Northrop Frye, *The Bush Garden: Essays on the Canadian Imagination*	

1972	• Margaret Atwood, *Survival: A Thematic Guide to Canadian Literature* • Governor General's Award for Fiction to Robertson Davies for *The Manticore* • Governor General's Award for Fiction (French language) to Antonine Maillet (Acadian author) for *Don l'Orignal*	• ERA (Equal Rights Amendment for women), first introduced in 1923, passes both houses of Congress and goes to states for ratification (thirty-eight states needed)
1973	• Governor General's Award for Fiction (French language) to Réjean Ducharme for *L'hiver de force* • Arab oil embargo	• Arab oil embargo • Wounded Knee occupation[5] • Roe v. Wade, a Supreme Court decision legalizing abortion

1974	• Governor General's Award for Fiction to Margaret Laurence for *The Diviners* • *The Fourth World: an Indian Reality*, an early manifesto about Aboriginal rights, by First Nations leader George Manuel • The World Council of Indigenous Peoples (WCIP), under the leadership of George Manuel, formed in Canada; dissolved in 1996	• National Book Award for Fiction to Thomas Pynchon, *Gravity's Rainbow* • President Nixon resigns in wake of Watergate scandal • President Gerald Ford, Republican (1974–1977) • The World Council of Indigenous Peoples (WCIP), formed in Canada; US represented; dissolved in 1996
1975	• Governor General's Award for Fiction (French language) to Anne Hébert, *Les enfants du sabbat*	
1976	• Margaret Atwood, *Lady Oracle* • Governor General's Award for Fiction to Marian Engel for *Bear* • Parti Québécois elected to government for first time[6]	• Nobel Prize Literature to Saul Bellow (born in Canada)

1977	• Governor General's Award for Fiction to Timothy Findley for The Wars • Governor General's Award for Fiction (French language) to Gabrielle Roy, *Ces enfants de ma vie* • Controversial Bill 101 in Quebec[7]	• President Jimmy Carter, Democrat (1977–1981)
1978	• Governor General's Award for Fiction to Alice Munro for *Who Do You Think You Are?*	• Nobel Prize for Literature to Isaac Bashevis Singer (born in then Russian Empire, now Poland)
1979	• Prix Goncourt (French literary prize) to Antonine Maillet (Acadian author) for *Pélagie-la-Charrette*. First recipient outside Europe. • PM Joe Clark, Progressive Conservative (1979–1980)	• Three Mile Island Nuclear Reactor Accident

1980	• PM Pierre Trudeau, Liberal (1980–1984 • Quebec Referendum[8]	• Nobel Prize for Literature to Czesław Miłosz, (born in then Russian Empire, now Lithuania) • National Book Award for Fiction to John Irving for *The World According to Garp* • Pulitzer Prize for Fiction to Norman Mailer for *The Executioner's Song*
1981	• Governor General's Award for Fiction to Mavis Gallant for *Home Truths: Selected Canadian Stories* • UN Convention on acid rain takes effect	• President Ronald Reagan, Republican (1981–1989) • UN Convention on acid rain takes effect • Reagan administration decertifies PATCO (Professional Air Traffic Controllers Organization) and breaks the union following a strike
1982	• Prix Femina to Anne Hébert for *Les fous de Bassan* • Constitution Act, "patriating" the Canadian Constitution; includes Canadian Charter of Rights and Freedoms[9]	• ERA (Equal Rights Amendment) fails state ratification by deadline • Centers for Disease Control names new disease "AIDS": Acquired Immune Deficiency Syndrome

1983		• National Book Award for Fiction to Alice Walker for *The Color Purple*
1984	• PM John Turner, Liberal (June 1984–Septemer 1984) • PM Brian Mulroney, Progressive Conservative (1984–1993) • Canada Health Act	• First woman (Geraldine Ferraro) nominated on a major party ticket (as Democratic vice-presidential candidate)
1985	• Governor General's Award for Fiction to Margaret Atwood for *The Handmaid's Tale* • Dany Laferrière, *How to Make Love to a Negro without Getting Tired* • Publication of first volume of *Selected Journals of L.M. Montgomery*	• National Book Award for Fiction to Don DeLillo for *White Noise*
1986	• Governor General's Award for Fiction to Alice Munro, *The Progress of Love* • Expo 86, World's Fair in Vancouver	• National Book Award for Fiction to E. L. Doctorow for *World's Fair*

1987	• Michael Ondaatje, *In the Skin of a Lion* • Governor General's Award for Fiction (French language) to Gilles Archambault for *L'obsédante obèse et autres aggressions* • Meech Lake Accord, failed[10] • Free Trade Agreement (FTA) between Canada and the US	• Nobel Prize for Literature to Joseph Brodsky (born in Russia) • Free Trade Agreement (FTA) between Canada and the US
1988		• Pulitzer Prize for Fiction to Toni Morrison for *Beloved*
1989		• President George H. W. Bush, Republican (1989–1993)
1990	• Jane Urquhart, *Changing Heaven* • Oka Crisis[11] • First Earth Day Canada	
1991	• Canada participates in First Gulf War • US–Canada Air Quality Agreement • Collapse of Soviet Union, end of Cold War	• First Gulf War, against Iraq after its invasion of Kuwait • US-Canada Air Quality Agreement • Collapse of Soviet Union, end of Cold War

1992	• Governor General's Award for Fiction to Michael Ondaatje for *The English Patient* • Man Booker Prize to Michael Ondaatje for *The English Patient* • Gays, lesbians, and bisexuals allowed to serve openly in Canadian Armed Forces • Charlottetown Accord, failed[12]	• National Book Award for Fiction to Cormac McCarthy for *All the Pretty Horses*
1993	• Governor General's Award for Fiction to Carol Shields for *The Stone Diaries* • Mavis Gallant, *Across the Bridge* • PM Kim Campbell, Progressive Conservative (Jun 1993–Nov 1993), first woman PM • PM Jean Chrétien, Liberal (1993–2003)	• Nobel Prize in Literature to Toni Morrison • President Bill Clinton, Democrat (1993–2001)

1994	• North American Free Trade Agreement (NAFTA) among Canada, the US, and Mexico • Alice Munro, *Open Secrets*	• North American Free Trade Agreement (NAFTA) among Canada, the US, and Mexico • "Don't Ask, Don't Tell" policy regarding gays in US Armed Forces; in effect until 2011
1995	• Pulitzer Prize for Fiction to Carol Shields for *The Stone Diaries* • Québec Referendum[13]	
1996	• Ottawa Declaration establishes the Arctic Council, with Canada, the US, and six other Arctic nations[14]	• Ottawa Declaration forms the Arctic Council, with Canada, the US, and six other Arctic nations[14]
1997	• Governor General's Award for Fiction to Jane Urquhart for *The Underpainter* • Carol Shields, *Larry's Party* • Canada proposes Ottawa Treaty to ban landmines; 161 signatories	• US does not sign Ottawa Treaty
1998	• Aritha van Herk, *Restlessness* • Robert Kroetsch, *The Man from the Creeks*	

1999	• Alistair McLeod, *No Great Mischief* • Governor General's Award for the Performing Arts to Michel Tremblay, Québec playwright • Creation of third Canadian territory, Nunavut, formerly part of Northwest Territories[15]	• Impeachment trial of President Clinton, resulting in acquittal
2000	• Alistair McLeod, *Island*	
2001	• Madeleine Thien, *Simple Recipes* • "Operation Yellow Ribbon" on 9/11: 255 aircraft due to land at US airports diverted to seventeen different airports across Canada • Canada participates in invasion of Afghanistan	• President George W. Bush, Republican (2001–2009) • September 11 ("9/11") terrorist attacks on US soil • Invasion of Afghanistan in response to 9/11
2002	• Immigration and Refugee Protection Act	
2003	• *Northrop Frye on Canada: Collected Works* • Canada refuses to participate in Iraq invasion • PM Paul Martin, Liberal (2003–2006)	• Iraq invasion begins
2004		

2005	• Civil Marriage Act, extending civil marriage rights to same-sex couples • Kelowna Accord with some First Nations; later cancelled by PM Harper	
2006	• Marie-Célie Agnant, *The Book of Emma* • Prix Femina to Nancy Huston for Fault Lines • PM Stephen Harper, Conservative (2006–incumbent) • Québec recognized as a "nation" within Canada by law, but not in the Constitution	
2007	• Governor General's Award for fiction to Michael Ondaatje, *Divisadero* • Official launch of WikiLeaks, a non-governmental, whistle-blowing organization; publication of many classified Canadian and US documents	• Pulitzer prize to Cormac McCarthy for *The Road* • Official launch of WikiLeaks, a non-governmental, whistle-blowing organization; publication of many classified Canadian and US documents
2008	• PM Stephen Harper makes Statement of Apology to former students of Indian Residential Schools on behalf of the Government of Canada[16]	

2009	• Man Booker International Prize to Alice Munro	• President Barack Obama, Democrat (2009–incumbent)
2010	• Jane Urquhart, *Sanctuary Line*	• Affordable Care Act ("Obamacare")
2011		• Man Booker International Prize to Philip Roth • Gays and lesbians allowed to serve openly in US armed forces • US troops withdrawn from Iraq
2012		• National Book Award for Fiction to Louise Erdrich for *The Round House*
2013	• Margaret Atwood, *MaddAddam* • Nobel Prize in Literature to Alice Munro, "master of the contemporary short story"	

Notes

1. **Quiet revolution.** Although French-speaking (francophone) Quebeckers had always been a majority in the province of Québec, at the beginning of the 1960s, their economic standing compared unfavorably to that of English speakers (anglophones), both in the province and elsewhere in Canada. They had long been under the strong influence of the Catholic Church and controlled few of the province's economic resources. The period of the Quiet Revolution (in French, "*révolution tranquille*") saw much progress in raising the level of economic and political participation of francophones in Québec, as well as a profound secularization of society. These changes led to even more sweeping changes, eventually leading to calls for sovereignty or separation from Canada (Fortin).

2. **Athabasca Oil Sands in Alberta.** Alberta has one of the largest untapped sources of crude oil in the world. Although people had been aware of this potential resource for years, extraction only began seriously in the late 1960s. The grade of crude oil, or bitumen, in the Oil Sands deposits, whose thick and tarry consistency has led to an alternate term, "Tar Sands," requires much more processing than lighter grades of crude oil in order to be useful and, therefore, creates more pollution and carbon releases. Energy companies and the governments of Alberta and Canada have met with fierce opposition to further development of the Oil Sands from environmental and some Aboriginal groups. The picture has recently become more complicated by the proposed Keystone XL Pipeline, which would bring Alberta oil to refineries in American Gulf of Mexico ports. As of mid-2014, the XL Pipeline issue was unresolved.

3. **Royal Commission on Bilingualism and Biculturalism.** In Canada the establishment of Royal Commissions is a common way to investigate pressing national problems. This one concluded "that French-speaking Canadians did not hold the economic and political place their numbers warranted. For example, in 1965, francophones in Québec made on average thirty-five percent less than anglophones, and over eighty percent of employers were anglophones. Representation within the federal bureaucracy and French-language services outside Québec were also a long-standing concern" (Hudon, Behiels, and Millette).

4. **October Crisis.** A group called the FLQ (*Front de Libération du Québec*, in English Quebec Liberation Front) formed with the aim

of pursuing the independence of Québec by all means available, including violence. In October 1970, they kidnapped two important government officials, one of whom was later found dead. Prime Minister Trudeau invoked the War Measures Act, which included the suspension of many civil liberties, in the only case of its use in Canada in peacetime. He also called in the Canadian Armed Forces. The FLQ was outlawed and hundreds of people were arrested. The incident remains controversial. For further details see Smith and Millette.

5. **Wounded Knee.** This site in South Dakota (where an infamous massacre by US government troops had taken place in 1890) was occupied in February 1973 by members of AIM (the American Indian Movement) and local Oglala Lakota (Sioux) activists. Their demands included action from the US government on treaties dating from the nineteenth and twentieth centuries. During a seventy-one-day siege, considerable violence and two deaths occurred. See Chertoff for a brief overview.

6. **Parti Québécois.** This Québec provincial political party, advocating increased political, economic, and social autonomy for Québec, was formed in 1968 and was elected to office for the first time in 1976. Over the years, it proposed numerous changes in language laws (see Note 7) and called for several referenda on Québec sovereignty.

7. **Bill 101.** Partly in response to the findings of the Royal Commission on Bilingualism and Biculturalism (see Note 3), a number of laws governing the use of the French language were passed in Québec. The most controversial of these is generally known as Bill 101 or Law 101, mandating the use of the French language in almost all contexts within Québec. Widespread resistance followed by English speakers, in particular a group known as the Alliance Québec (Quebec Alliance), formed to protect English language rights.

8. **Québec Referendum 1980.** The first of an important series of provincial referenda on the subject of Québec's relationship with the rest of Canada, sponsored by the Parti Québécois, was about "sovereignty association," which the Party supported. Sovereignty association is a vague term proposing greatly expanded sovereignty, or autonomy, for Québec, while at the same time retaining certain ties with Canada ("association"). The exact nature of that association has never been satisfactorily specified. It was defeated by about sixty percent of voters in the province.

9. **Patriation of the Constitution and Constitution Act of 1982.** The original Constitution Act of 1867, or British North America Act, established Canada's independence from Great Britain, but left amending power in the hands of the British Parliament. In 1982, the Canadian Constitution was "patriated," or put solely into the hands of the Canadian Parliament. Among other sections the Act includes the Charter of Rights and Freedoms, modelled after the US Bill of Rights (explicitly including equality on the basis of sex), and an Aboriginal rights clause. Negotiations leading to this Constitutional reform were importantly affected by the sovereignty movement in Québec, and Québec became the only province not to ratify it. The Meech Lake Accord (see Note 10) was an attempt to persuade Québec to ratify. For further details, see Snyder, and Sheppard and Azzi.

10. **Meech Lake Accord.** Although Québec was bound by the terms of the new Constitution, in 1981 the province rejected formal ratification. Attempts to bring Québec on board resulted in the so-called Meech Lake Accord, an agreement between the federal government and all ten of the provinces. It included amendments particularly desired by Québec, such as declaring Québec a "distinct society" and strengthening provincial powers. Although at first favored by the Canadian public, the "distinct society" clause became controversial and the agreement unraveled. Québec perceived the rejection of the Meech Lake agreement by the rest of the country as a rejection of Québec itself. As one historian has said, "Minorities forget less easily than majorities. A Quebec City commentator recalled that in his province 'the collapse of Meech was as close to an apocalyptic event as can be imagined in peacetime'" (Hillmer).

11. **Oka Crisis.** The Oka Crisis was a seventy-eight-day standoff between Mohawk protesters, Québec police, and the Canadian army. At the heart of the crisis was the proposed expansion of a golf course and development of condominiums on disputed land that included a Mohawk burial ground. A local police officer was killed and the situation was only resolved after the army was called in. The golf course expansion was cancelled, but the disputed land has not yet been transferred to the community.

12. **Charlottetown Accord.** This agreement was another attempt, following the failure of the earlier Meech Lake Accord (see Note 10) to amend the Constitution in a way that would satisfy the federal government and all the provinces, including Québec. After intensive

efforts, including input from Aboriginal peoples, the Charlottetown Accord was reached in 1992. The "Québec as a distinct society" clause was once again a source of dissension. For more details of what was included in an extensive constitutional reworking, see the discussion in Gall, et al. The Accord was put to a national referendum and was voted down.

13. **Québec Referendum 1995.** October 30, 1995, the date of the referendum on sovereignty held in Québec, has been called "the day when Canadians almost lost their country" (Hillman). The failures of the Meech Lake and Charlottetown Accords, and growing dissatisfaction in Québec over resistance to the "distinct society" concept by the rest of Canada, led to the return to power of the Parti Québécois. The Premier immediately announced that a provincial referendum would be held, with one question, in essence, "Do you agree that Québec should become sovereign?" The referendum campaign was emotional and the vote was incredibly close, with a winning percentage for the No side (the side against Québec sovereignty) of just a little over fifty percent. To date, the province of Québec has not ratified the 1982 Constitution Act. In 2006, however, Québec was recognized as a "nation within Canada" by legislative, rather than constitutional, means.

14. **The Arctic Council** was formed as "a high-level intergovernmental forum to provide a means for promoting cooperation, coordination and interaction among the Arctic States, with the involvement of the Arctic Indigenous communities and other Arctic inhabitants on common Arctic issues; in particular, issues of sustainable development and environmental protection in the Arctic" (*ArcticCouncil.org*) The Arctic Council's members are Canada (inaugural Chair), the United States, Finland, Iceland, Russian Federation, Norway, Denmark, and Sweden. The Chairmanship rotates every two years. The Council includes permanent representation from a number of Aboriginal organizations.

15. **Nunavut.** Nunavut is the newest territory in Canada. Besides the ten Canadian provinces (Newfoundland, Prince Edward Island, Nova Scotia, New Brunswick, Quebec, Ontario, Manitoba, Saskatchewan, Alberta, and British Columbia), there are now three territories: Yukon, Northwest Territories, and Nunavut. Over three-quarters of Nunavut's sparse population is Inuit and four official languages are

recognized: Inuktitut, Inuinnaqtun, English, and French (Craufurd-Lewis).

16. **Residential schools apology.** A deliberate policy of separating Aboriginal children from their families and sending them to sometimes distant residential schools run by religious groups was in effect for many years in Canada and the United States. The overt goal was to educate all Aboriginal children, but there was also an underlying agenda, that of encouraging loss of language, religion, and culture, and promoting or enforcing assimilation. This policy led to generations of disrupted families and communities, and the schools themselves were often sites of physical and sexual abuse. In 2008, Prime Minister Harper publicly apologized, recognizing the profound damage done to Aboriginal communities. The similar schools in the United States are referred to as Indian Boarding Schools; to date, no apology has come from the US government. For more on the residential schools in Canada and current projects for reconciliation, see the article by J. R. Miller and Tabitha Marshall.

Works Cited

Arctic-Council.org. Arctic Council Secretariat, Tromsø, Norway, n.d. Web. 29 June 2014.

Chertoff, Emily. "Occupy Wounded Knee: A 71-Day Siege and a Forgotten Civil Rights Movement." The Atlantic 23 Oct. 2012. Web. 29 June 2014.

Craufurd-Lewis, Michael. "Nunavut." Canadian Encyclopedia Online. 6 Aug. 2014. Web. 1 July 2014.

Fortin, Pierre "Quebec's Quiet Revolution, 50 years later." Inroads Journal 29: 90–99. Summer–Fall 2011. Web. 30 June 2014.

Gall, Gerald L., Gord Mcintosh, & Richard Foot. "Charlottetown Accord." Canadian Encyclopedia Online. 30 Jun. 2014. Web. 01 July 2014.

Hillmer, Norman. "Death of the Meech Lake Accord." Canadian Encyclopedia Online. 16 Dec. 2013. Web. 01 July 2014.

Hudon, R., & Dominique Millette. "Québec referendum, 1980." Canadian Encyclopedia Online. 9 Apr. 2014. Web. 28 June 2014.

_____, M. D. Behiels, & Dominique Millette. "Bill 101." Canadian Encyclopedia Online. 8 Aug. 2014. Web. 29 June 2014.

Miller, J.R., & Tabitha Marshall. "Residential Schools." Canadian Encylopedia Online. 2 Sept. 2014. Web. 28 June 2014.

Sheppard, Robert, & Stephen Azzi. "Patriation of the Constitution." Canadian Encylopedia Online. 16 Dec. 2013. Web. 01 July 2014.

Smith, Denis, & Dominique Millette. "October Crisis." Canadian Encylopedia Online. 27 Jan. 2014. Web. 27 June 2014.

Snyder, Tim. "Constitution Act, 1982." Canadian Encylopedia Online. 16 Dec. 2013. Web. 01 July 2014.

Learning How to Read in Atwood's *MaddAddam*___
Sharon R. Wilson

Margaret Atwood, winner of the Booker Prize for *The Handmaid's Tale* and *The Blind Assassin* and the Giller Prize and Premio Mondello for *Alias Grace,* is published in more than thirty-five countries and is the author of more than forty books of fiction, poetry, and essays. Some of her best-known volumes of poetry are *The Circle Game, Power Politics,* and *True Stories.* Recently, she has been writing speculative fiction, also referred to as dystopian (nightmarish) and ustopian (interconnected dystopian and utopian).

The third volume of Margaret Atwood's trilogy, *Oryx and Crake, The Year of the Flood,* and *MaddAddam,* not only teaches us how to read literature, but how to tell and write stories and, thus, to begin the process again. The title of the third volume is a palindrome, reading the same from the end as from the beginning, just as each book finishes with a new beginning, underlining the importance of cycle when we expect apocalypse. It's not literally the same beginning, nor can the trilogy actually begin with *MaddAddam,* as Debrah Raschke suggests, since Snowman-the-Jimmy, and possibly Toby and Zeb, die in the third volume. The three books are what Atwood has termed "simultane-quels" rather than sequels to one another, with events overlapping and often occurring simultaneously. In *Oryx and Crake*, Jimmy tells us the story of how Crake and Oryx created numerous hybrid species, such as Wolvogs, Rakunks, Liobams, Pigoons and Crakers, to replace the human beings he exterminated, but it is unlikely that, by the end of *MaddAddam,* Pigoons are approaching full "personhood," as Canavan implies. In *The Year of the Flood,* Toby and Ren take over as main narrators when Snowman-the-Jimmy is immobilized with illness. In *MaddAddam,* with help from Zeb, Toby trains the Craker Blackbeard to tell and write stories, and he teaches Jimadam, Pilaren, Medulla, Oblongata, and probably other Crakers, who may have altered what we've read, to hear the voices in the written word.

Although some readers think the trilogy is about America's colossal ignorance and egotism that will cause apocalypse, the locations are not exclusively in the United States. Santa Monica, Seattle, Jersey, and New York are mentioned, but other settings just in *MaddAddam* are Mexico, Columbia, Whitehorse, and Calgary; and the university and Beaches areas of Toronto seem suggested. The point is that whatever disaster Atwood seems to predict is global and not limited to particular geographies. The Paradice Dome is an eggshell "half-eye," conceivable anyplace that is breakable and lacks vision. The reviews of *MaddAddam* are excellent, but as *Kirkus* puts it, *MaddAddam* is "by no means her finest work" (400).

The stories are of various kinds, recalling the evolution from oral tradition of myths, folklore, fairy tales, religion, sermons, oral history, history, and fiction with closely related jokes, songs, and other performances. Toby has to follow the ritual of eating a fish, wearing the red hat, listening to the broken watch, and requesting constantly that the Crakers do not sing because, not only is it distracting, but singing is close to, even a part of, a different story. The often parodic hymns of God's Gardeners in *The Year of the Flood* illustrate this (Wilson 347–49). Earlier volumes use creation, flood, biblical and other myths, vegetable folklore, Craker lore, the stories of Frankenstein, Faust, Bluebeard, and a number of other fairy tales about Jimmy (Wilson 335–47). *MaddAddam* alludes to fairy tales and popular culture, such as Jimmy's nursery rhyme pictures on his quilt (151), Zeb as the ogre with treasure (127), Zeb as the hundred-eyed giant Argus (184), as Smokey the Bear (294), and as the Wizard of Oz without a yellow brick road or an Emerald City (78). Annalee Newitz says the book, a blend of satiric futurism and magic realism, "almost resemble[s]" a fairy tale ("Atwood Imagines").

As *MaddAddam* begins with an overview of the chapter similar to those in eighteenth- and nineteenth-century literature, Toby tells the Crakers the story of creation as she imagines it, somewhat differently from the way Jimmy or Genesis envisaged it. Like the Talese/Doubleday cover, the story is about the hand-imprinted Egg in which Crake made the Crakers, edible food, and rain. It is in a nest and surrounded by chaos and people with "two" skins, some of whom are "bad" to animals and people (Atwood, *MaddAddam* 3–5). In *Oryx and Crake,* however, Jimmy uses less detail: "In the beginning, there was chaos." When the Crakers request pictures, Jimmy stirs dirt and water with a stick in an orange plastic pail to show chaos. By pouring the water of chaos away, he does the Great Rearrangement and makes the Great Emptiness (Atwood, *Oryx and Crake* 102–03). In both cases, evil is combatted and peace created.

Patrocinio Schweikart's Reader-Response theory is useful for investigating how Toby teaches Blackbeard to read and write and her larger audience, including readers of the books, to listen, read, tell stories, write them, and ultimately read and write ourselves. In "Reading Ourselves: Toward a Feminist Theory of Reading," Schweikart insists that we cannot overlook differences of race, class, and gender (122). By implication, we could assume that age, religion, nationality, and even species are also important. Reading is dualistic: "Reading becomes a mediation between author and reader, between the context of writings and the context of reading" and this occurs in a reading community. "To read a text and then to write about it is to seek to connect not only with the author of the original text, but also with a community of readers" (Schweikart 133, 135, 137). As Stanley Fish, another Reader-Response critic, says, "the production of the meaning of a text depends upon the interpretative strategy one applies to it, and the choice of strategy is regulated (explicitly or implicitly) by the canons of acceptability that govern the interpretative community" (Schweikart 133). Jimmy, Toby, Ren, Zeb, and then Blackbeard do speak to a community of readers and thus establish community even beginning to include Pigoons, the large pigs with human genes implanted in their brains. Unlike the patriarchal canons assumed to exist in the human world outside the trilogy, however, the characters in this novel seem to begin reading and writing in a fresh new world. Jimmy in *Oryx and Crake* recalls fragments of colonial and androcentric (male-centered) texts, but we do not see the characters in this community reading or writing such texts. In complex texts such as Atwood's, narrators also interact with the author and readers in the community.

In addition to myths, Toby's stories communicate basic information about what is going on in the cobb house and with Zeb, and she attempts to answer the many questions the Crakers have about the meaning of words and of existence. Because she has used the word *fuck,* she must tell the story of Zeb and Fuck. Fuck is explained as an invisible friend and helper (Atwood, *MaddAddam* 164–65). In other cases, such as with the phrase "suck it up" or the smelly bone, she manages to shift the story to another time, and she doesn't necessarily tell all the stories she thinks or discovers. Her old journals left in AnooYou are "whispers from the past" (Atwood, *MaddAddam* 282–83). Toby makes up part of "The Story of Zeb and the Snake Women" in her head to have it ready for the Crakers (Atwood, *MaddAddam* 256–57), since Zeb is in the middle of his story about Zeb. Even though she leaves out the death of Chuck, the Crakers cry as Toby tells them "The Story of Zeb and the Bear," when Zeb eats the bear. There's the story, the real story, the story of how it came to be told, and what you leave out, which is part of the story, too (Atwood, *MaddAddam* 56). As in the fairy tales "The Three Snake Leaves" and "The White Snake," about eating snake leaves or a snake, which bestows knowledge and regeneration (Grimm 95, 98), Zeb wonders whether, after eating the bear's heart, he would now be able to speak the language of animals (Atwood, *MaddAddam* 81). But apparently, he and the other humans are not yet able to do so. "The Story of Zeb and Thank You and Good Night" explains the death of the bear, fish, and all living beings, why Zeb thanked the bear, and Toby thanks the Crakers, and that she needs to go to bed. Aware that "she skirts the darker and more tangled corners of reality" (Atwood, *MaddAddam* 105), Toby strives to invent and transform rather than to lie. "The Story of the Birth of Zeb" reveals that, like the Crakers, he was born from a bone cave and his mother was secretly buried under the rock garden. "The Story of Zeb and the Snake Women" states the general principle that stories need not be directed and that important matters may come into stories non-chronologically.

Although Toby is uncertain that readers will exist in the future, she believes in the value of stories such as Pilar's folklore about an afterlife: "however dark, a darkness with voices in it is better than a silent void" (Atwood, *MaddAddam* 154). She teaches Blackbeard that he needs to be the voice of the writing: "*Reading* is when you turn these marks back into sounds." Although she worries that she and Zeb may be only a footnote and that rules and laws may follow for the Crakers, she decides to "take what the moment offers" (Atwood, *MaddAddam* 202–4). "The Story of the Two Eggs and Thinking" continues to clear away the chaos for the Great Rearrangement and Great Emptiness. In the story, Oryx, in the form of an owl, laid two small eggs inside the giant one, one full of animals and birds and fish and insects and the other full of words, some of which the Crakers and Pigoons ate. Oryx made singing for the Crakers. Because people in the chaos could not learn, if they killed the earth, including trees, flowers, animals, and fish, there would be nothing, not even people. Rather than giving people yet another chance, Crake made tasty little seeds and scattered them over the earth, causing nearly everyone but the Crakers to die.

Because Toby is too upset to tell "The Story of the Battle," Blackbeard puts on the Red Sox hat, which speaks its name, puts the fish briefly in his mouth until he gets sick, and, adding the names of Gardeners' festivals and positions of the moon, tells the story as Toby's helper. He wore shoes with wings and a light into the egg structure of the Paradice Complex, protecting him from danger as he symbolically returned to the beginning of the creation story. Initially, when he sees the dead bodies of Oryx and Crake, he insists they should be beautiful, as in the stories, and that the egg should be for making, not for killing. But Blackbeard realizes that the bodies are only husks, as the egg is only eggshell, so the stories supersede and are truer than "reality" (Atwood, *MaddAddam* 360). After Jimmy, Adam, and a Pigoon are killed in the battle, the community engages in "interspecies cooperation," including Craker singing, for the funeral. The book ends with "Book," the complete story that Toby made so that the end self-reflexively includes the beginning, creating the worm ouroboros design of a snake with its tail in its mouth.

Schweigart poses several questions relevant to our reading of *MaddAddam*. Strangely, she does not consider narrators, which in any of Atwood's books make a tremendous difference in the reading experience. Toby, Zeb, and Blackbeard are very different humanids, with different life experiences and are, thus, different narrators. To oversimplify, Toby is generally a considerate person who cares about others. Her judgment is impaired when Zeb is around. Zeb is macho, swears, and enjoys making Toby jealous. Blackbeard, ironically named after a bloodthirsty pirate, is a Craker child, the first to learn reading, writing, and telling stories. If the other readers who are learning to write—Jimaden, Pilaren, Medulla, and Oblongata—change the manuscript, as *The Handmaid's Tale* may have been altered by one or two narrators, the text begins to disappear as a tangible entity, much as many Reader-Response critics suggest is always the case since, to varying degrees, the reader creates the text. Thus, the text, *MaddAddam,* is in process and changes as we read. Atwood's epilogue to *The Handmaid's Tale* and the passages in *MaddAddam* about other readers and writers make readers aware of Atwood's knowledge of Reader-Response theory and thus affect this novel as we read. Blackbeard has already written down Toby's instructions for making ink, for taking care of the manuscript, and what has happened since Toby left. He has his own pen, pencil, and book: "This is my voice, the voice of Blackbeard that you are hearing in your head. That is called *reading.* And this is my own book, a new one for my writing and not the writing of Toby" (Atwood, *MaddAddam* 378). The new readers/writers will continue, constructing different stories and identities.

An important question raised by Schweigart is "What does it mean for a woman, reading as a woman, to read literature written by a woman writing as a woman?" (133). Although we could debate whether Atwood is writing as a woman and whether her texts are ever feminist, it seems pointless to examine the other alternatives. Dating the usefulness of her theory, Schweigart seems to forget that male readers can also be feminist. Her discussion of feminist readers and texts is still apt in raising the question of whether this text, which seemingly silences female Crakers, can be feminist. Some readers get the impression that the comic handling of the Crakers' rape of Amanda and Ren implies the approval of "Atwood" or the text. Not overly concerned, Toby, who may have been considered a reliable narrator in *The Year*, understates the incident by referring to it as a cultural misunderstanding, even though she is unsure whether Crakers have a culture. She tells the male Crakers that they have to ask permission in future, which they do. We never hear, however, what the female Crakers—who have, of course, grown up with singularly biological inducements for sex—think of the tradition of blue sex organs or suitors' bowing and presenting flowers followed by intercourse, which appears to be a male's idea of a courting ritual that males think females might like. What female Crakers think of this ritual is not expressed and not a topic of a *MaddAddam* story. Since writers imagine characters of different sexes and even species than themselves, however, Atwood—and we—might prefer to investigate the writing and reading of a human or humanid reader reading and writing as a humanid.

Of course, without the plot detail of the Crakers raping the women who have just been raped by Painballers, the cross-species breeding that insures the continuation of both humans and Crakers, leading to the "happy ending"[1] some readers create, would seem less likely. This is where we must recognize that ignoring the difference between narrators and authors is fatal to the reading experience. Like most postmodern authors, Atwood does not speak her thoughts through narrators and leaves moral decisions to readers. Rather than assuming that Atwood favors rape or does not find it objectionable, we can recognize that her narrator Toby, in love and obsessed with Zeb's faithfulness, is somewhat unreliable. As is usual in Atwood texts, Atwood tends to satirize "true love" ("True Romance," *True Stories;* "True Trash," *Wilderness Tips*), which sometimes blinds characters and, in this case, shows Toby's insecurity. Similarly, Zeb's shocking murder of Adam's father reveals how deeply he has been marked by childhood abuse and how he, too, is unreliable. As a child, Blackbeard is, by definition, unreliable, but since he seems sincere in wanting to be a good reader and writer and will be fathering a child soon, he is becoming more reliable. But do unreliable narrators explain why we never hear any real opinion from female Crakers and why Atwood seems to present the same events—Amanda and Ren's rapes—both tragically and comically?

In reference to *The Year of the Flood,* Carol Osbourne speaks of the "dynamic tension" Atwood maintains between opposite ideas at the same time (30–42), and the same technique recurs in *MaddAddam* and many postmodern novels, which are typically non-resolved, questioning even their own hierarchies of dominance. Toby admits that she cannot remember the Crakers' names, and this means that we readers have trouble as well. The fact that female Crakers are not particularly individualized in *MaddAddam* does not necessarily mean that they are silenced. At least one of the hybrid children learning the reading/writing process is female, and we do not know the sex of all the hybrids. If they are not named after famous humans, their names may be gender neutral. Feminists distinguish between sexual difference and gender roles. Roles are performed by the different sexes exaggerating sexual differences, as in differentiating clothing, jobs, behavior, hair styles, and family roles. Rather than being biological, these differences are social and may vary from culture to culture (see Humm). Nor do we know much about gender roles of the Crakers, who seem to have none, perhaps boding well for the future: they have few household duties, since they live outside; do not wear clothes; and do not cook food. Instead of once spending time and money on porno and glamour at places like Scales and Tails and AnooYoo, both males and females heal and heal others by purring.

Although they are exposed to human gender roles and biases, there is little evidence that Crakers are influenced by these roles or that they are beginning to feel the jealousy and anger that Crake genetically attempted to eradicate in sexual relationships. As far as we know, the hybrid and human children are exposed to egalitarian parental roles as Crozier, Manatee, Shackelton, Ivory Bill, and the Crakers offer help. With Zeb and Toby gone from the group, perhaps the other humans will be able to begin again, with less jealousy. Crakers are not, of course, human beings, and a hybrid society is just beginning, so we cannot determine the likelihood of a feminist

Craker society or even the likelihood of a continuing mixed humanid one. Nevertheless, Reader and Feminist theories offer some useful perspectives. According to the feminist Hélène Cixous, the originator of *L'Ecriture Feminine* (writing through the body), both women and men must write, and they must write through their bodies: "I write woman: woman must write woman. And man, man" (348). Rather than being silenced by male-dominated or other castrating traditions and fearing Freud's emphasis on what females "lack," we must invent language that will wreck codes (Cixous 355) and teach us to write and read and write again.

Perhaps the most important technique of reading we can learn from *MaddAddam* and the trilogy is the significance of the multiplicity of voices, of who tells the story at a particular moment, of what that narrator's biases, short-sightedness, and fallibilities may be, of how the views reflect, refract, and even contradict one another, and of how that affects our construction of the story and of ourselves. Ironically, the trilogy's apocalypse began largely because technology forgot human issues; science people outnumbered and overcame "word" people, and violence ensued. All three novels end on the beach[2] as they began, with singing and the beginning of a cycle: *Oryx* and *The Year* with new moons and *MaddAddam* with a full moon, as well as childbirth and Blackbeard's story of Toby. Whatever else we may worry about, words and stories remain and promise to structure the blended Craker—Pigoon—Human society.

Notes

1. See McEuen, Seaman, Heer. On the other hand, Sean Andrew Greer of the *New York Times* and James Kidd from *The Independent* think that *MaddAddam* does not hold much hope for human survival.

2. Carol Beran thinks that Atwood may be referring to Nevil Shute's *On The Beach* in these scenes (email to author).

Works Cited

Atwood, Margaret. *MaddAddam: A Novel.* New York: Nan A. Talese/ Doubleday, 2013.

_____. *Oryx and Crake: A Novel.* New York: Nan A. Talese/Doubleday, 2003.

_____. *The Year of the Flood.* New York: Nan A. Talese/Doubleday, 2009.

_____. *True Stories.* Poems. New York: Simon & Schuster, 1981.

_____. "True Trash." *Wilderness Tips.* Toronto: McClelland and Stewart, 1991.

Beran, Carol. Email to author. 29 February 2014.

Canavan, Gerry. "Roundtable on Atwood's Trilogy." *Margaret Atwood Society Session.* MLA.

Chicago, Marriott Hotel. Jan. 2014. Paper.

Cixous, Helene. "The Laugh of the Medusa." *Feminisms: An Anthology of Literary Theory and Criticism.* Ed. Robyn R. Warhol & Diane Price Herndl. Rev. ed. New Brunswick: Rutgers UP, 1997.

Greer, Andrew Sean. "Review of *MaddAddam,* by Margaret Atwood." *New York Times.*

6 Sept. 2013. n.p. Web. 17 Jan. 2014.

Grimms, Brothers. "The Three Snake-Leaves." *The Complete Grimm's Fairy Tales.* Ed. James Stern. Trans. Margaret Hunt. New York: Pantheon, 1972. 94–97.

_____. "The White Snake." *The Complete Grimm's Fairy Tales.* Ed. James Stern. Trans. Margaret Hunt. New York: Pantheon, 1972. 98–101.

Heer, Jeet. "Mirth Found in Apocalypse; Atwood's Vinegary Wit Helps Drive the Plot in Enjoyable MaddAddam." *Edmunton Journal.* 6 Sept. 2013, C11. Web. 24 Feb. 2014.

Humm, Maggie. "Glossary." *Modern Feminisms: Political, Literary, Cultural.* Gender and Culture Series. Ed. Carolyn G. Heilbrun & Nancy K. Miller. New York: Columbia UP, 1992.

Kidd, James. "Review: *MaddAddam*, By Margaret Atwood." *The Independent*, 10 Aug. 2013. Web. 20 Sept. 2014.

McEuan, Paul L. "Science Fiction: A Post-pandemic Wilderness." *Nature.* 500 (22 Aug. 2013): 1–3. Web. 18 Jan. 2014.

Newitz, Annalee. "Atwood Imagines Humanity's Next Iteration in *MaddAddam.*" *NPR Books,* 13 Sept. 2013. Web. 17 Jan. 2014. <http://www.npr.org/2013/09/9/13/215749337/atwood-imagines-humanitys-next-iteration-in-maddaddam./>

Osborne, Carol. "Compassion, Imagination, and Reverence for All Living Things: Margaret Atwood's Spiritual Vision in *The Year of the Flood.*" *Margaret Atwood Studies.* 3.2: 30–42.

Raschke, Debrah. "Atwood's *MaddAddam.*" *Margaret Atwood Society Roundtable.* MLA. Jan. 2014. Chicago, Marriott Hotel. Paper.

_____. "Review of *MaddAddam,* by Margaret Atwood." *Kirkus Reviews* 81.14 (15 July 2013). *Proquest.* 16 February 2014.

Seaman, Donna. "Review of *MaddAddam,* by Margaret Atwood." *Booklist.* 109 (Sept. 2013): 19–20. Web. 24 Feb. 2014.

Schweickart, Patrocinio. "Reading Ourselves: Toward a Feminist Theory of Reading." *Contemporary Literary Criticism: Literary and Cultural Studies.* Ed. Robert Con Davis & Ronald Schlefer. 2nd ed. New York & London: Longman, 1989. 118–141.

Wilson, Sharon R. "Post-Apocalyptic Vision: Flood Myths and Other Folklore in Atwood's *Oryx and Crake* and *The Year of the Flood.*" *Critical Insights: Margaret Atwood.* Ed. J. Brooks Bouson. Ipswitch, MA: Salem Press, 2013.

Cultural Heroines and Canadian Imaginaries:
Evangeline and Anne_____

Rita Ross

Two of Canada's iconic literary heroines are Evangeline, the central figure in a narrative poem published in 1847 by Henry Wadsworth Longfellow, and Anne Shirley of L. M. Montgomery's *Anne of Green Gables*, published in 1908. Although there are many differences between the two, in other ways, these characters and their stories have had a remarkably similar impact upon Canadians and others around the world. Though coming from pre-modern works, they are far from being mere literary footnotes. To this day, Evangeline and Anne remain important literary and cultural figures.

Both are still in print in their original English texts and in numerous translations into other languages, both have entered the world of popular culture, where they are represented by such things as dolls, coloring books, and decorated plates, and both are presented in dramatic offerings, like plays and pageants. Both heroines have important roles in Canadian National Parks that are eagerly visited by tourists wanting to see the actual places where Evangeline or Anne lived—even though they are both fictional. Both figures have given rise to economically and culturally important tourist industries. Both heroines embody elements thought to be either typically Acadian (in the case of Evangeline), or Canadian (in the case of Anne). Both are intimately connected with ideas of national identity and pride. In the literary realm, they have inspired imitators, followers, and critics, and are the subject of lively debates to this day. And despite what elite literary and cultural critics have to say about them, both are still loved by ordinary people.

Evangeline
Evangeline tells the story of separated lovers set against the backdrop of the 1755 Deportation of the French-speaking Acadians from Nova Scotia. This event, in which the British forcibly removed

the Acadians from their homeland, has become a defining event in Acadian history.[1] In the first part of Longfellow's poem, the fictional young woman Evangeline and her fiancé Gabriel are at home in their idyllic village of Grand-Pré, Nova Scotia, on the eve of their wedding. Longfellow describes the peaceful rural life of the village:

Columns of pale blue smoke, like clouds of incense ascending,
Rose from a hundred hearths, the homes of peace and contentment.
Thus dwelt together in love these simple Acadian farmers,
Dwelt in the love of God and of man. Alike were they free from
Fear, that reigns with the tyrant, and envy, the vice of republics.
Neither locks had they to their doors, nor bars to their windows;
But their dwellings were open as day and the hearts of the owners;
There the richest was poor, and the poorest lived in abundance.
(Longfellow 40)

Within this Paradise-like setting lives the saint-like Evangeline, a character of gentleness, goodness, and religious devotion. As she walks down the street on Sunday morning to church "a celestial brightness—a more ethereal beauty—/Shone on her face and encircled her form, when after confession,/Homeward serenely she walked with God's benediction upon her,/When she had passed, it seemed like the ceasing of exquisite music" (Longfellow 41).

This vision of life in a golden age village[2] is shattered when the British troops arrive. Grand-Pré is destroyed, and Evangeline and Gabriel are put on separate ships that carry them away from their homeland and each other. Part II of the poem follows Evangeline as she wanders through what is now the United States in search of her fiancé. They are reunited only in old age, when she finds him gravely ill, and he dies in her arms.

Although little read today except by specialists, Longfellow was once a giant of American letters in a time when Americans were just beginning to create an "American" literature (Ruland 666). When the poem appeared in 1847, it was an enormous success, inspiring the devotion of Acadians and others around the world. As Edward Wagenknecht, the noted Longfellow scholar, says:

It was the first long poem in American literature to live beyond its own time, and it would be impossible to exaggerate its vogue, either at home or abroad. Its popularity cut through all class distinctions. It was read and loved and pondered over in humble cottages, and both the Honorable Mrs. Norton and King Leopold I of Belgium admired it . . . . In 1947 Hawthorne and Dana counted over 270 editions and at least 130 translations. (85–86)

Longfellow's intent in writing this poem was almost certainly to present a picture of pure and devoted womanhood, but the Acadians of the late nineteenth century embraced it instead as a poem about the tragic central event in their history: the Deportation. When Longfellow wrote his poem, the Acadians had been virtually lost to history for more than a century. The poem's 1847 publication was just in time for it to become part of the "Acadian Renaissance" of the late nineteenth century. During that time, a relatively small group of educated Acadian elites became eager to reestablish a uniquely Acadian identity and sense of "nationhood." (Nationhood, in this sense, means a sense of shared heritage and belonging that sets off people from others. It does not necessarily imply an independent geographical and governmental identity.) Longfellow's poem furnished them with a national story and national heroine to complement other symbols, such as a new flag and national anthem. According to the Acadian historian Léon Thériault, "A myth and a legend had been created in which the Acadians recognized themselves. The couple Gabriel and Evangeline symbolized their progress as a people, both in their dispersal to the four winds and in their eventual reunion" (56–57). And as the historian Naomi Griffiths says, "the poem was the most powerful cultural tool available to those constructing an Acadian identity in the late nineteenth century" (37). She, among others, has pointed out the significance of the existence of such a ready-made "founding myth," encapsulated in *Evangeline,* which celebrates an idyllic golden age disrupted by the Deportation, over which the Acadians triumphed by the very fact of their survival.

The original poem, written in a language that most Acadians could not read, came to them indirectly, mainly through a series of translations into French by the French Canadian Pamphile Le May.

His first version appeared in his *Essais poétiques* (1865). Le May's translations often exaggerated the misfortunes of the Acadians and the brutality of the English, contributing to a widespread misunderstanding of Longfellow's true motives in writing the poem. Because it was through Le May's translation that *Evangeline* became best known to the Acadians, one may say that Evangeline is, in some sense, a Canadian work. Evangeline herself is certainly a Canadian and Acadian heroine.

It is impossible to overstate the very high regard once felt for Longfellow's poem. As one early critic said, "I do not wonder that the French Canadians treasure *Evangeline* as a sacred book; it will, indeed, be a holy gospel as long as human hearts beat with love" (Walters 28). *Evangeline* has also been referred to as the "odysée acadien" ("Acadian Odyssey") and "épopée nationale" ("national epic") by Robert Rumilly (II: 715).

Evangeline the poem and Evangeline the literary heroine helped create an *imaginary* of Acadians, helping to fill a large blank spot in Canadian and world history. In a famous quotation about the concept of imaginary, the Canadian sociologist Charles Taylor explains: "I'm talking about the way ordinary people "imagine" their social surroundings, and this is often not expressed in theoretical terms; it is carried in images, stories, and legends" (106). Imaginaries may be thought of as "widespread, shared and largely unconscious sets of understandings about the world" (Ross, "Evangeline, Acadians" 2). The imaginary of the Acadians was not built on history or any other kind of academic study, but almost solely on the power of the images, emotions, and story described by Longfellow.

Non-Literary Effects: Popular Culture, Commodification, and Tourism

Although Evangeline soon became extremely popular as a literary figure, her continuing importance in the cultural imaginary of Acadia would not be so great if she had not also gained fame thorough her physical image. The original edition of Longfellow's poem was not illustrated, but a small portrait of Evangeline by the professional artist James Faed (a Scot) appeared soon afterwards and was widely copied by both professional and folk artists (Robichaud 3–4). Images of Evangeline soon crossed over into popular and commercial art as well, appearing widely in illustrations, souvenirs, postcards, and advertisements (LeBlanc *Postcards*, "Grand-Pré"). Chocolates manufactured by the Ganong company featured her picture on the box and were marketed as exhibiting the same "purity, excellence, constancy, romance, and sweetness" as Evangeline herself (Rudin 22).

As image, story, and symbol, Evangeline was also involved in the reclaiming of Grand-Pré by the Acadians in the 1920s, in part spurred by literary and later cultural tourism (Neilson; Ross, "Evangeline Acadians"). Originally this tourism was the kind of "literary tourism" prompted by a widespread desire by readers to see in person the landscapes described in favorite books (Robinson), or the sites described by them, or their homes. Evangeline brought together all these impulses. As Ingalls says, "Nineteenth century love of sentimental narrative, and pastoral scenery peopled by rustic, but virtuous peasants was embodied in *Evangeline* and reflected in the landscape and people of Nova Scotia" (27).

Although the great popularity of the poem had been drawing visitors, especially Americans, to Grand-Pré to see Evangeline's village for some time, the earliest tourists were disappointed when they got there, for the pre-Deportation village had been completely destroyed and the area had been taken over by newcomers from New England. Eventually the Dominion Atlantic Railway, which owned the property, became interested in the tourist possibilities of the Evangeline connection. They commissioned the now famous statue of Evangeline at the site, attracting even more tourists to travel there on the railway. The site continued to develop over the years, eventually adding a memorial church. Ian McKay notes that:

> The most impressive attempt to exploit [Nova Scotia] history in the interests of tourism was the Dominion Atlantic Railway's "Evangeline" promotion, in which American tourists were enticed to the Annapolis Valley with images of Longfellow's imaginary heroine (commemorated in a park after 1917), and by the quintessentially antimodern appeal of an unspoiled region of romance. (106)

A Canadian National Historic Site since 1982 and a UNESCO World Heritage Site since 2012, the Grand-Pré complex remains an important cultural and tourist site (Bergman; De Jonge; LeBlanc; Neilson; Rudin 185–187). As may be expected, Evangeline has a prominent place in the gift shop. The park is thus a successful combination of what Valene Smith calls the "4 H's of tourism—habitat, history, heritage, and handicrafts" (112). It is clear that Evangeline in her many manifestations—literary, ethnic, and economic—remains a powerful and persistent symbol that lies at the center of the Acadian imaginary for Acadians and non-Acadians alike.

Literary Heritage

Evangeline has had a significant impact on the literary world as well (Cowan; Keefer). Writing about what she calls the "Evangeline sisterhood," Judith Cowan traces stories of 'Evangeline' and 'Gabriel' types separated by the Deportation and later reunited after many hardships. Quite a few of these claim to be based on family traditions dating back to the years of exile, but few are of literary value. There were also many retellings of the Evangeline story in plays, musical entertainments, and even operas.

The eminent twentieth century Acadian novelist and playwright Antonine Maillet has been influenced by Evangeline as well, not in homage to her but in reaction against her. Among Maillet's creations is a recurring figure who is a conscious alternative to the romanticized character created by Longfellow and traditionally associated with the Acadian people. Perhaps her most beloved character is La Sagouine (1986), an elderly washerwoman who speaks in Acadian dialect and is uneducated, funny, and outspoken. She has strong ideas about the survival of the Acadian people, a favorite theme of Maillet's. With the play *Evangéline Deusse* (*Evangeline the Second*) (1986), the author puts on stage her own anti-Evangeline, a corrected version of the traditional archetype (Usmiani; Dairon 59–62), a character who once again emphasizes that the real Acadians didn't wander about passively after the Deportation, but courageously struggled to return and rebuild. Another of Maillet's famous Evangeline alternatives is Pélagie of *Pélagie-la-Charrette* (*Pélagie of the Cart*) (1979), who is a leader of her people on the long journey home.

To say that Maillet's heroines are anti-Evangelines is not to say everything about them. But many Acadians have taken La Sagouine, Pélagie, and Evangéline Deusse to their hearts, and have thereby learned an alternative image of the Acadian woman to Longfellow's Evangeline—one who is tough, earthy, capable, funny, passionate, and proud. Although for many Acadians, Evangeline is still a beloved figure, for others, she represents an outmoded image of Acadians, one that today's Acadian elite would like to leave behind (Ross, "Evangeline, Acadians" 13). In any case, though published in 1847, the poem *Evangeline* is by no means an obscure literary relic. By her persistence as a cultural icon, Evangeline has become a contemporary Canadian fiction. Despite controversy, she is still alive and remains at the heart of the Acadian imaginary.

Anne

The novel *Anne of Green Gables,* published in 1908 by Lucy Maud Montgomery, "the darling of Prince Edward Island" (Siourbas 133), tells the story of a red-haired, eleven-year-old orphan girl who gets mistakenly sent to an elderly brother and sister who want a boy to help on their farm. The book recounts her adventures, her relationships, and her increasing attachment to her new family, home, and community. Anne is an enchanting creation, spirited, good-hearted, and given to amusingly flowery language based on romantic books she has read. The book was meant as children's literature and has flourished with this audience, but unlike most children's books, it continues to hold a special place in the hearts of adults as well. "It is a particular gift of *Anne of Green Gables*, the novel, and Anne of Green Gables, the character, to have been adopted by generation after generation over a century. Anne engages scholarly reading, children's reading, teachers' choices, translators' voices, and adults' re-reading" (Ledwell & Mitchell 5). Anne, like Evangeline, is alive today.

Anne's success was immediate. It was Canada's first international bestseller and was translated into more than thirty languages (Ledwell & Mitchell 3). It is still read and fiercely loved all over the world, even in some surprising places, including Iran (Samigorganroodi), Turkey (Tunc), and Uruguay (Coll). "Red-Haired Anne" is so wildly popular in Japan that Japanese tourists visit Prince Edward Island in droves and, at home in Japan, have created popular Anne clubs and online groups (Akamatsu; Allard; Baldwin; Rea).

In contrast to Longfellow, who based his descriptions of Grand-Pré (which he had never visited) on travelers' accounts, Montgomery set her story in a place she knew very well. The countryside was the one she had grown up in, and the house called Green Gables was based on a neighbor's. Her descriptions of landscapes, people, and everyday life are much more accurate than Longfellow's. Yet they also are idealized. De Jonge mentions that Montgomery didn't hesitate to alter the details of her landscape to make them more appealing (255), and Waterston notes that the world of the Anne books is a highly romanticized one of "red earth, green meadows, blue sea and sky, golden sands" (27) .

Montgomery herself wrote in her diary that "[Anne] belongs to the green, untroubled pastures and still waters of the world before the war" (qtd. by Fiamengo 237). And according to Saul, "In her novels she puts forward the world almost as it should be, and this world somehow speaks to people across borders and across time" (xiii). Like Evangeline, Anne lives in a golden world of the past. The noted Canadian critic Northrop Frye cites her world as an example of the "pastoral myth."[3]

Montgomery's descriptions of the physical features of Anne's world, as well as the social relationships of the fictional village of Avonlea, idealized as they are, have made a lasting impression on readers and helped form an imaginary of the Maritimes and even Canada as a whole. Yet the attraction of this rural Prince Edward Island landscape, evoking a benign bucolic milieu, is strikingly different from the more typical Canadian landscapes often discussed by Canadian writers and considered representative of Canada—

the rugged Canadian Shield, the vast prairies, and especially the forbidding North (Hamill 68). None of these is as immediately appealing to a reader as a landscape featuring pleasant woods, fields, and flowers, like the one Anne encounters when she arrives in the fictional Avonlea. But *Anne of Green Gables*, as Faye Hammill says, is one of a number of books offering a different vision of the Canadian land, "presenting a much more alluring vision of landscape" (69), and thereby perhaps more immediately appealing to readers and potential visitors. Anne's surroundings are made even more memorable by her habit of renaming. Very early in *Anne of Green Gables*, she renames the local "Avenue" of flowering apple trees "the White Way of Delight" and transforms the prosaic "Barry's Pond" into the "Lake of Shining Waters" (18). These exaggeratedly romantic names have further endeared the locality to readers. As Fiamengo has commented, Montgomery transformed the fictional Avonlea into a "cultural myth . . . in which all of nature seems an enchanted park" (233).

Anne of Green Gables became so popular around the world that it was soon associated with the very idea of Canada, not only in terms of landscape, but also in terms of values and way of life. Just as earlier readers had formed an imaginary of the Acadians based on Evangeline, later ones formed an imaginary of Canada largely through their familiarity with Anne.

Like earlier admirers of Evangeline, fans of the Anne books soon sought a tangible place to visit. Responding to the demands of literary tourism, the farmhouse in Cavendish that had served as the model for Green Gables was made into a small museum, and later, this "shrine" (Pike 247) was gradually expanded to include other sites in the "Avonlea" neighborhood. In the 1930s, Parks Canada incorporated all these sites into Prince Edward Island National Park, a major tourist attraction in the province as well as a significant contributor to its economy (De Jonge; Pike). In the Park bookstore, visitors may choose from a dizzying array of Anne souvenirs, including dolls, plates, coloring books, and the ubiquitous straw hat with attached red braids, which can instantly transform any little girl into Anne. These Anne souvenirs are available throughout Canada as well, often showing up in such tourist venues as airport shops as quintessentially Canadian memorabilia. As in the case of Evangeline, there is a large component of commercialization and commodification, in addition to literary fandom, in "Anne tourism" (Lynes; Neilson; Pike; Sheckles).

Lucy Maud Montgomery and the Canadian Canon

While both Longfellow and his creation had been highly praised to begin with, only to be devalued later as new generations of Acadians began to reexamine the meaning of Acadian identity, the reputation of Montgomery's work has proceeded more unevenly. Initial reception of her work was mixed, with some readers and critics dismissing *Anne* and others, including Mark Twain, praising it highly. As Siourbas writes, "For three decades after her death, Montgomery's status was ambiguous: though she held a special place in the popular heart, literary critics refused to write about, and thus to recognize, her achievements" (135).

In part, this is because Montgomery fell victim to what Jane Urquhart has called a "boys' club" (56) of male scholars who actively attacked her work. One of her most vocal critics was an eminent scholar of the day, William Arthur Deacon, who was "ruthless in his scorn toward Montgomery and her writing" (Urquhart 55). He wrote about Montgomery that "Canadian literature could go no lower" (Gerson 18). Another male literary critic, Arthur Phelps, a colleague and supporter of Deacon's, joined in the attacks upon Montgomery. He "asserted that Montgomery's work was naïve and provincial" and denigrated her readers for enjoying it (Urquhart 56). And, as Urquhart points out, Montgomery was not connected to any academic institution that might have supported her, and she was even forced out of the Canadian Authors Association by Deacon, depriving her of any kind of a literary home. "Most damning of all was the notion that she wrote only for an audience of young girls" (Urquhart 54).

Beginning in the 1950s, feminist literary scholars started to confront this unfair criticism of "girls' books"—doubly devalued because they are for children and, in particular, girls. The field of "domestic literature," which focuses on ordinary everyday lives, especially of families, women, and children, has helped to bring girls' books into literary respectability (Urquhart; Gerson). Montgomery's books about Anne and about Emily of New Moon often take center stage in these discussions.

The reevaluation of Montgomery's work was also prompted by several pivotal turning points, discussed by Carole Gerson in her article "*Anne of Green Gables* Goes to University: L.M. Montgomery and Academic Culture" (2002), in which she details Montgomery's changing academic fortunes over the years (see also Garner). An especially important year was 1985, which saw both the publication of the first edited volume of Montgomery's journals, drawing increased attention from scholars, and the appearance of the Megan Follows film on television, which introduced the Anne books to a new audience (Gerson).

While her creator's status has recently increased in academic circles, there has never been a time when Anne was not loved by ordinary readers everywhere. In a perceptive discussion of the difference between *literary canon* (the "great books" deemed important by academics) and *cultural capital* (meaning those works that are a part of a general cultural awareness and appreciation by people at large), Helen Siourbas states that "Montgomery's value as cultural capital is very high, and has been so for decades, though her value as institutional capital has, until recently, been quite low" (131). Her institutional capital has been steadily rising since the founding of the L. M. Montgomery Institute at the University of Prince Edward Island in 1993. The Institute has become an important site for academic conferences devoted solely to her, which have resulted in the publication of several important scholarly collections (Gammel 28–29). By the time of the centennial of Anne's publication in 2008, a new wave of Lucy Maud Montgomery studies was well established, and Anne is now something of a literary industry in Canada. Academic studies are continuing to appear about Montgomery and Anne into her second century, for example *Anne's World: A New Century of Anne of Green Gables* (Gammel & Lefebvre).

It is now recognized that "the pervasive influence of Montgomery and Anne on Canadian writers and their characters, as well as on Canadian critics and readers, is remarkable" (Steffler 154). Steffler also notes that, "When Canadian women writers are asked about formative literary influences, almost all of them begin their responses with L.M. Montgomery" (153). Two of Canada's literary stars, Margaret Atwood and Jane Urquhart, have written appreciations of *Anne of Green Gables* (Atwood, Urquhart). Anne now seems to have gained as secure a place in the Canadian canon as she has always had in her readers' affections (Gerson 2010).

Imaginaries of Past, Place, and Home

Why are *Evangeline* and *Anne of Green Gables*, in their different ways, still so powerfully alive to today's readers, despite their relative antiquity in terms of Canadian literature? This essay has shown that both these unlikely heroines have had effects far beyond the audience for the original poem and novel, as can be seen in the items of popular culture, souvenirs, and stage performances that are associated with them and that continually attract new fans. The mixture of cultural and commercial appeal represented by tourist literature continues to draw visitors to see where Evangeline and Anne actually "lived." The demand for contact with these still-beloved characters has resulted in the original small visitors' destinations having been raised to the status of National Heritage Sites. So there is much to see and to buy, to remind people today about Evangeline and Anne continually.

Another connection between the two heroines is that they both evoke powerful imaginaries of land and home, but in a particularly idealized and romanticized way. Both harken back in time to a world that had ceased to exist even at the time of their writing. In Evangeline's case, the Acadian Deportation had occurred almost one hundred years earlier, and the Acadians who returned had been forced to make very different lives for themselves under British rule. The romanticism of Longfellow's poem furnished the Acadians with a "founding myth" and a heroine in the figure of a devoted and saintly woman living in a community of peace and tranquility. They made good use of this golden age myth in their efforts to reimagine an Acadian identity and a sense of Acadian nationhood.

In the case of Anne, Montgomery was writing about scenes from her childhood, so when *Anne of Green Gables* appeared, it was already a representation of a past life. As previously discussed, Montgomery's Avonlea, like Longfellow's Grand-Pré, is an idealization harkening back to a romanticized past. This idealization seems to be a strong attraction for readers and visitors from Canada and elsewhere. Both the landscape and the people seem to exist in a better, pre-modern age, which appeals to tourists. As Tom Selwyn suggests, tourists are seeking "to recover—mythologically—those senses of wholeness and structure that are missing from modern life" (2). Fiamengo notes that a "shared discourse of revitalization and repose" in both the Anne books and in the tourist literature of Prince Edward Island "contributes to the popular appeal of both kinds of writing" (23).

Perhaps one of their greatest similarities is the focus in both works on specific places previously unknown to most outsiders, Grand-Pré, Nova Scotia, and Cavendish, Prince Edward Island. These locations, previously obscure even to most Canadians, were given meaning through the imaginaries created by the original writings and, later, through the multiple offshoots that grew from them. Fiamengo quotes a passage in Montgomery's journal, in which she writes about Cavendish, "Everything is so green and fresh, the ripe but not over-ripe luxuriance of midsummer without as yet a hint of decay. And beyond the green field and slopes was the blue girdle of the gulf, forever moaning on its shining shore" (Fiamengo 231).

Both *Evangeline* and *Anne* embody an imaginary of the landscapes and social relations of the Maritimes that continues to appeal to readers, visitors, and consumers. Evangeline has remained a symbol of the essential Acadian heritage. Anne, on the other hand, has grown to represent qualities that are felt by many to reflect Canada as a whole. Both heroines exist, though, in an unchanging past golden age that their fans never tire of revisiting.

Another, related, basis for the still-powerful attraction that these works exert upon so many is that both are built around an imaginary of "home." As Rosemary Ross Johnston has written, the concept of home includes "the idea of home, and the powerful associations of coming home, finding home, making home . . . and at the rim of home is nation—not just a geography but a history, shared views of the world, shared codes of relationships, shared values and concerns" (411). For the Acadians, the loss and then reclaiming of their homeland, *Acadie*, is the central event in their history. The shared nature of that recognition is a validation of their claim to be a separate "nation" within the Maritimes and Canada. Anne's story, which touches us on a personal rather than ethnic level, is about a homeless orphan girl finding a home and then making it her own: Anne arrives in Avonlea hardly hoping that she will be allowed to stay, then gradually finds and makes her home in a family and community. In both works, the search is intimately connected to a deep attachment to past, place, and home, which together create a sense of belonging.

The quest for identity is a continuing one for Canada. *Evangeline* by Longfellow/Le May and *Anne of Green Gables* by Montgomery have tapped into this quest in ways that may not have been apparent to their creators. Their enduring popularity tells us something about an idealization of a past that is in some ways outmoded, yet in other ways continues to represent a powerful component of the Canadian imaginaries of home.

Notes

1. The Acadians, originally from France, had begun settling in *Acadie*, or Acadia (now Nova Scotia) beginning in 1604. They are a different group from those who settled in Québec, called the Québécois, or French Canadians. The Acadians had the misfortune to be caught between the French and the British in their struggle over North America. They were willing to swear that they would not fight against the British, but also insisted that they would not fight against the French or the Indians. Their claim to exist as the "Neutral French" was ultimately rejected by the British, and in 1755, they were forcibly deported from the land they had lived on for over a century. They were allowed back to Canada beginning in 1763, only to find that their lands had been taken over by Loyalist settlers from the United

States. The Acadians went into a "dark age" for over a century due to years of cultural, religious, and linguistic subjugation by the British. A good English-language source on the Deportation is Griffiths, *The Acadian Deportation*. For a discussion of Evangeline in Louisiana, where some of the deported Acadians eventually settled (to become known as Cajuns), see Ross, "Evangeline in Louisiana."

2. Longfellow is clearly referring here to myths of a past "golden age" that had been familiar in Western culture since Greek and Roman times. A representative quotation from the Roman poet Ovid expresses some of the same sentiments as Longfellow:

> This was the Golden Age that, without coercion, without laws, spontaneously nurtured the good and the true. There was no fear or punishment: there were no threatening words to be read, fixed in bronze, no crowd of suppliants fearing the judge's face: they lived safely without protection. No pine tree felled in the mountains had yet reached the flowing waves to travel to other lands: human beings only knew their own shores. There were no steep ditches surrounding towns, no straight war-trumpets, no coiled horns, no swords and helmets. Without the use of armies, people passed their lives in gentle peace and security. (I: 89–112)

3. The "pastoral myth," which is related to the concept of the "Golden Age" mentioned above is explained by Frye as:

> the vision of a social ideal. The pastoral myth in its most common form is associated with childhood, or with some earlier social condition—pioneer life, the small town, the *habitant* rooted to his land—that can be identified with childhood. The nostalgia for a world of peace and protection, with a spontaneous response to the nature around it, with a leisure and composure not to be found today, is particularly strong in Canada. *It is overpowering in our popular literature, from Anne of Green Gables* to Leacock's Mariposa, and from *Maria Chapdelaine* to *Jake and the Kid*. (238–9, emphasis added)

Works Cited

Akamatsu, Yoshiko. "Japanese Readings of *Anne of Green Gables*." *L.M. Montgomery and Canadian Culture*. Ed. Irene Gammel & Elizabeth Epperly. Toronto: U Toronto P, 1999. 201–212.

Allard, Danièle. "*Taishu Bunka* and Anne Clubs in Japan." *Making Avonlea: L.M. Montgomery and Popular Culture*. Ed. Irene Gammel. Toronto: U Toronto P, 2002. 295–309.

Atwood, Margaret. "Revisiting Anne." *L.M. Montgomery and Canadian Culture. L.M. Montgomery and Canadian Culture*. Ed. Irene Gammel & Elizabeth Epperly. Toronto: U Toronto P, 1999. 222–226.

Baldwin, Douglas. "L.M. Montgomery's *Anne of Green Gables*: The Japanese Connection." *Journal of Canadian Studies* 28.3 (1993): 123–33.

Bergman, Brian. "Sad Land of Broken Dreams." *Maclean's* 110.32 (1997): 18.

Coll, Dorely Carolina. "Reading *Anne of Green Gables* in Montevideo." *Anne Around the World: L.M. Montgomery and Her Classic*. Ed. Jane Ledwell & Jean Mitchell. Montreal: McGill-Queen's UP, 2013. 192–99.

Cowan, Judith Elaine. *Outcasts from Paradise: The Myth of Acadie and Evangleine in Canadian Literature in English and in French*. Ph.D. Thesis. University of Sherbrooke, Québec, 1983.

Dairon, Pierre. "Evangeline: American and Acadian Icon." *Jefferson Journal of Science and Culture* 1 (2011): 35–70. Web. 08 February 2014.

De Jonge, James. "Through the Eyes of Memory: L.M. Montgomery's Cavendish." *Making Avonlea: L.M. Montgomery and Popular Culture*. Ed. Irene Gammel. Toronto: U Toronto P, 2002. 252–67.

Fiamengo, Janice. "Towards a Theory of the Popular Landscape in *Anne of Green Gables.*" *Making Avonlea: L.M. Montgomery and Popular Culture*. Ed. Irene Gammel. Toronto: U Toronto P, 2002. 226–37.

Frye, Northrop. "Conclusion to a Literary History of Canada." *The Bush Garden: Essays in the Canadian Imagination*. Toronto: Anansi, 1971. Web. 28 May 2014.

Gammel, Irene, ed. *Making Avonlea: L.M. Montgomery and Popular Culture*. Toronto: U Toronto P, 2002.

Gammel, Irene, & Elizabeth Epperly, eds. *L.M. Montgomery and Canadian Culture*. Toronto: U Toronto P, 1999.

Gammel, Irene, & Benjamin Lefebvre, eds. *Anne's World: A New Century of Anne of Green Gables*. Toronto: U Toronto P, 2010.

Garner, Barbara Carman. "A Century of Critical Reflection on *Anne of Green Gables.*" *Anne Around the World*. Ed. Jane Ledwell & Jean Mitchell. Montreal: McGill-Queen's UP, 2013. 63–79.

Gerson, Carole. "Anne of Green Gables Goes to University: L.M. Montgomery and Academic Culture." *Making Avonlea: L.M. Montgomery and Popular Culture*. Ed. Irene Gammel. Toronto: U Toronto P, 2002. 17–31.

_____. "Seven Milestones: How *Anne of Green Gables* Became a Canadian Icon." *Anne's World: A New Century of Anne of Green Gables*. Ed. Irene Gammel & Benjamin Lefebvre. Toronto: U Toronto P, 2010. 17–34.

Griffiths, N.E.S. *The Acadian Deportation: Deliberate Perfidy or Cruel Necessity?* Toronto: Copp Clark, 1969.

_____. *The Acadians: Creation of a People.* Toronto: McGraw-Hill Ryerson, 1973.

_____. "Longfellow's *Evangeline*: The Birth and Acceptance of a Legend." *Acadiensis* 11.2 (1982): 28–41.

Hammill, Faye. *Canadian Literature.* Edinburgh: Edinburgh UP, 2007.

Ingalls, Sharon. "Mad about Acadians." *The Beaver: Exploring Canada's History*, 69 (June–July 1989): 21–27.

Johnston, Rosemary Ross. "L. M. Montgomery's Interior/Exterior Landscapes." *Anne of Green Gables: A Norton Critical Edition*. Ed. Mary Henley Rubio & Elizabeth Waterston. New York: Norton, 2007. 409–413.

Kulyk Keefer, Janice. "The Ideology of Innocence: Anglophone Literature and the Expulsion of the Acadians." *Revue de l'Université Sainte-Anne* (1984–5): 39–46.

LeBlanc, Barbara. *Postcards from Acadie: Grand-Pré: Evangeline & the Acadian Identity.* Kentville, NS: Gaspereau Press, 2003.

_____. "Grand-Pré in Acadie." *Encyclopedia of French Cultural Heritage in North America*, 2007. Web. 2 Feb. 2011.

Ledwell, Jane, & Jean Mitchell, eds. *Anne Around the World: L.M. Montgomery and Her Classic.* Montreal: McGill-Queen's UP, 2013.

_____. Introduction. *Anne Around the World: L.M. Montgomery and Her Classic.* Ed. Jane Ledwell & Jean Mitchell. Montreal: McGill-Queen's UP, 2013. 3–24.

Le May, Pamphile. *Essais poétiques*. Québec: G. E. Desbarats, 1865.

Longfellow, Henry Wadsworth. *Evangeline, a Tale of Acadie.* 1847. Halifax: Nimbus, 1951.

Lynes, Jeanette. "Consumable Avonlea: The Commodification of the Green Gables Mythology." *Making Avonlea: L.M. Montgomery and Popular Culture.* Ed. Irene Gammel. Toronto: U Toronto P, 2002. 268–279.

McKay, Ian. "History and the Tourist Gaze: The Politics of Commemoration in Nova Scotia, 1935–1964." *Acadiensis* 22 (1993): 102–38.

Maillet, Antonine. *Pélagie-la-Charrette*. Paris: B. Grasset, 1979.

_____. *Evangéline Deusse*. Montreal: Leméac, 1975.

_____. *La Sagouine*. Montreal: Leméac, 1986.

Neilson, Leighann. "Marketing the 'Forest Primeval: The Development of Romantic Tourism in the Land of Evangeline, 1847 to 1920." *The Romance of Marketing History, Proceedings of the 11th Conference on Historical Analysis and Research in Marketing (CHARM)* (2003): 234–45. Web. 04 February 2014.

Ovid. *Metamorphoses.* Trans. A.S. Kline. Book 1. *The Ovid Collection, University of Virginia Library.* Web. 08 June 2014.

Pike, E. Holly. "Mass Marketing, Popular Culture, and the Canadian Celebrity Author." *Making Avonlea: L.M. Montgomery and Popular Culture.* Ed. Irene Gammel. Toronto: U Toronto P, 2002. 238–51.

Rea, Michael H. "A *Furusato* Away from Home." *Annals of Tourism Research* 27.3 (2000): 638–60. Web. 4 Feb. 2014.

Robichaud, Deborah. "Images of Evangeline: Continuity of the Iconographic Tradition." *River Review-Revue Riviere* 3 (1997): 97–107. Web. 4 Feb. 2014.

Robinson, Mike. "Between and Beyond the Pages: Literature-Tourism Relationships." *Literature and Tourism.* Ed. Mike Robinson & Hans Christian Andersen. London: Continuum, 2002. 39–79.

Ross, Rita. "Evangeline in Louisiana: the Acadian-Cajun connection." *Canadian folklore canadien* 13.2 (1991): 11–23.

_____. "Evangeline, Acadians, and Tourism Imaginaries." *Tourism Imaginaries: Place. Practice, Media.* Ed. Maria Gravari-Barbas & Nelson Graburn. Surrey, England: Ashgate, 2015.

Rudin, Ronald. *Remembering and Forgetting in Acadie: A Historian's Journey Through Public Memory.* Toronto: U Toronto P, 2009.

Rumilly, Robert. *Histoire des Acadiens.* 2 vol. Montréal: Fides, 1955.

Samigorganroodi, Gholamrez. "Teaching and Reading Anne of Green Gables in Iran, the Land of Omar Khayyam." *Anne Around the World: L.M. Montgomery and Her Classic.* Ed. Jane Ledwell and Jean Mitchell. Montreal: McGill-Queen's UP, 2013. 181–99.

Saul, John Ralston. Introduction. *L.M. Montgomery.* By Jane Urquhart. Toronto: Penguin, 2009. ix–xiii. Extraordinary Canadians Ser.

Selwyn, Tom. Introduction. *The Tourist Image: Myths and Myth Making in Tourism.* Ed. Tom Selwyn. Chichester: Wiley, 1996.

Sheckels, Theodore. "Anne in Hollywood: The Americanization of a Canadian Icon." *L.M. Montgomery and Canadian Culture.* Ed. Irene Gammel & Elizabeth Epperly. Toronto: U Toronto P, 1999. 183–91.

Siourbas, Helen. "L.M. Montgomery: Canon or Cultural Capital?" *Windows and Words: A Look at Canadian Children's Literature in English.* Ed. Aïda Hudson & Susan-Ann Cooper. Ottawa: U Ottawa P, 2003. 131–141.

Smith, Valene L., ed. *Hosts and Guests: The Anthropology of Tourism.* Oxford: Blackwell, 1977.

Squires, Shelagh J. "Ways of Seeing, Ways of Being: Literature, Place, and Tourism in L.M. Montgomery's Prince Edward Island." *A Few Acres of Snow: Literary and Artistic Images of Canada.* Ed. Paul Simpson-Housley. Toronto: Dundern, 1992. 137–145.

Steffler, Margaret. "Anne in a 'Globalized' Word: Nation, Nostalgia, and Postcolonial Perspectives of Home." *Anne's World: A New Century of Anne of Green Gables.* Ed. Irene Gammel & Benjamin Lefebvre. Toronto: U Toronto P, 2010. 150–65.

Strauss, Claudia. "The imaginary." *Anthropological Theory* 6 (2006): 322–44.

Taylor, Charles. "Modern social imaginaries." *Public Culture* 14.1 (2002): 91–124. Web. 19 Sept. 2014.

Thériault, Léon. "Acadia, 1763–1978: An Historical Synthesis." *The Acadians of the Maritimes.* Ed. Jean Daigle. Moncton, New Brunswick: Centre d'études acadiennes, 1982. 47–86.

Tunc, Tanfer Emin. "Teaching *Anne* and *Antonia* in Turkey: Feminist Girlhood in L.M. Montgomery's *Anne of Green Gables* and Willa

Cather's *My Antonia.*" *Anne Around the World: L.M. Montgomery and Her Classic.* Ed. Jane Ledwell & Jean Mitchell. Montreal: McGill-Queen's UP, 2013. 200–15.

Urquhart, Jane. *L.M. Montgomery.* Toronto: Penguin, 2009. Extraordinary Canadians Ser.

Usmiani, Renate. "Recycling an Archetype: the Anti-Evangelines." *Canadian Theater Review* 46 (1986): 65–71.

Wagenknecht, Edward. *Henry Wadsworth Longfellow: His Poetry and Prose.* New York: Ungar, 1986.

Walters, Frank. *Studies of Some of Longfellow's Poems.* 1892. Folcroft, PA: Folcroft Press, 1969.

Warnqvist, Åsa. "I Experienced a Light That Became a Part of Me: Reading *Anne of Green Gables* in Sweden." *Making Avonlea: L.M. Montgomery and Popular Culture.* Ed. Irene Gammel. Toronto: U Toronto P, 2002. 228–42.

Waterston, Elizabeth Hillman. "*Anne of Green Gables*—and Afterward." *Anne Around the World: L.M. Montgomery and Her Classic.* Ed. Jane Ledwell & Jean Mitchell. Montreal: McGill-Queen's UP, 2013. 27–34.

CRITICAL
READINGS

MacLeod's Men

Shannon Hengen

The stories and novel of Alistair MacLeod often trace the maturing of boys into men. While the works are frequently set on Cape Breton Island—at the northeastern point of the province of Nova Scotia, on the Atlantic Ocean—and usually in the latter part of the twentieth century, they point beyond those settings of time and place to motifs dating back at least three centuries to the Highlands of Scotland. Forebears of the central male characters in MacLeod's fiction are men who fought the British in battles for independence, or who uprooted their families during the period of Scottish history referred to as the Clearances (when land was cleared of human habitation to make room for lucrative sheep farming; see educationscotland. gov.uk), moving them to Cape Breton. These events occurred in the eighteenth century and, in the case of the Clearances, into the nineteenth century.

By studying a number of short stories and MacLeod's only novel, this essay will argue that his male characters carry the burden of familial and cultural traditions in uneasy, but ultimately necessary ways, creating for each character his soul. As such, the stories of those characters exceed national boundaries and are indeed most fruitfully read in reference to the maxims that they contain, short statements of belief rooted in historical times and places, a "rule of conduct expressed in a sentence" ("Maxim"). The harsh climate of Cape Breton Island and its ruggedly beautiful land, repeated with emphasis in every story, provide a physical space that, in its unique challenges and rewards, reflects the male characters' inner struggles. Those struggles, however, are not uniquely Canadian or postmodern, but rather of the human spirit beyond boundaries of time and place.

Analysts of Canadian literature in the early years of its canonization labored to show how that literature defined the country. In the point of view of Robert Lecker in his *Making It Real: The Canonization of English-Canadian Literature*,

> the formation of the English-Canadian literary institution was driven by the desire to see literature as a force that verified one's sense of community and place. . . . Implicit in this view is the assumption that valuable writing underwrites a national-referential aesthetic. This assumption inspires most Canadian criticism written up to the 1980s. (4)

Rooted in a specific "community and place," MacLeod's stories nevertheless spread into the wider issue of belief itself: what it is, how it affects the soul, and the ways in which it shapes the whole man. Their spirit, paradoxically, comes to acknowledge its ultimate lack of control, while celebrating and using its great strength. Coming to know their ultimate powerlessness, MacLeod's men are nevertheless led to intuit where strength truly lies.

Forged in struggle, and beyond a man's physical or emotional strength, the soul is that which gives each man his spiritual energy, his unique calling. Necessarily deeply rooted in tradition and family ties, the individual's soul must still grow beyond them in MacLeod's fiction. His men suffer in that growth, but also find themselves. Worse suffering ensues when the suffering is ignored, for without the resulting sense of soul, a man is never himself.

The emphasis of Canadianist and theoretical literary criticism on the construction of identity by material conditions prevents emphasis on immaterial, or spiritual, conditions that MacLeod implies shape individuals just as powerfully. Canadian novelist Jane Urquhart writes that, as such, "MacLeod's stories have been called . . . traditional, even conservative, by a literary world cluttered with theories and 'isms'" (37). Significantly, however, his work is admired and popular in his home country, has received numerous literary awards in Canada and beyond, and has been translated into many languages.

While the critical reception of his work has, rightly, placed it within the contexts of Canadianist literary discourse and international literary theory, it has, with some notable exceptions, ignored what can be called the spiritual contexts. One such exception is James O. Taylor's article that acknowledges, though in passing, the power of immaterial forces in MacLeod's work. Taylor writes about "a deep sense of the . . . spiritual" and a "fundamental spirituality" that is "the informing principle of MacLeod's vision" (62). But Taylor names this principle as fate, "an inexplicable controlling power" (62–3), whereas the power cannot really be named. Rather, it inheres in the unavoidable struggle between familial obligation and personal fulfillment, a struggle that provides MacLeod's men with their uniquely described souls. Both the familial obligation and the personal achievement in MacLeod's work pull mightily. In understanding that they cannot respond equally to both pressures, they change.

Other notable exceptions include Andrew Hiscock's theoretically informed critique, in which he writes that "Gaelic referents furnish MacLeod's narrators with the possibilities of self-evaluation and spiritual meditation" (56), those referents being grounded in Scottish language, history, and culture. David Creelman asserts that "When the protagonists make . . . gestures toward freedom . . . [the moment] constitutes an instance of grace. Although he [MacLeod] is not developing or advocating a particular theological framework, he views such moments of choice with a kind of awe" ("Hoping To Strike"). Francis Berces comments that "the human spirit is seen striving to affirm its most basic values" ("Existential Maritimer") in a collection of MacLeod's stories. Berces continues that, "Although there is no explicit religious discourse in [the collection] . . . there is much that generates analogous implications" ("Existential Maritimer").

What do these men—whose complex and often conflicting beliefs shape them in important ways—in fact believe? Unlike MacLeod's men (and, significantly, most of his main characters are male), his women and the many loyal, hard working farm animals in his stories experience no spiritual dilemmas. Almost always, the women escape the world of these stories altogether or, less often, preach in word and deed a simple ethic of survival; the horses and dogs remain exceptionally, intensely teachable and helpful. The men attempt to reconsider maxims that have guided clan thinking for generations.

In his own commentary on "The Canadian Short Story," MacLeod discusses the importance of writing that comes from Canada's diverse geographical and cultural regions, stating: "All of these people [from diverse regions] worry, however, about the universal subjects. They worry about love and death and betrayal and the welfare of their children" (164). He sees in the best of that writing a "Finding [of] the vastness of the universal in the apparently small and comparatively isolated" (MacLeod, "Canadian Short Story" 165). Of his own stories, he states in an interview about a particular episode that "it seems to resonate with some people as a very specific experience, and, hopefully, it resonates with others as a kind of universal experience" (Baer 350). But really, the experiences he writes about concern not "people," but men.

What shifts MacLeod's fiction from the specific to the universal is the recurring theme of belief. He states: "I think of people who live their lives according to folklore as being somewhat similar . . . to people who live their lives by certain strict religious principles" (Kruk). In another interview, he clarifies that "I was interested in . . . people with a belief, whatever their belief is. If they are inside the circle of belief, that is reality, and people who are outside their circle of belief think of them as strange" (Collinge & Sohier). And so, occasions for disagreement and conflict necessarily arise.

Urquhart writes about the men in MacLeod's short fiction that "I am struck by the largeness of . . . [the] main characters. This is not only a largeness of physical stature but also, and more important, a largeness of soul, a generosity of spirit. Reflective and emotional without being self-conscious, his men are intimate . . . with life itself" (36). But they achieve that "generosity of spirit" at a cost. And they are "intimate" with violent death.

As hard rock miners, farmers, and fishermen, they do demanding physical work that could, at any time, maim or kill them. The older mining figures in the fiction often suffer from amputations or diseases; one younger family member dies in a mine shaft. The farmers raise livestock with tremendous skill and care, then butcher and eat it. The fishermen often face life-threatening weather conditions. But their belief in the strength of centuries of courageous forefathers sustains them. As the congenial MacDonald grandpa in MacLeod's novel, *No Great Mischief*, claims, "half rising tipsily from his chair . . . [:] 'Never was a MacDonald afraid'" (89). Whether or not he means "never was a MacDonald *man* afraid" remains unclear, but what is abundantly clear is that clan MacDonald has a heavy burden placed upon it—never to be afraid.

Living through those conflicting beliefs, his male characters grow up. The conflicts are not resolvable, and so, as critic Colin Nicholson writes, "there is, co-existing with his lyrical celebration of living, a pervasive sense of sadness" (197), adding that a "tone of regret . . . suffuses these stories" (198). MacLeod himself says about growing up that "you realize that adults can't do everything and now you are one of them and there is no one to run to, because this is what it means to be an adult. So I was interested in that kind of moment" (Collinge & Sohier). Critic Christian Riegel, writing about an often anthologized story in the collection, "The Boat," asserts that "the narrator documents a period in his life where he must choose between upholding old beliefs and forging his own path in life. In this sense, the story he tells is effectively a coming of age tale—stories that document a period frequently associated with troubled identity and competing life choices" (234).

Adult males in MacLeod's fiction are held by folklore traditions and ancestral beliefs that fit awkwardly in contemporary contexts. In an interview, MacLeod reflects on a recurring value in his fiction, said explicitly by characters or implied by their actions: "'Always look after your own blood' is a maxim that is almost a threat . . . [and that] borders upon a strong religious belief," (Rogers 33). Looking after your own extended family, upholding traditions and customs from another era, and assuming your father's life's work recur as motifs in most of the sixteen pieces in *Island*, a book that includes all of MacLeod's stories published previously in two volumes as well as two previously uncollected stories, and from which all quotations here arise. They are indeed all "coming of age" stories.

In MacLeod's novel, *No Great Mischief*, the grandmother voices the "maxim that is almost a threat" as she raises the narrator, her grandson, and his twin sister after their parents drown: "'Always look after your own blood'" (14 and throughout). Models of looking after their own blood are the working dogs that appear often throughout this fiction. Border collies that descend from the original dog that refused to stay in the Scottish Highlands when its family emigrated, swimming out to sea after their boat and eventually being brought on board for the journey, these animals are described from time to time as ones who "care too much" and "try too hard" (MacLeod, *No Great Mischief* 57 and elsewhere). Intelligent and capable, they often risk their lives for their people. His men, being thoughtful, are frequently placed in situations where they must choose between their own plans and dreams and those of their families. While usually not life-threatening, these situations are nevertheless defining in dramatic ways, their outcomes always painful. The men themselves could often be described as caring too much and trying too hard.

In MacLeod's novel, the narrator's older brother, Calum, kills a man in a brawl at a northern Ontario mining camp, defending his younger brothers as he has done constantly and effectively since the death of their parents. In the present time of the novel, he is dying of alcoholism, after having served time in an Ontario penitentiary and then having worked at odd jobs in Toronto. The brothers recall their lives on Cape Breton Island, when they meet occasionally in the dingy upstairs room where Calum stays. In one reminiscence, they lament having lost their father when they were too young, for it had "seemed unfair" to both of them (MacLeod, *No Great Mischief* 127). The normal way in this traditional culture should instead be: "Fathers helping sons and sons helping fathers in the mysteries of ability and time" (MacLeod, *No Great Mischief* 127), not only in this story but throughout.

The grandmother figure in this novel voices another maxim, one that balances the more challenging and threatening, "always look after your own blood." And her words end the novel: "'All of us are better when we're loved'" (MacLeod, *No Great Mischief* 283). How these often strikingly inarticulate men show love, though, is complex. The narrator in the story "The Closing Down of Summer" reflects on "a certain eloquent beauty" in the difficult and dangerous mining work at which he and his crew excel and for which they are in demand around the world, an unsung beauty. When at their work sites, they revert to talking and singing in their first language: Gaelic. And one summer, during what he refers to as a Celtic Revival in his home area, he and his crew are invited to sing at a concert under the name, MacKinnon's Miners' Chorus. Of the experience he says: "It was as if we were parodies of ourselves . . . mouth[ing] our songs to batteries of tape recorders and to people who did not understand them "(MacLeod, *Island* 195). He continues to lament that they are "Men . . . huge and physical . . . ; polished and eloquent in the propelling of their bodies toward their desired goals and in their relationships and dependencies on one another [like professional athletes], but often numb and silent before the microphones of sedentary interviewers" (MacLeod, *Island* 200).

But numbness and silence are not restricted in his male characters to the situation of facing a microphone. As MacLeod states in an interview about the characters in this story in particular, but applicable to all of his men: "if you're in a completely verbal situation . . . and you're not a verbal person . . . [your silence] may be mistaken for lack of intelligence or lack of feeling" (Kruk 2). Working in occupations that are isolated or extremely noisy, or both—and having done so for several generations—his men act, often with strength and purpose, but they very rarely emote. His fiction seems to imply that the rugged, ever-changing, spectacularly beautiful, and at times treacherous natural world in which his characters live, so carefully described in the fiction, would be as likely to express how it "feels" about itself as these men would be. They are simply compelled by centuries of intense physical struggle. Yet they remain, to quote Urquhart, remarkably "intimate" (36).

Turning to the collection of stories, in the retrospective voice that MacLeod often uses, a now mature narrator in "The Boat" recalls the summer in which his life changed. At age sixteen, it was "that kind of moment" the author refers to in which a boy realizes he has, with great anguish, become a man. He is faced with a most wrenching decision: to stay in school, where he excels, or to quit school and fish with his otherwise incapacitated father, earning a living for the family. He thinks to himself: "I wished that the two things I loved so dearly did not exclude each other in a manner that was so blunt and too clear" (MacLeod, *Island* 19). In the fall, he decides not to return to school, knowing that his father disapproves, as his father has said to him: "'It is best that you go back'" to school (MacLeod, *Island* 18). The young man must then acknowledge "that perhaps my father had never been intended for a fisherman . . . . [H]e had never really loved it. . . . And I thought then to myself that there were many things wrong with all of us and all our lives" (MacLeod, *Island* 21).

Later in his rumination, he remembers that "then there came into my heart a very great love for my father and I thought it was very much braver to spend a life doing what you really do not want rather than selfishly following forever your own dreams and inclinations" (MacLeod, *Island* 21). The completion of high school becomes, for him, "a silly shallow selfish dream" (MacLeod, *Island* 21). The "braver" choice is to follow the traditional pattern for these Cape Breton men: "Fathers helping sons and sons helping fathers." But as MacLeod clarified in an interview about the fathers and sons in his stories: "by encouraging them [their sons] to do something different, they [the fathers] have lost them. It is a kind of ironic situation" (Collinge & Sohier 6). Ironic and deeply sad, but resulting in the creation of a man's soul.

In "The Return," a ten-year-old boy visits Cape Breton for the first time with his parents from their home in Montreal where his father, a Cape Bretoner, works at his wife's father's law firm. The boy's grandfather, ignoring the fastidiousness and barely concealed revulsion of the boy's mother, offers the boy a sip from his glass of rum, hot water, and sugar as the boy, his dad, and his dad's father sit together. The grandfather says to his own son what any one of the other fathers in MacLeod's stories would say: "a man always feels a certain way about his oldest son," ruminating further that "I guess in some ways it is a good thing that we do not all go to school. I could never see myself being owned by my woman's family" (MacLeod, *Island* 85). At age seventy-six, the grandfather is still mining alongside four of his sons.

And so this boy, who enjoys his two weeks outdoors on Cape Breton immensely, watching a cow and bull mate, for example, appreciating the island's unique natural beauty, comes to realize that as an only child "perhaps I have been lonely all of my short life" (MacLeod, *Island* 89). The grandmother in this story, like other grandmothers in MacLeod's work, gives voice to the story's maxim, which in this story is about not leaving home. Of her eight sons, she says to the lawyer son: "'it seems that we can only stay forever if we stay right here. And we have stayed to the seventh generation. Because in the end that is all there is—just staying. I have . . . four [sons] who still work the coal like their father and those four are all that I have that stand by me. It is these four that carry their father now that he needs it" (MacLeod, *Island* 87). Her lawyer son can only reply, no doubt with some regret, that "we just can't live in a clan system any more. We have to see beyond ourselves and our own families" (MacLeod, *Island* 88). The boy in this story has only begun to realize the cost to him of a life apart from the Cape Breton family clan, a cost that however provides him with a soul.

"The Vastness of the Dark" opens in the year 1960 on the narrator's eighteenth birthday when, as the oldest of eight children, he has made up his mind to leave "this grimy Cape Breton coal-mining town whose prisoner I have been all my life" (MacLeod, *Island* 33): "For I must not become as my father . . . . And I must not be as my grandfather who . . . in his moments of clarity remembers mostly his conquests over coal" (MacLeod, *Island* 33). But in a startling irony, as the result of an encounter with a repellant man who offers him a ride, he comes to see that he has misjudged his family and indeed himself.

On the road again, hitchhiking west, he thinks of his parents and grandparents as "Different but in some ways more similar than I had ever thought" (MacLeod, *Island* 56). Recognizing "a soul that I did not even know that I possessed" (MacLeod, *Island* 57), the young man thinks: "perhaps I have tried too hard to be someone else without realizing at first what I presently am" (MacLeod, *Island* 57). What he presently is, almost certainly, will be a miner. Accepting a ride from a carload of other young men leaving the area because the mines are "playing out" (MacLeod, *Island* 58) there, he does not reject their offer to continue to Ontario or Colorado or wherever miners are needed. He may, in fact, come to accept his grandfather's parting words to him, that "It is in all of our blood. We have been working the mines here since 1873" (MacLeod, *Island* 35). The prison in which he senses himself in the story's opening pages transforms itself, shockingly to him, into a kind of home.

In "The Golden Gift of Grey," a story set in the Midwestern United States, another eighteen-year-old narrator again finds himself by distinguishing himself from his family, only to return to them in the end. Jesse, the oldest of six children of parents displaced to Indiana from their mining community in eastern Kentucky, does well in school and on the football field. Unknown to his family, however, he has learned the game of pool by watching older men play at a local bar. One night he takes up a cue and plays for hours, winning game after game in "a type of dream . . . [in which] you do not quite know if the feeling is one of ecstasy or pain, or if the awakening is victory or defeat, or if you are forever saved or yet forever doomed" (MacLeod, *Island* 60). In that conflicted state in which MacLeod's maturing young men often find themselves, Jesse—having defeated a man he admires in the night's final game—"was overcome by a mingled feeling of loneliness and sorrow, regret and anger and fierce exultant pride that made him almost ashamed" (MacLeod, *Island* 69). In short, he has found his soul.

To his strictly religious, hard working parents, who, according to him, are also uncouth, he naively plans to give the money he has won at pool, thereby returning something "to those from whom he had always taken. And he was filled with a great love for the strange people that were his parents" (MacLeod, *Island* 73–4). More, "he was ashamed now of the times he had been ashamed of them" (74). In this single experience of defying his parents, and reflecting throughout a sleepless night on real adult struggles, he has moved from a boy's view of adulthood to a young man's. The "type of dream," from which this character awakens, has taken him through "loneliness and sorrow, regret and anger and fierce exultant pride." Has he been "saved or yet forever doomed"? That is, in order to continue into manhood, must he continue to act in ways that appall those about whom he cares most, or accept their beliefs, or find another way?

"In the Fall" has another boy, James, as narrator, this one "almost fourteen" (MacLeod, *Island* 100), his brother David ten. A loyal, capable old horse is being sold that November so that it will not use feed that should be given to healthier, more useful farm animals. But the man who has worked with the horse for many years at different jobs has grown to care deeply for it, as have his two young sons. And yet the wife and mother, who raises chickens annually for the Christmas market, insists that it be sold that day. In the ensuing painful struggle between husband and wife, James reflects: "I think I begin to understand for the first time how difficult and perhaps how fearful it is to be an adult and I am suddenly and selfishly afraid not only for myself now but for what it seems I am to be" (MacLeod, *Island* 111–2).

As the good old animal is being trucked away, the younger son in a frenzy of mad sadness commits brutally fatal acts against his mother's chickens. While husband and wife are, paradoxically, brought closer together as a result of David's acts, James decides that "I will try to find David, that perhaps he may understand" (MacLeod, *Island* 117)—understand as James now does "how difficult and perhaps how fearful it is to be an adult."

A dying man in his "twenty-sixth year" (MacLeod, *Island* 145) in "The Road to Rankin's Point" returns to the Cape Breton home of his grandmother, "hoping to find such strength [as hers] for the living of my life and the meeting of my death" (MacLeod, *Island* 172). He realizes that "I have never thought of my grandmother so much in terms of love as in terms of strength. Perhaps, I think now, because the latter has always been so much more visible" (MacLeod, *Island* 163). Ninety-six years old and still living alone in her own home, still playing "Gaelic airs" on her violin (MacLeod, *Island* 158), having lost her husband when she was the narrator's age and having raised seven children on her own, the grandmother survives the many requests of her family to move into a nursing home by repeating the motto: "*I will not be defeated*" (MacLeod,

Island 171). But the motto that has served her so well during her hard life does not offer the adequate "perception of death" that the narrator has come to her for. "I would like to realize and understand now my grandmother's perception of death in all its vast diversity" (MacLeod, *Island* 160), he states. In fact, "deep down I know that I will find only the intensity of life" (MacLeod, *Island* 158). Taught by his grandmother about strength and survival, he struggles to understand their absence.

"To Every Thing There Is a Season" recounts a Christmas when the male narrator was eleven. Taking place on a small farm on the west coast of Cape Breton Island in the year 1977, the story centers around the boy's not wanting to relinquish his belief in Santa Claus—a stage in growing up—for "without him [Santa Claus] . . . it seems our fragile lives would be so much more desperate" (MacLeod, *Island* 210). Six young children, their mother, and a seriously ill father await the arrival of the family's eldest child, a young man of nineteen who works on the large transport boats in the Great Lakes and sends packages home from such places in Ontario as Toronto, St. Catharines, and Sault Ste. Marie.

On this Christmas Eve, the young narrator is asked, for the first time in his life, to stay up with the other adults after the younger five children have gone to bed, in order to help prepare the gifts for them. His own gifts no longer say "'from Santa Claus'" (MacLeod, *Island* 217), he sees: "Yet I am not so much surprised as touched by a pang of loss at being here on the adult side of the world. It is as if I have suddenly moved into another room and heard a door click lastingly behind me. I am jabbed by my own small wound" (MacLeod, *Island* 217).

Simultaneously, the father's imminent death at age forty-two becomes clear, such that the young boy seems to understand that he will be losing hope in him soon, as well as in Santa Claus. "'Every man moves on,' says my father quietly . . . , 'but there is no need to grieve. He leaves good things behind'" (MacLeod, *Island* 217). "[J]abbed by his own small wound" and "touched by a pang of loss," this narrator—like the others—comes to conflicting, incompatible realizations in the story. Delighted by his big brother's return home and the Christmas Eve celebrations described here with such care, he is nevertheless at the same time saddened by the loss of comfort of a benevolent and helpful figure in his and his family's "fragile lives."

A seventy-eight-year old widower, Archibald, is the main character in "The Tuning of Perfection," a man who has lived all of his adult life in the house he built on original family ground of Cape Breton Island. Implicated in his large family's invitation to sing at a Scots Around the World Festival in Halifax, Nova Scotia, that summer in the 1980s, Archibald insists to the visiting TV producer that the family be allowed to sing all of the verses of all of the "mournful" (MacLeod, *Island* 301) songs he recalls perfectly in Gaelic. He is refused, and instead a group of young island men is chosen—a group who will sing "a bunch of nonsense syllables strung together" (MacLeod, *Island* 303) because neither they nor the majority of the large audience knows, or cherishes, the original language of the island. Having greatly disappointed his extended family with his unwillingness to adapt to the TV producer's demands, Archibald feels, surprisingly, "that he was 'right' in the way he had felt so many years before when he had . . . decided to build their house near the mountain's top . . . . And he felt as he had felt during the short and burning intensity of their [his and his wife's] brief life together. He began almost to run" (MacLeod, *Island* 305).

Difficult decisions, often fraught with lasting emotional consequences, recur for MacLeod's men throughout their lives. Archibald in this story, "betrayed by forces he could not control" (MacLeod, *Island* 290), nevertheless accepts a gift from the young male singers with whom he, finally, feels connection: "He . . . envied them their closeness and their fierceness and . . . their tremendous energy. And he imagined it was men like them who had given, in their recklessness, all they could think of in that confused and stormy past" of their shared Scottish heritage (MacLeod, *Island* 309). These young men are "'*adjustable*'" to what the producer demands, that word becoming this tale's fatal maxim.

In the collection's final story, "Clearances," another aged male narrator faces the dilemma posed by a maxim that has guided his family for generations: "We will have to go forward" (MacLeod, *Island* 418 and elsewhere) by, for example, learning English at an earlier time. Now this man must decide whether or not to sell to German tourists the house his grandfather built, in which he lives, and the prime Cape Breton land on which it stands. Accompanied by one of the famously loyal border collies of MacLeod's fiction, hearing his own son quote the maxim minutes earlier—"We have to go forward" (MacLeod, *Island* 429)—this elderly man and his dog are about to be attacked by a neighbor's escaped pit bull at story's end. Like the Scottish ancestors centuries earlier, who left their homes and sailed to Canada because of government Clearances of their land, this man and his collie are victims of an uncontrolled and soulless greed that resembles the madness of an attacking pit bull. "'Neither of us was born for this,'" he thinks as the mad dog approaches (MacLeod, *Island* 430). What they were born for he seems, at this critical juncture, unable to name. It would seem to be the finding of their souls.

Works Cited

Baer, William. "A Lesson in the Art of Storytelling: An Interview with Alistair MacLeod." *Michigan Quarterly* 44.2 (2005): 334–52. *Literature Online*. 8 Feb. 2014.

Berces, Francis. "Existential Maritimer: Alistair MacLeod's *The Lost Salt Gift of Blood*." *Studies in Canadian Literature/Études en littérature canadienne* 16.1 (1991): n.p. *Érudit*. 7 Feb. 2014.

Creelman, David. "Hoping To Strike Some Sort of Solidity": The Shifting Fictions of Alistair Macleod." *Studies in Canadian Literature/Études en littérature canadienne* 24.2 (1999): n.p. *ProQuest*. 7 Feb. 2014.

Collinge, Linda, Jacques Sohier. "Alistair MacLeod – b. 1936 [interview]." *Journal of the Short Story in English*. 41 (Autumn 2003): n.p. *revues. org.* 2 Feb. 2014. Educationscotland.gov.uk.

Hiscock, Andrew. "'This Inherited Life': Alistair MacLeod and the Ends of History." *Journal of Commonwealth Literature* 35.2 (2000): 51–70. *Scholars' Portal.* 8 Feb. 2014.

Kruk, Laurie. "Alistair MacLeod: The World Is Full of Exiles [Interview]." *Studies in Canadian Literature/Études en littérature canadienne* 20:1 (1995): n.p. *ProQuest.* 8 Feb. 2014.

Lecker, Robert. *Making It Real: The Canonization of English-Canadian Literature.* Concord, Ontario: House of Anansi P, 1995.

MacLeod, Alistair. "The Canadian Short Story." *Dominant Impressions: Essays on the Canadian Short Story.* Ed. Gerald Lynch & Angela Arnold Robbeson. Ottawa, Ontario: Ottawa UP, 1999. 161–166.

_____. *Island: The Collected Stories.* Toronto: McClelland & Stewart, 2000.

_____. *No Great Mischief: A Novel.* 1999. Toronto: McClelland & Stewart, 2001.

"Maxim." *The Concise Oxford Dictionary.* Ed. Robert E. Allen. 8th ed. 1990.

Nicholson, Colin. "Alistair MacLeod: Interviewed and Assessed by Colin Nicholson." *The Journal of Commonwealth Literature* 21.1 (January 1986): 188–200. *Scholars' Portal.* 7 Feb. 2014.

Riegel, Christian. "Elegy and Mourning in Alistair MacLeod's 'The Boat.'" *Studies in Short Fiction* 35 (1998): 233–40. *Literature Online.* Web. 7 Feb. 2014.

Rogers, Shelagh. "An Interview with Alistair MacLeod." *Alistair MacLeod: Essays on His Work.* Ed. Irene Guilford. Toronto: Guernica, 2001. 11–35.

Taylor, James O. "Art Imagery and Destiny in Alistair MacLeod's Fiction: 'Winter Dog' as Paradigm." *The Journal of Commonwealth Literature* 29.2 (1994): 61–9. *Scholars' Portal.* 7 Feb. 2014.

Urquhart, Jane. "The Vision of Alistair MacLeod." *Alistair MacLeod: Essays on His Work.* 36–42.

Race Roulette: Hierarchy, Hypersexuality, and Hyperbole in Marie-Célie Agnant's *The Book of Emma* and Dany Laferrière's *How to Make Love to a Negro without Getting Tired*_____

Holly L. Collins

> The great roulette wheel of the flesh. That's how it turns. Red,
> Black, Yellow. Black, Yellow, Red. Yellow, Red, Black. The Great
> Mandala of the Western World.
> (Dany Laferrière, *How to Make Love to a Negro without Getting Tired*)

This image from Haitian-Québécois writer Dany Laferrière underscores the ever-present leitmotif of the man of color as object. Indeed, objectification is a key theme of Laferrière's first novel, one which sketches the life of a young, black immigrant living inescapably in the gaze of the white society that surrounds him. Montreal society's reaction to the young author vacillates between fear and a taste for the exotic. But whence does this Otherness come? How was the "Black man," or people of African descent in general, invented in the white, North American imagination?

North America's present cannot be separated from its past, and this not merely a recent past, but a past several centuries old. The present outlined by Laferrière in *How to Make Love to a Negro without Getting Tired* (1985) stems directly from the history that Marie-Célie Agnant reexamines in her 2001 novel *The Book of Emma*. Laferrière and Agnant share a common homeland and immigration story. Both were born in Haiti in 1953 and subsequently moved to Montreal at a relatively young age, in 1976 and 1970 respectively. As Mary Jean Green puts it, both authors "play an important role in defining a bipolar diasporic identity oscillating between Haiti and Montreal" (327). Their backgrounds give Agnant and Laferrière particular insight into the history of race in North

America, including slavery in the Caribbean and its consequences, which continue to play out centuries later.

By examining the themes of hierarchy, hypersexuality, and hyperbole in Agnant's *Book of Emma* and Laferrière's *How to Make Love . . .* we gain a clearer picture of the historical context that shaped the racial paradigm in which contemporary North Americans live. Gendered representations of the experiences of racism figure prominently and make these two works complementary expressions of postcolonial Otherness. Both Agnant and Laferrière examine color and color hierarchy, colonial history, and the persisting specters of this period. Within the hierarchy of color created in a slave-era Caribbean, both the black woman and black man were assigned many characteristics, presumed to be essential or innate, of which sexuality or hypersexuality was prominent. This essay will examine how this characteristic actually coincides with the racial hierarchy, as Laferrière explains that each race and sex had a hypothetical superior, whom he or she was supposed to please. While the metaphor of sexuality implies a certain hierarchy among the slaves and colonists, the slaves also lived within a very real system of sexual exploitation. Finally, both authors employ hyperbole in their novels in order to emphasize and ridicule the invented and exaggerated nature of racial stereotype and racism itself.

Before embarking upon this study, it is necessary to briefly introduce and contextualize the two novels. *The Book of Emma* tells the story of a Haitian woman who pursued doctoral studies in France before settling in Montreal. The novel takes place with Emma confined to a mental institution in Montreal, being interrogated by a doctor because she has apparently murdered her young child. Emma's bilingual, Creole- and French-speaking character refuses to speak to the French–speaking doctor and chooses instead to only speak to his translator Flore. The story of Emma navigates the history of slavery and oppression via Emma's personal and familial history. Emma's own life provides an illustration of the consequences of the slave epoch in today's society. This gut-wrenching, yet intriguing novel takes the reader on an intimate journey through the history of the Caribbean, from a personal rather than official perspective.

How to Make Love to a Negro without Getting Tired is the first novel of prize-winning author and member of the prestigious Académie Française Dany Laferrière, and the first installment in what he calls his "American autobiography." It chronicles his experience of moving to Montreal and encountering North American racism for the first time. Though a sexually explicit novel, with strong and often racist language, *How to Make Love . . .* capitalizes on sexual metaphor, not in a gratuitous manner, but as an important trope that itself stems from sexual exploitation of slaves. Further, the racists whom the young Laferrière encounters pull no punches of their own. Laferrière must fight fire with fire, so to speak. In this novel, he boldly treats the themes of racism, stereotype, hierarchy, and exploitation in the postcolonial world in a simultaneously humorous and critical manner. According to one *Le Devoir* critic, the novel encourages both "laughing and thinking at the same time." *La Presse* insists that this novel "has a terrorist side to it [. . .] It's a little grenade, designed by a conscientious, clever demolitions expert." However, while translator David Homel calls the title a "come-on title that plays both sides of racial and sexual stereotypes," he also insists that "in this book sex is mostly an indicator of class, ethnic, and historical conflict" (4).

I should also mention Homel's struggle with the translation of the French word *nègre*. The word in French often has a derogatory connotation, though in varying degrees. He explains that it would be inappropriate to use the politically-correct "black" in English because this term rings "simply too free of stereotypes and too politically cool to be used in social satire" (Homel 6). For Homel, it was important to faithfully translate "Laferrière's dynamic between the sexes and colors, in which blacks will always be *nègre*" (6). For this reason, the reader will usually encounter the word "Negro," alternating at times with "Black" and the highly offensive *N-word*, as the context dictates.

Racial/Racist Hierarchy

Rather than meeting an open and welcoming society that would afford him the opportunities to live out his own American dream, the young narrator of *How to Make Love* . . . abruptly encountered a North American racism all too prevalent in societies with a predominantly white, European, Christian heritage. Likewise, when Agnant's Emma moved to France to pursue her studies, she encountered what she called the "Bordeaux colonists" (56). Emma's boyfriend Nicolas describes the African and West Indian students who were "constantly denouncing the racism or discrimination that they had to endure throughout their studies" in France (Agnant 56). Further, after moving to Montreal, Emma would also encounter similar prejudice: many doubted that she had undertaken doctoral studies in France (Agnant 16) and the hyperbolic headlines after the death of her child, which read "Black Woman Sacrifices Her Child . . . A Voodoo Act?" (Agnant 18).

Laferrière explains that "People want so badly to put you in different categories . . . In my books, people examine with a magnifying glass everything that comes from Haiti, and that's what they find extraordinary, whereas the rest . . ." (Chouinard).[1] This tendency towards labelling and classifying everyone leads to an explicit Otherization of anyone seen to be "different" by the majority culture of a society. Many migrant authors of Québec consistently endure this type of prejudice.[2] The "Black person" as the North American imaginary sees him or her does not exist. Laferrière explains, "On the human level, the black man and the white woman do not exist" (145). They are "American inventions, like the hamburger or the drive-in" (Laferrière 145).

Contemporary racism has not emerged simply as a phenomenon of recent history. In fact, most of the labels and stereotypes that fed twentieth-century racism have their origins in the first encounters between Europeans and Africans. Indeed, Franca Bernabei classifies the "persistence of racism, colourism, and sexism in the circumatlantic world as an unresolved consequence of slavery" (486). Louis XIV's *Code noir*, signed in 1685 and revised in 1724, delineated the rules, regulations, and conditions of slavery within the French Empire. Though it would be slowly abandoned throughout the early 1800s, its tradition and influence would continue to mark the perceptions of race that developed in France during the nineteenth century, the second great imperial era leading up to and including the Scramble for Africa.

It was the *Code noir* that promulgated an official conception of black people as inferior or even subhuman. According to Article 44 of the *Code noir*, slaves were considered to be objects of possession, portable property (*meubles*), like furniture, and as such their emotions, goals, desires, and points of view were irrelevant (*Code noir* 32–33). Often black slaves were even considered incapable of such expressions of humanity. Into the nineteenth century, and coupled with the budding sciences of biology and genetics, the tradition of the black person as subhuman took on a new, pseudo-scientific air. An evolutionary hierarchy was created in which black people were considered to be closer to apes than to white men. They were thus supposedly of a more savage or animal-like nature. A veritable color scale was thought to coincide with evolutionary development, ranging from black as the least evolved and most inferior human to white as the superior human specimen. All other "colors" fell in-between. The closer to white, the nearer to perfection a person was seen to be.

Sue Peabody explains that these were not simply ideas held by a racist public. Rather, people of color were institutionally excluded from a Republic that was supposed to protect the ideals of *liberté, égalité*, and *fraternité* for all men. According to Peabody, rights were legally restricted for "blacks," "mulattoes," and "other people of color" (509). She gives several examples of these color-based racial exclusions: in 1762, all "negroes and mulattoes" in France were ordered to register with the Admirality; another ordinance, issued in 1778, "required 'blacks, mulattoes and other people of color' to carry identification papers;" also, marriages between "whites, blacks, mulattoes and other people of color" were prohibited, and "all priests, notaries, land surveyors and other public officials [were prohibited] from giving any people of color the title of sir or dame" (Peabody 509). Such language within the written law supported the cultural mythology of racial difference and hierarchy and even gave them a legislative legitimacy.

In *The Book of Emma*, Agnant brings together the history of objectification and the present-day life of a black woman in North America. Indeed, Maria Adamowicz-Hariasz characterizes Agnant's novel as "an intersection of personal and collective history" (149), and Bernabei likewise underscores the personal and transgenerational trauma of the protagonist (488). Both French and Québec society see Agnant's protagonist as an object. For her doctor, Flore explains, "she is like the wood of the table, like the bed, just an object" (38), which seems to be a clear allusion to *Code noir*-type language. Like her ancestors brought to the slave plantations who were given names that could be "shout[ed] in a single breath, one or two syllables spit out of [the] mouth like a seed, that cracked like the blows of a whip" (Agnant 165–6), those around her efface Emma's name and simply call her "the negro lady in 122" (Agnant 29, 191). Likewise, in the same way that Kilima, the first of Emma's ancestors to come to America, was literally labeled as property with a mark on her cheek, "the *C* of the word 'Count,' like a crescent moon" (Agnant 166), Emma's humanity also disintegrates. Flore writes that "Emma was no longer a human being, but a case, a file, perhaps even an object in room 122" (Agnant 197). Emma's confinement and objectification echoes loudly the slave-era insistence that black people were sub-human, that they "were nothing but beasts" (Agnant 176).

According to Emma, society only accepts a black woman, especially one with dark skin, when face down in submission. She whispers to Flore: "Nothing provokes as much hate as a stand-tall black woman. They want to see all of us prostrate" (Agnant 74). Emma's own attempt at writing history, her doctoral thesis on slavery, was "trampled on" by both the "Bordeaux colonialists" (Agnant 56) and those at the university she attended in Montreal. It was shortly after her second attempt to defend the thesis that she murdered her child. Emma's attempts to rewrite a "truncated, lobotomized, excised, chewed on, ground up, then spat out" history were crushed, in her words, "so that they alone will continue to write for us" (Agnant 29). According to Emma, the world sees the "word of a black woman" as worthless (Agnant 71). Agnant underscores this fact in an interview with Florence Ramond Jurney by insisting that "Slave women were submissive to white men—their masters, they were submissive to black men—their companions, they were submissive to white women—their masters' wives, submissive to everyone. They found themselves on the bottom rung, subjected to racism and sexism of all kinds, rape and violence of all kinds" (Jurney 388).

Just as Emma fights an identity imposed on her by those around her—"black," "mad," "negro"—Laferrière also battles the stereotyped notions that seek to define him, most of which are a throwback to colonial perceptions of race. He found himself subjected to the white gaze of his host society and thus subject to all of their myths and stereotypes. Throughout *How to Make Love . . .* , Laferrière explores the various stereotypes about black men and shows how ridiculous and laughable they can be, though certainly not innocuous. As Mireille Rosello insists, "it is impossible not to be traversed by the flow of stereotypes" (64). Laferrière adds that, "In America, one encounters myth on every street corner" (Gagnon). In exile, Laferrière went to North America in pursuit of the "American Dream." Montreal, the French–speaking metropolis of North America should have afforded him the opportunities to succeed. However, like Emma in France, he found himself subjected to the heavy North American racism that has plagued it for so long.

Laferrière also refers to the tradition according to the *Code noir*, which saw the black person as a piece of moveable property. He cites Article 44 of the *Code noir* before the first chapter of *How to Make Love . . .* , signaling to the reader early on the important role played by tradition and perceptions of the "Black man" in the designation of his being. As Frantz Fanon writes, "Je suis sur-déterminé de l'extérieur"—he lives as a slave of his appearance (Fanon 93). Fanon also insists that, "color is the most visible external sign of race," and because of this, persists as "the criteria by which one judges people without taking into account their [particular situation and knowledge]" (95). Though society may no longer be consciously racist, there remains an underlying centuries-old racism that otherizes and inferiorizes black people.

Beyond the myth of the primitive Negro, we also see many examples in *How to Make Love . . .* of the supposed savage nature of the "Black man." While in the nineteenth century, this stereotype tended to a more animalistic interpretation, in the later twentieth and twenty-first centuries, it has had more of a criminal interpretation, with black men being feared as aggressors prowling the city streets. Throughout the book, those who surround him often look upon our narrator with a suspicious eye. He references the "the myth of the animalistic, primitive, barbarous black who thinks only of fucking" (Laferrière 42) and the complaints that they are "all maniacs, psychopaths and hassle-artists who are always coming on to women" (Laferrière 48). As an intellectual, the narrator constantly encounters those who see him as a *surprisingly* intelligent black man. With seething sarcasm, Laferrière underscores the ridiculous nature of these absurd ideas that somehow black humans are less capable and less likely to be educated: "a black with a book denotes the triumph of Judeo-Christian civilization! Proof that those bloody crusades really did have some value. True, Europe did pillage Africa but this BLACK IS READING A BOOK" (Laferrière 35).[3] Such justification of the civilizing mission has allowed the West to ignore and forget the detriment it has caused. Places like Canada and the United States can, therefore, continue to put forth an image of a bountiful and welcoming society while still harboring a racist attitude, whether consciously or unconsciously.

The Stereotype of Black Hypersexuality

The exploration and exploitation of myth by Laferrière in *How to Make Love to a Negro without Getting Tired* begins with the title. Already from the cover of the book, he signals the myth of black hypersexuality: believed to be physically well-endowed and of sexual talents and appetites that are greater than average, one could easily wear oneself out making love to the mythological, hypersexed black man. Laferrière points out, however, that behind this myth hides the perpetuating cycle of white hierarchy that places the white man above the black man, all relations being unequal: "White women must give white men pleasure, as black men must for white women. Hence, the myth of the Black stud" (40–41). This order signals an exoticized view of the black man, a part of the myth of the primitive nature of blacks, itself a vestige of the evolutionary hierarchy and of the sexual exploitation of enslaved men and women in the Caribbean.

The violent sexual abuse of women and men of African descent is an all too often forgotten or ignored aspect of American history. Agnant's reappraisal of history via Emma and her great-aunt Mattie tells the story of the forced mating the slaves underwent and the horrifying punishment for refusal. Emma describes the "days when the black men had been transformed into animals in the cane fields" (Agnant 88). They were "ordered with a whip to service the women one after the other. In those days, black men were led to fornicate, just as beasts were led to water" (Agnant 88–89). Still worse was the fate of women "who refused the matings ordered by the commanders" (Agnant 90). They were forced "to dig a big hole and pour cane syrup into it. Then, they had to get into the hole and wait, wait for the ants to do their work" (Agnant 91).

Laferrière illustrates the way in which this past creeps into the present with what seemed to the narrator a simple conversation while waiting in line at the post office. His perception contrasts greatly with what was seen by all of those around him as "the Negro attacking the white woman" (Laferrière 48). In reply to a simple question about reading, the woman, whom he describes as "over-cruised" and "sick of it," forcefully asks him to leave her alone, and the majority of the people in line "turn around to watch the spectacle [. . .]" (Laferrière 48). Because of their preconceived notions about black men, in their eyes, the narrator becomes something outside of his control. His actions are converted, perverted even, into a stereotyped role. This manifestation of racialized sexuality[4] according to Daniel Coleman mythologizes the black man as a sexual predator, a mythology that was created in order to move the focus away from the white slave owners' transgressions with their female slaves: "the red-herring story of the black rapist's lust for the white virgin deflects attention away from the hidden deeds of the white master rapist" (59).

Indeed, this type of sexual abuse was prevalent on the plantations of the Caribbean and the US South. The Count, Kilima's master, lusted after his slaves. Mattie describes him as an "insatiable being, a caricature of a man that power and lust had transformed into a monster" (Agnant 179). He had an "obsessive vision that had lingered in him for a long time, that of his hands buried in that mass of tobacco-colored flesh, of his fingers kneading the flabby breasts, of her vagina, overcoming without consideration the presumptuousness of that slave, much younger than she claimed" (Agnant 180). After having been forced to serve completely nude at a dinner party for the master, the young Kilima soon became an object in the hands of three men, including the Count. Agnant describes how the young Kilima's attempts to resist were punished by the cutting off of her nose—a mutilation usually reserved for women to deprive them of their beauty. Cecile, her adoptive mother, lost her hands for trying to protect her.

The Use of Hyperbole as a Tool

In order to push back against these antiquated and invented conceptions of people of color, both Agnant and Laferrière employ hyperbole as a tool, albeit in different ways. By infecting present-day Emma with what seems, on a superficial level, to be a centuries-old madness, Agnant draws attention to the immanence of the past in the present. Flore, Emma's doctor, and others label Emma, on many occasions, as mad. At their first meeting, Flore describes the "unusual excesses [Nature] indulged in when she created Emma" (Agnant 12). Flore can see that "Emma's soul is imprisoned in the madness that has taken over her body" (Agnant 13). The doctor struggles to "interpret the metaphors, the exaggerations, these images of unusual violence" put forth by Emma (Agnant 79). She has an "unhealthy obsession with ships" and an "obsessive delirium" (Agnant 80, 197). Emma's madness and the excesses with which Agnant creates her serve to draw the reader's attention not to the ramblings of a so-called madwoman, but rather to a history not forgotten by the descendants of slaves. Though some "prefer silence as a way of pretending we have forgotten," as Aunt Mattie says, Agnant provides a brightly flashing caution light that cannot be ignored (182).

The "madness which is supposed to have come over in the holds of the slave ships" consumes Emma (Agnant 10). She struggles with "the curse of our blood," "the self-destruction which she had inherited," and an "ancient sadness" (Agnant 30, 53, 57). In the end, Emma murders her daughter to save her from this curse and from the condemnation of life as a black woman. While her actions may seem hyperbolic, Agnant uses Emma's story to draw attention to the truth of what occurred in America's past. In her interview with Jurney, Agnant explains that in *The Book of Emma*, she wanted to understand Emma's present by examining the past (388). Many enslaved women murdered their children to rescue them from slavery, a tragic reality that should not be forgotten. Yet, as Agnant notes, the slave era in Haitian novels remains totally absent, if not repressed (Jurney 388). Emma asks if we know "how much sugar, how much blood, how many slaves, how much black women's milk had been needed to construct just one European city" (Agnant 145). While the West continues to forget that our societies were built on the backs and by the blood of slaves, Agnant puts this history center stage, makes it present, and embodies it in Emma.

Laferrière's hyperbole, on the other hand, comes in the form of what Coleman classifies as metaparody because of the multiple ways and on multiple levels in which he rejects racialized discourse: "Laferrière's text is not a simple one-to-one parody [. . .] it is a metaparody because it re-sites and ridicules not just the original discourse of racialized sexuality, but also its many responses and variation throughout its etiology, including its opponents and resisters" (Coleman 65). That is, Laferrière's metaparody mocks not just one image or stereotype, but rather the many layers of stereotype and response that weave the fabric of our current understanding of race.

Throughout *The Matter of Images*, Richard Dyer explains that stereotypes maintain boundaries and limits between those who see themselves in the center and those whom they classify as being peripheral. The tight grip on these stereotypes, which define the world of those in a so-called center and make them feel safe, cannot be loosed by simply proclaiming the falsehood of these ideas. Myth persists by being deeply ingrained in their memory. Rather, suggests Rosello, those who reappropriate stereotypes and myth steal what made this old system function smoothly and use it for laughter and derision (64). The humorous aspect of Laferrière's *How to Make Love to a Negro without Getting Tired* makes it no less powerful a statement against white cultural myth about black men. By getting to know the narrator intimately through his writing and thoughts, we see him as a man, as a human and not as a "black man." From this point, the reader can see how ridiculous and inconsistent with reality that myth and stereotype can be. As Rosello reiterates, it is impossible to escape the onslaught of the many stereotypes that are taught and reinforced by dominant culture and its institutions, but knowing what they are and how they work can allow for their reappropriation (64).

Laferrière's exploitation of myth and stereotype allows him to combat the popular perceptions about black men living in white society. Though repetition of myths and stereotypes poses a certain amount of danger, Laferrière's form of resistance against them, whether it be sarcasm or repetition in order to ridicule, hopefully accomplishes two goals. First, he seeks to make those who may unconsciously perpetuate myth aware of its constructed nature, and second, he helps to deconstruct and destroy the cycle that perpetuates myth and stereotypes in society.

Of the various strategies available in the fight against the stereotypes that compose myth, reappropriation can be deployed as a very powerful tool, as we see in *How To Make Love . . . .* Instead of trying to rewrite stereotypes, Rosello suggests that reappropriation offers a better form of resistance. Trying to rewrite a stereotype creates another construction or posits an exception to the stereotype, which itself reinforces the so-called rule. For example, Laferrière opposing the "myth of the black stud" by saying that "Black men are not studs," would both create a new stereotype, that black men are not "studs," and would also reinforce the grouping together of black men in a homogenizing fashion. Instead, reappropriation in humorous ways is, as Rosello describes it, adding fuel to the fire (64). Putting out a fire leaves the fire still under control: it can (and will be) reignited. Contrarily, if we take Rosello's image to its logical conclusion, throwing fuel on a fire makes it burn wildly and out of control.

Once Laferrière reappropriates these myths, he can then deconstruct them and make them crumble from within. Through his reappropriation of the *Negro myth*, Laferrière adds his own fuel to the fire in an effort to destroy the constructed ideas of the past that created and reinforced racialized and racist discourse. Laferrière cannot control myth, but by hyperbolically making the foundation of the myth rage out of control, he may just be able to make it crumble into a pile of ridiculous notions that are now recognizable as the rubble that they are.

Conclusion

Reiterating Frantz Fanon's declaration that "the black soul is a white construction" (11), Laferrière concludes *How To Make Love . . .* with a short chapter entitled "You're Not Born Black, You Get That Way" (153), a clear allusion to Simone de Beauvoir's statement in *The Second Sex* that "One is not born, but rather becomes, a woman" (301). Labels and stereotypes that were "written" throughout history are in serious need of rewriting. Laferrière makes many allusions to writing within his novel and also exploits the fact that his narrator seeks success as a writer. Creating a work of fiction takes on great significance in Laferrière's strategy of dismantling stereotype. This metafiction, a fiction within a fiction, and his many allusions draw attention to the importance of text, textuality, and discourse, the tools with which much of existent stereotype and myth were built. By becoming a successful author within the novel, Laferrière "highlight[s] his role as a creator taking control of the discourses that seek to constrain him" (Ireland 73). Susan Ireland suggests that Laferrière's metafictional dimension "is used primarily to emphasize the constructed nature of stereotyping discourses" (68). Laferrière's exploitation of writing and his many references to other texts throughout the novel highlight the extent to which text and discourse have served to create the representation of the black man. Ireland affirms that, through this emphasis on writing and text, Laferrière seeks to "draw attention to the constructed nature of black identity and to the possibility of rewriting it" (71). Our knowledge of the past, according to Ireland, is inevitably linked to textuality, and by keeping the focus on colonial discourse in its many forms, Laferrière reminds his reader "that these 'texts' could have been written differently" (71) and that there exists "the possibility of creating a new text" (72).

Likewise, while Emma fails to rewrite history through historical writing in the form of her dissertation, Mattie, Emma, Flore, and Agnant succeed in making the unofficial story known through writing reimagined oral history and historical fiction. Emma recalls that "Living with Mattie was like living in a big book, a book that she constructed each day, page after page" (Agnant 136). Mattie understood the importance of passing on their story: "we must know how to sustain it," she teaches Emma and explains that "after me, you will pass on this memory" (Agnant 147, 163). Like Mattie, though Emma will die, she also passes on the story to Flore who recognizes she was "left alone to carry the burden of her terrifying tale" (Agnant 197). In this way, their stories are not forgotten, even though they have been excluded from official history and memory. Patrice Proulx contends that "These stories, disseminated from generation to generation by way of a female narrative chain, offer a counter-discourse to official history" (42).

Emma recognizes the importance of writing: she derides the idea that "great books were written by great men" (Agnant 71) and makes several lamentations to Flore about what she knew of her own past being limited by those books. Emma explains that "They have written so much garbage, so much nonsense," but that "in spite of all their great books, they are ignoramuses" (Agnant 199). For this reason, Agnant has undertaken a rewriting of history, and as Scott W. Lyngaas puts it, "Emma's life is a struggle to express the history of slavery to a world that refuses to hear" (969). For Agnant, "writing functions as a mode of resistance" (Proulx 36).

In conclusion, Laferrière and Agnant rely on similar tactics to convey their message that, as Laferrière puts it, "a human being, even a black one (especially a black one!) is made of flesh and blood, muscle and piss" (130). Everyone and their experiences differ, but these novels highlight the human element; everyone thirsts, for basic needs, for a chance to thrive, to chase one's dreams. The narrator of *How To Make Love . . .* exclaims, "Shit, I've got a thirst for a decent life. I am thirsty. The Gods are thirsty. Women are thirsty. Why not Negroes? THE NEGROES ARE THIRSTY" (Laferrière 150).⁵ Laferrière wishes to dwell on this human experience as a citizen of the world and of humanity and exhorts his reader to do the same. He explains "The paths are all laid out to define you, the culture shock they want to hear me talk about, it isn't from leaving Port-au-Prince that I experienced it, it was in leaving childhood!" (Chouinard).

Agnant reexamines the history that created today's racial, racializing, and racist discourse, showing how "the past is past in name only" (192). Laferrière addresses the resurgence of this past first by seeking to ridicule and thus dissolve racist myth and stereotype, then by insisting on the human experience, the commonality of what we all live. Despite how different this experience may be for each individual, Laferrière challenges his readers to consider him and everyone else as fellow citizens of the world and not as "black," "white," "red," or "yellow," the latter being merely figments of Western constructed myth. Similarly, Agnant posits the necessity of this world citizen, the "man from every continent that the world needs to cure it of the chaos into which hate has plunged it" (53).

Notes

1. Translation mine for all quotations originally in French unless otherwise stated.
2. See Chouinard, Marie-Andrée. "Ecrivains d'ailleurs ou écrivains tout court."
3. The all caps were in the original French version, though not in Homel's translation.
4. On racialized sexuality, see Abdul R. JanMohamed's "Sexuality on/off the Racial Border: Foucault, Wright, and the Articulation of

'Racialized Sexuality'" in *Discourses of Sexuality: From Aristotle to AIDS* (94–116).

5. Again, the capital letters are in the original French version, but not Homel's translation.

Works Cited

Adamowicz-Hariasz, Maria. "Le Trauma et le témoinage dans *Le Livre d'Emma* de Marie-Célie Agnant." *Symposium* 64.3 (2010): 149–168.

Agnant, Marie-Célie. *The Book of Emma*. Trans. Zilpha Ellis. Toronto: Insomniac Press, 2006.

Balibar, Étienne, & Immanuel Maurice Wallerstein. *Race, nation, classe : Les identités ambiguës*. Paris: Découverte, 1988.

de Beauvoir, Simone. *The Second Sex*. New York: Vintage Books, 1973.

Bernabei, Franca. "Transatlantic poetics of haunting." *Atlantic Studies* 8.4 (2011): 485–506.

Chouinard, Marie-Andrée. "Ecrivains d'ailleurs ou écrivains tout court." *Le Devoir*. 22 Mar. 1999: B-8.

Le Code Noir. Ed. Robert Chesnais. Paris: L'Esprit Frappeur, 1998.

Coleman, Daniel. *Masculine Migrations: Reading the Postcolonial Male in "New Canadian" Narratives*. Toronto: U of Toronto P, 1998.

Dyer, Richard. *The Matter of Images: Essays on Representation*. London: Routledge, 2002.

Fanon, Frantz. *Peau noire, masques blancs*. Paris: Éditions du Seuil, 1965.

Gagnon, Katia. "Danny [sic] Laferrière à la chasse aux mythes de l'Amérique." *La Presse*. 21 (Nov. 1993): B-6.

Green, Mary Jean. "Accenting the French in Comparative American Studies." *Comparative Literature* 61.3 (2009): 327–334.

Homel, David. "How to Make Love with the Reader . . . Slyly." *How to Make Love to a Negro without Getting Tired*. By Dany Laferrière. 2010. Vancouver: Douglas & McIntyre, 2010. 1–6.

Ireland, Susan. "Declining the Stereotype in the Work of Stanley Lloyd Norris, Max Dorsinville, and Dany Laferrière." *Quebec Studies* 39 (2005): 55–77.

JanMohamed, Abdul R. "Sexuality On/Of the Racial Border: Foucault, Wright and the Articulation of 'Racialized Sexuality.'" *Discourses of Sexuality: From Aristotle to AIDS*. Ed. Domna C. Stanton. Ann Arbor: U Michigan P, 1995.

Jurney, Florence Ramond. "Entretien avec Marie-Célie Agnant." *The French Review* 79.2 (2005): 384–394.

Kazemipur, Abdolmohammed, & Shiva S. Halli. "Immigrants and 'New Poverty': The Case of Canada." *International Migration Review*. 35 (Winter 2001): 1129–56.

Laferrière, Dany. *How to Make Love to a Negro without Getting Tired.* Trans. David Homel. Vancouver: Douglas & McIntyre, 2010.

Lyngaas, Scott W. "Confronting Haitian History in the Novels of Marie-Célie Agnant." *The French Review* 84.5 (2011): 967–977.

Peabody, Sue. "Race, Slavery and the Law in Early Modern France." *The Historian* 56.3 (1994): 501–10.

Proulx, Patrice. "Bearing Witness and Transmitting Memory in the Works of Marie-Célie Agnant." *Québec Studies* 39 (2005): 35–53.

Rosello, Mireille. *Declining the Stereotype: Ethnicity and Representation in French Cultures*. Hanover, NH: Dartmouth, 1998.

Margaret Atwood's Comedy: The Fat Lady and the Gendered Body in *Lady Oracle*

Charlotte Templin

The comic is central to Margaret Atwood's imaginative vision. Her dominant voice is impish and satirical—nowhere more so than in the comic novel, *Lady Oracle*. Atwood has been called a "connoisseur of pain" (Maddocks 77), but one response to pain is humor, and I would argue further that the comic mode of *Lady Oracle* permits the hopefulness—in Atwood's case, largely a suggestion of hope—that is a generic feature of comedy. Few would dispute that *Lady Oracle* is a comic novel, but critics of the novel have often ignored the generic characteristics of comedy that influence its meaning.

In fact, the novel has often been interpreted in ways that contradict the generic features of comedy. Reading *Lady Oracle* squarely within the paradigm of comedy resolves certain problems of interpretation, including how to view the protagonist and how to interpret the ending of the novel, matters of crucial importance since they relate to an important issue in this and other Atwood novels: the possibilities for women in a sexist society. This essay argues that a central concern of the novel is the subordination of women, with the "fat woman" standing in for women in general.

In the mainstream of comic tradition, Atwood's 1976 novel employs both satire and humor. Satire, which is often distinguished from a more benign form called humor, holds up institutions, human traits, and sometimes individuals to ridicule, while "humor" connotes a more accepting attitude toward human failings, with the suggestion that we should forgive ourselves for our human nature (Heilman 71). Atwood's satire is hilarious and spirited, but Atwood has a way of combining hilarity with a critique that is biting in the extreme. Atwood's targets include fringe movements of the political left, avant-garde art and the publishing industry. But her more pointed barbs are directed at the sexist cultural values that her protagonist Joan Foster and all women are subject to—and particularly social control of women through control of the body. The ideology of romance, which limits women's autonomy and self-development, also comes in for mockery.

The most significant humor and the basis of much of the satire in the novel is Atwood's treatment of the "Fat Lady Joke," a tradition in popular comedy that presents the fat woman as inherently funny. The protagonist and narrator, Joan Foster, starts life as an overweight child. She eventually loses one hundred pounds in her late teens. Although she becomes a slim beauty (with flaming red hair, no less) she is haunted by her childhood fat. The image of the fat lady is central to the novel. When Joan and her Aunt Lou attend a carnival, Lou does not allow Joan to view the Fat Lady or the other freaks, but the Fat Lady continues to haunt Joan throughout the novel. She reminds Joan that she has fallen short, and she appears whenever Joan is in an anxiety-provoking situation. She also becomes the subject of fantasies for Joan.

Atwood turns the Fat Lady Joke to her uses, appropriating it for feminist purposes. By confronting the joke head-on, Atwood makes a joke of making the fat lady a joke. Atwood uses the image of the fat lady to create comedy about society's expectations for women and about women's internalization of society's values. She also makes Joan, the fat woman (eventually the slender woman who is haunted by her youthful fat), a trickster figure, giving her agency, and making her subject instead of object. Besides rehabilitating the fat woman as subject, she also reinvents the victims of comedy, the butts of the jokes. Atwood's butts include those things that are the norms of traditional comedy: society's normative values and the young, marriageable men who traditionally are bearers of the oppositional values of comedy.

Joan is taught by her society (including pop culture, an important influence in the novel) to view herself as destined to serve and please others, to look to lovers and husbands to give her life meaning. She takes little responsibility for who she is, looking to men for rescue and validation. Trying to fit herself into the gender roles that have been laid out for her, she seeks escape through fantasy and becomes a creator of a fantasy product herself—costume gothics. But there is another side to Joan, one that links her to a long tradition of comic heroes. She is certainly flawed and sometimes mocked in the novel, but she is also passionate, creative, and unconventional (Fee 69). Uneasy with the restrictive and the customary, she is a skeptic, an improviser, a trickster. Ultimately, she gains self-knowledge and takes the first steps away from the role of victim.

Let's look more closely at the Fat Lady Joke. Max Sennett is supposed to have said that "The whacking of Fat Lady's behind is the basis of all true comedy" (Fussell 246). One of the jokes or comic incidents involves the rotund Joan getting hit in the rump by an arrow while she is employed as a carnival worker, whose job it is to pick up arrows around the target. Perhaps it was an accident, but Joan thinks some wise guy simply could not resist the temptation. Whacking somebody's behind brings about the fall of dignity, B. H. Fussell explains in "A Pratfall Can Be a Beautiful Thing." It is comedy's role to deflate pretension and authority: "Comedy poses the question, 'Is nothing sacred?' and answers with a fart" (Fussell 246).

But I don't think Fussell's reasoning explains adequately why the Fat Lady is the most humorous object. The Fat Lady Joke must be analyzed in terms of the tradition of misogynist humor and specifically in the light of mechanisms of social control of the female body. Western culture has a long history of controlling and shaping the female body as a tool for male dominance, as Susan Bordo explains in *Unbearable Weight: Feminism, Western Culture and the Body*. Bordo writes, "Viewed historically, the discipline and normalization of the female body . . . has to be acknowledged as an amazingly durable and flexible strategy of social control" (166). In misogynist humor, women and their bodies are jokes: the mother-in-law, the dumb blonde, the woman driver. The most eligible butt of humor, the fat lady, is a joke because she so clearly falls short of a feminine ideal. Fat on a male comic character can signify good living and a hearty appetite for life, as we see in the example of Falstaff and numerous more recent comics. A fat woman signifies a grotesque failing, a lack of something. Humor can be used for social control, as illustrated in misogynist jokes and stereotypes. But it can also be used to liberate, and Atwood has chosen this tack, like other women who have created comedy (Barreca 9).

Joan, as a disempowered fat female, does not qualify as a person of value; her role is to enable the preferred type of femininity. As a non-subject, Joan is invisible, something she is aware of. When she is thrust upon people's attention, they can't tell her age—all fat women look middle-aged, Joan says. In *Lady Oracle*, Atwood exposes the arbitrary meanings attributed to gender and body shape and thus calls attention to the constructed nature of the gender norm—and its coercive effect. Through the character of the fat-thin Joan, Atwood makes us aware of how the female body is policed and scrutinized.

In her satire, Atwood destabilizes the categories of the funny and the unfunny, the normal and the abnormal. She undertakes parody of the so-called desirable types of femininity in her descriptions of "normal" women and through the costume gothics that Joan writes. Larraine Porter asks, "Is there something intrinsically funny about the female form in its exaggerated state with large breasts, buttocks and thighs when it becomes it becomes a parody of heterosexual desire?" (92). She answers by noting that the "desirable" female form is a construct of male fantasy, and, as such, "ripe for parody, comic abuse, and loss of dignity" (Porter 92). Atwood's effects depend on such parody.

Satire is directed at women acting in characteristic feminine ways that would generally be the norm against which the fat woman is measured. The high school girls, for whom Joan acts as sympathetic listener, are presented as grotesque in their own way. In their sweaters (ornamented with poodle pins) and matching plaid skirts, flirting with athletic stars and avoiding unattractive boys labeled "pills," they are shallow and mindless. Joan's neurotic and destructive mother always appears in Joan's imagination, even when deceased, as slim and well-groomed, in a navy suit and white gloves, a suggestion that she is trapped by the social role she has adopted.

The women in Joan's gothic novels are parodies of the female stereotypes. Some are pure, circumspect, obedient; others are vampish—sexual and daring. They are characterized by the clothes they wear. Joan learns that the secret to success in pulp romance is to get the costumes right. She learns the vocabulary of "pelisse" and "fichu," spending days in costume room of the Victoria and Albert Museum to master the details. It seems the approved female subject exists by virtue of her wardrobe. She participates in what Larraine Porter calls a masquerade, "the masquerade of a fragile physical decorum: of cosmetic fakery, upholstery and physical support, corsetry and prosthetics" (92). Readers of the novel will recall Joan's flagrantly transgressive wardrobe, including a chartreuse car coat with toggles. In the end, the novel is less about the plight of the fat female than about the constructed nature of the ideal of femininity and the inherent absurdity and amenability to parody of gender roles.

Claiming the subject position for the Fat Lady, Atwood makes Joan the narrator of the novel. While satire dominates the novel, Atwood also employs humor to give the fat woman humanity and to destabilize the subjects and objects of traditional comedy. As Joan tells her life story, she finds humor in fat. Fat is funny, as we know from the history of comedy. Sennett said that a pie in the face is much funnier if the face is a fat face (Fussell 248). Laughing at fat— an oddity, a divergence from the norm—is one way of laughing at our common human feet of clay.

As narrator, Joan is capable of laughing at herself. Trying to move quickly to escape the "bad man" in the ravine, Joan runs down the hill like a "trundled barrel" (Atwood, *Lady Oracle* 50). Imagining herself from her mother's point of view, Joan describes herself as "a teenage daughter who looked like a beluga whale and never opened her mouth except to put something in it" (Atwood, *Lady Oracle* 70). As a child in a school program, she looks grotesque in the butterfly costume, and she is assigned the role of a mothball instead. She eats half a layer cake, knowing that she would get the same scolding if she ate just one piece. When the Brownie leader asks the child Joan to control herself, the narrator comments on the amount of territory that would have to be covered. Repudiation and disgust are not the only possible responses to female fat, Atwood suggests. She shows us how to laugh sympathetically at the indignities of the body all people are subject to, extending her sympathy even to the fat woman.

In her use of the fat female body to create sympathetic laughter at the inescapable features of the human condition, Atwood draws on an old tradition. We must remember that "the body is a vital source of comedy," as Maurice Charney says in *Comedy High and Low: An Introduction to the Experience of Comedy* (7). We all live in bodies and endure the inconveniences and betrayals of the body. Basic jokes in comedy are things like falling down, farting, dandruff, as lovers of comedy from the era of silent films are aware. Humor about the body goes back to ancient Greek comedy, which modern comedy would be hard to match in vulgarity.

Atwood's comedy makes ample recognition of the grounding of comedy in the body, but she laughs with, instead of at, the fat female. Comedy is not afraid to address physical functions usually deemed unmentionable: Joan's Aunt Lou, who is built "like an Eaton's Catalog corset ad for the mature figure, but doesn't seem to mind" (Atwood, *Lady Oracle* 77), does public relations for sanitary napkins (which embarrasses Joan's mother). In one episode, Joan's mother tempts Joan with cake frosted with Ex-Lax, causing Joan a lot of misery.

The people who love and accept Joan—and these happen to be women who are strong enough to choose their own values—know that her identity is not determined by the extra fat. To her Aunt Lou, Joan is a beloved niece, whom she regards as normal. Aunt Lou, an independent spirit with a boyfriend, has a laugh that sounds like "an enraged walrus" (Atwood, *Lady Oracle* 80) and likes telling jokes on herself, even though she has a tendency to choke when she roars with laughter. Leda Sprott, an eccentric medium who turns out to be one of the most sane people in the novel, regards Joan as a normal teenager, not a grotesque.

The characters Atwood mocks have characteristics that are normative for the butts of satire. They are what Edward Galligan calls "willful" characters: "comedy consistently mocks willfulness, pride of purpose, and self-centered design . . ." (32). Totally lacking flexibility or a sense of humor and unable to accept the inevitable constraints all human beings have to deal with, these characters are obsessed with control.

One such "willful" character is Joan's mother. Although as a doctor's wife, she seems to live a comfortable life, she is dissatisfied. Her problem is anger at what she considers being trapped in a life she does not want. (Joan finds out that her mother regards her as an "accident.") She wants something she has not got and not knowing herself what it is, she strives for status and gentility, the only possible goals in her unimaginative vision. Although the Lady-of-Shallot image has shaped Joan's sensibility, she comes to see her mother as the Lady of Shallot, unable to look on reality, to enjoy life, to be herself, to give herself to other people. Like other characters from comedy, such as the colonels and generals in Joseph Heller's *Catch-22* or Jane Austen's Lady Catherine in *Pride and Prejudice*, Joan's mother is a controlling character. Joan comments that her mother views herself as "creator, manager, agent" and Joan as "product" (Atwood, *Lady Oracle* 63). Joan eats to defy her mother, who considers a fat daughter an obstacle to her ambitions. Joan comments, "The war between myself and my mother was on in earnest; the disputed territory was my body" (Atwood, *Lady Oracle* 66).

From one point of view, Joan's mother is doing her female work as a bearer of culture, and although we can't clear her of personal responsibility, Atwood lets us know that it is quite true that, in a way, she is merely the primary conduit for social control of the female body. Of course, she has help. She sends Joan to a psychiatrist, who asks her, "Don't you want to get married?"(Atwood, *Lady Oracle* 79). Joan's psychiatrist earns a place on a list of psychiatrists who figure in feminist fiction as aligning themselves with social forces that control women, for example, the one in Alix Kates Shulman's *Memoirs of an Ex-Prom Queen.*

Joan's rebellion through eating shows a desire for self-empowerment, an attempt to escape her mother's control: "It was only in my relation to my mother that I derived a morose pleasure from my weight; in relation to everyone else, including my father, it made me miserable. But I couldn't stop" (Atwood, *Lady Oracle* 74). She also acknowledges she ate from panic:

> Sometimes I was afraid I wasn't really there. I was an accident. I'd heard her call me an accident. Did I want to become solid, solid as a stone so she wouldn't be able to get rid of me? What had I done? Had I trapped my father, if he really was my father, had I ruined my mother's life? I didn't dare to ask. (Atwood, *Lady Oracle* 74)

Joan's large body is an unspoken rebellion against mechanisms of control, but she places herself in a position that is hardly a solution to the problem, as she intuitively recognizes.

The other major butt of comedy in the novel is Joan's husband, Arthur. Joan fails to see the Arthur that she unwittingly reveals to the reader. Rigid, dour, controlling, he is a classic comic butt. Joan notes that he arranges his face before he enters a room, not wanting to be taken by surprise. He is obsessed with germs and spends an inordinate amount of time gargling with Listerine. He is ineffectual and without ideas as a political activist: the only protest he ever manages is to spit on a policeman. The butt of comedy turns out to be the young political activist and lover, a development that represents a departure from a centuries-long comic tradition. That tradition would have placed such a figure on the side of the positive values associated with comedy: rebellion against oppressive forces, change, and renewal. Atwood, turning comedy to feminist uses, has reinvented the butts and heroes or subjects and objects of comedy. Joan's first lover, Paul, has a psychological profile similar to Arthur's. He leaves home at exactly the same time each morning, arranges Joan's activities, and lectures her incessantly. Comedy is on the side of flexibility. Those who lack it are often skewered in comic works.

However, Joan invests Arthur with the qualities of a romantic hero, and through Joan's attachment to Arthur, Atwood satirizes the ideology of romance. Joan fantasizes about a mysterious male figure in a cloak and falls first for Arthur, the young political radical and failed knight, and then for the Royal Porcupine (who actually wears a cloak). She does not mind Arthur's aloofness because she thinks it covers hidden depths: "His aloofness was intriguing, like a figurative cloak. Heroes were supposed to be aloof" (Atwood, *Lady Oracle* 195). She sees in him a "melancholy fighter for lost causes, idealistic and doomed, like Lord Byron" (Atwood, *Lady Oracle* 164). She is smitten as soon as she sees him: Atwood mocks the ideology of romance by the construction of her sentence: "We finished collecting the pamphlets, I fell in love, and we went for a drink at the pub" (Atwood, *Lady Oracle* 164). The romance plot limits women's self-development, while social ideas of femininity enable the romance plot. J. Brooks Bouson identifies as one of Atwood's purposes the effort "to construct a feminist reading position by exposing and resisting the romance ideology that attempts to fix women in a rigid, culturally established order and literary structure" (64).

Joan's attempts to assume the role of fitting consort to Arthur makes for some hilarious satire about the internalization of society's requirement for gendered bodies. Unable to forget that she once was fat, she comments on her "shadowy twin, thin when I was fat, fat when I was thin" (Atwood, *Lady Oracle* 245). Her first lover says she has the body of a goddess, but she carries the fat teenager around with her. The thin woman who is afraid people will find out she was once fat is a very effective comic device. Deeply ashamed of once having been fat, Joan is determined to conceal her past as a fat child and adolescent. Atwood brings off a very funny bit of satire when Joan accompanies Arthur by commuter train to the address of the person he has found to perform their marriage ceremony. Joan notices they are journeying toward her old neighborhood and fears that the person who marries them will be someone who knows her past. Her terrible secret will be out—not that she lived with a man before she met Arthur, as she did (he knows and does not care), and not anything that most people would want to conceal, e.g., that she had committed a crime or that her background is insufficiently genteel. She is afraid Arthur will find that she was a fat teenager, bordering on the obese, and not, as she told him, a cheerleader who was in the running for prom queen.

Atwood makes clear the cultural relativity of the approved female form. In one of her many part-time jobs, Joan is a waitress and encounters a cook from the Mediterranean, perhaps Greece.

He sees the rotund Joan as desirable, since she is the shape that wives eventually assume in his culture. Furthermore, she has a good command of English and, as a wife, could assist him in his ambition of owning a restaurant. When Joan flees to Italy, she sees many socially-approved matrons who have the body shape she had formerly.

The trajectory of the novel follows Joan's journey toward self-knowledge and self-acceptance. Like many other comic heroes, from Jane Austen's Elizabeth Bennett to Erica Jong's Isaadora Wing, Joan must learn to know and accept herself. A lesson about self-knowledge comes to Joan in a fortune cookie: "It is often best to be oneself" (Atwood, *Lady Oracle* 230). Lack of self-knowledge is a major theme of comedy, and the journey to self-knowledge is one the hero must take.

The largest debate in the critical literature on the novel is whether or not Joan gains self-knowledge and embarks on a new life marked by a greater acceptance of responsibility and the refusal to be a victim. Many critics think that Joan is still stuck in her victim role (Fee 75). Sherrill Grace says that Joan "remains locked within her own story, not having progressed at all" (117). Barbara Hill Rigney offers the view that "the reader's hopes for [Joan's] regeneration are not rewarded" (79). Robert Lecker says, "the final vision Joan offers us is one of despair at being caught in a world of artifice with no relief in sight" (198).

More helpful are the interpretations of Sharon Rose Wilson and Lisa Marie Hoagland. Wilson reads Atwood's novel in the context of fairy-tale intertexts and argues that, at the end of the novel, Joan "ironically experiences a fairy-tale transformation" (134) and emerges as a strong person: "she frees herself to be more than a 'dancing girl,' and to open doors to Arthur, the reporter, her Demeter self, and the future, thereby becoming the real artist who writes the book we read" (132). Tracing Atwood's use of goddess allusions in the novel, Wilson asserts that "Joan recovers her wholeness in the Great Mother" (134). Hoagland sees the fake suicide as relating to the feminist project of "interrogating cultural assumptions about women writers (that writing—like any other achievement—is fatal to women . . .)" (15). Atwood shows that Joan is no Sylvia Plath: she is alive at the end of the novel and on the threshold of a career. She has become the butterfly, the figure in the novel of the self-actualized person. I would argue that Joan follows the designated path of the comic hero, who normally moves from the self-destructive to the self-nourishing (Galligan 85). Joan's position on the threshold of a life of self-knowledge and responsibility at the end of the novel is a dénouement in keeping with comic form.

Joan repudiates (or begins to) the female role of selfless nurturer. Contemplating the statue of Diana of Ephesus ("draped with breasts from head to toe") in Tivoli, she acknowledges that her ability to give is limited: "I wanted things for myself" (Atwood, *Lady Oracle* 233). She learns from the success of her pop feminist poems (entitled "Lady Oracle") that she enjoys being taken seriously. Her life as a celebrity was not a bed of roses, but "unpleasant as it had been, I discovered it was much better than not being taken seriously" (Atwood, *Lady Oracle* 287).

Joan's costume gothics take a strange turn toward reality in the last chapters of *Lady Oracle*: the stereotypes self-destruct and the characters make known their own desires. Joan finds that the story she is writing is her own story, with the two female characters different aspects of herself. She becomes more sympathetic to Felicia, the redhead, who embodies her own energetic and assertive side (Fee 67). In her new view of her male characters, Joan begins to appreciate the threats to her autonomy. Throughout *Lady Oracle*, Joan has hidden behind various disguises, but at the end of the novel, with her faked suicide in danger of being exposed and her friends in trouble on her account, she will go home and live more honestly. In a way, she ends up "back where she started but with more experience" (Atwood, *Lady Oracle* 257), but that formulation does not adequately reflect substantial changes in her attitude toward herself and the world. We could say of Joan what she once said about the circus Fat Lady of her fantasies: "One day she would rebel. She would do something; meanwhile she made her living from people's curiosity" (Atwood, *Lady Oracle* 86).

Atwood has always been uneasy with an ideology that permits people to think of themselves as victims. (See Atwood's *Survival*). Not really a victim, Joan is more a comic hero of the type illustrated by Henry Fielding's Parson Adams in *Joseph Andrews* or Joseph Heller's Yossarian in *Catch-22*. Galligan identifies the defining characteristics of the comic hero as "self-negligence," a blurred sense of one's own identity (which works against any sense of superiority or self-pity); a strong sense of play, with the focus on the doing; and an "odd sort of passivity that combines a flexible yet stubborn resistance to being pushed around with a general reluctance to pull" (83). These heroes find a way of being human that avoids the willfulness of self-assertive acts fueled by aggressive emotions, in short those things that are criticized in the butts of satire. A sloppy housekeeper, Joan copes well with the messiness of life. She doesn't understand theories and is forced to nod dumbly when Arthur talks political theory.

Joan's history as a fat woman has enabled her to maintain an outsider status with an ability to see, however intuitively, the constructed nature of gender roles. Joan is, in fact, a trickster figure. An escape artist, her biggest escape is the faked drowning at the center of the novel. Self-protective, she flees first her mother, then her first boyfriend Paul, then Arthur. Among her impressive tricks are the foiling of Fraser Buchanan—the blackmailer of celebrities— by stealing his little black book and hoodwinking Sam and Marlene into going along with her plot for a faked drowning. Her largest trick is side-stepping the rules that confine women. She does so guiltily and secretly through most of the novel, but will do so more openly and confidently after the close of the novel, the reader is given to believe. Joan's comments in the last chapter reveal that, in her dealings with the reporter who discovered who she is, she adopted truthfulness instead of lies and evasions. "I didn't tell any lies" she says and does not run away, though she could have.

Atwood's ending, emphasizing survival, change, and growth, is a classic comic ending. Joan, consistently a survivor, describes herself as "at heart an optimist with a lust for happy endings" (Atwood, *Lady Oracle* 209). Atwood follows (or agrees with) many students of comedy (including her mentor at the University of Toronto, Northrop Frye) who connect the comic with growth and new beginnings. Frye writes that the form involves "dispelling illusion" and movement toward "pragmatic freedom" (169–70). As a comic work, Atwood's novel celebrates courage and holds out the possibility of positive change, however difficult that may be. Heilman notes that we should not overemphasize the happiness or perfection of comic resolution. Living a life with a commitment to change and growth is not easy. A comic ending has a measure of hope, but also a measure of acceptance, of "coming to terms with a wayward world" (Heilman 236). Joan's story embraces both. She seems ready to "rebel," however tentatively, or "to do something," as she predicted of the circus Fat Lady. Intuitively, or perhaps more consciously, she seems savvy to the cultural forces that would confine and limit her.

Works Cited

Atwood, Margaret. *Lady Oracle*. 1976. New York: Bantam Doubleday, Dell, 1998.

_____. *Survival: A Thematic Guide to Canadian Literature*. Toronto: Anansi, 1972.

Barreca, Regina. "Introduction." *Last Laughs: Perspectives on Women and Comedy*. New York: Gordon & Breach, 1998.

Bordo, Susan. *Unbearable Weight: Feminism, Western Culture, and the Body*. Berkeley: U of California P, 1993.

Bouson, J. Brooks. *Brutal Choreographies: Oppositional Strategies in the Narrative Design of Margaret Atwood*. Amherst: U of Massachusetts P, 1993.

Charney, Maurice. *Comedy High and Low: An Introduction to the Experience of Comedy*. London: Oxford UP, 1978.

Fee, Margery. *The Fat Lady Dances: Margaret Atwood's* Lady Oracle. Toronto: ECW, 1993.

Frye, Northrop. *The Anatomy of Criticism: Four Essays by Northrop Frye*. New York: Atheneum, 1968.

Fussell, B. H. "A Pratfall Can Be a Beautiful Thing." *New Perspectives on Comedy*. Ed. Maurice Charney. New York: New Literary Forum, 1978. 243–57.

Galligan, Edward L. *The Comic Vision in Literature*. Athens: U of Georgia P, 1994.

Grace, Sherrill. *Violent Duality: A Study of Margaret Atwood*. Ed. Ken Norris. Montreal: Vehicle P, 1980.

Heilman, Robert Bechtold. *The Ways of the World: Comedy and Society*. Seattle: U of Washington P, 1978.

Hogeland, Lisa Marie. *Feminism and Its Fictions: The Consciousness-Raising Novel and the Women's Liberation Movement*. Philadelphia: U of Pennsylvania P, 1998.

Lecker, Robert. "Janus Through the Looking Glass: Atwood's First Three Novels" *The Art of Margaret Atwood*. Ed. Arnold Davidson & Cathy Davidson. Toronto: Anansi, 1981. 177–203.

Maddocks, Marvin. "Out of the Woods: Review of *Surfacing*, by Margaret Atwood." *Time* 19 Mar 1973: 77–78.

Porter, Laraine. "Tarts, Tampons, and Tyrants: Women and Representation in British Comedy." *Because I Tell a Joke or Two: Comedy, Politics and Social Difference*. Ed. Stephen Wagg. London: Routledge, 1998. 65–93.

Rigney, Barbara Hill. *Margaret Atwood*. London, Macmillan, 1987.

Wilson, Sharon Rose. *Margaret Atwood's Fairy-Tale Sexual Politics*. Jackson: UP of Mississippi, 1993.

Alice Munro's 1994 "A Wilderness Station": Storytelling and Retelling of Historic, Biblical, Gothic, and Grimm Stories_____

Judith McCombs

Alice Munro, the preeminent storyteller who, in 2013, won Canada's first Nobel Prize for Literature, has spoken of her art as intuitive and mysterious: "When you start to write a story many things come from distant parts of your mind and attach themselves to it" (Ross 86). Munro has also called her art deliberate and controlling: "What I want, you see, is a lot of overlay. I want things to come in as many layers as possible, which means the stories have to come from as many people as possible, with their different baggage of memories" (Ross 88).

"What Munro wanted in all of the eight stories she included in *Open Secrets* were new qualities of suggestion, deliberate suggestion without certainty," her biographer Robert Thacker wrote (454), and discussed the immediate high praise for these "'bold, ambitious, risky short stories [that] . . . reach for difficult truths.'" "'The careful ordering of these works, the casual reappearances of characters in various entriesthe layering of time, the unity of place . . . [make Munro's fiction seem] as infinitely startling as life itself'" (Thacker 454).

Ann Hurlbert's *New York Review of Books* essay acclaimed Munro's "'disconnections and unpredictable, implausible reconnections between then and now, . . . [town and beyond] . . . . the jaggedness of the juxtaposition doesn't feel predictably post-modern; more than a sense of relativist muddle, there is a sense of miracle in the transformations . . .'" (Thacker 458).

If these critics are right, we need to read and re-read, to weigh and ponder memories, gaps, connections, lies—so as not to miss the layered, truthful, difficult and transforming art of Munro's storytelling.

"A Wilderness Station," after its 1992 *New Yorker* appearance, became the sixth story in Munro's 1994 book, *Open Secrets*. That book's title reads two ways: adjective modifying noun, meaning known/unknown secrets: but also verb and object: tempting/advising us to open up secrets.

Munro's masterfully imagined, four-part, mostly epistolary "Wilderness Station" is pieced from three sequences of nineteenth-century letters and from two lengthy twentieth-century reminiscences—one published locally in 1907, one a 1959 letter to a historian. Seven different persons, from 1852 to 1959. What we readers can piece together from Munro's seven fictive letter writers and reminiscers is a primary tale of hidden nineteenth-century domestic murder and madness, plus a parallel, mirroring secondary story of a minister's disintegration. Or was it accident, not murder? Truth, or lies, or madness? What follows is one reader's search for baggage and memories, interests and blind spots, lies and other secrets, in "A Wilderness Station."

The letters and reminiscences in parts I, II, and IV contain plausible-sounding stories that, on quick reading, may well seem acceptable to the letter writers and/or their recipients. In I, the Toronto Orphanage Matron, replying to letters from Simon Herron and Minister McBain, recommends the eighteen-year-old orphan Annie McKillop to Simon as a wife "suited to the hard work of [his] life in the bush"; Annie is lean, but hardy, wall-eyed but clear-sighted, not silly or timid (Munro, *Open Secrets* 191).

Early in 1852, according to George Herron's 1907 published reminiscence, part II, Annie married George's "good-looking" brother (Munro, *Open Secrets* 194), the nineteen-year-old orphan Simon Herron, who brought her to the snowbound North Huron bush (wilderness), where he and his fourteen-year-old brother George were clearing their land. Simon, being minded to accept no one's help, wanted to raise their cabin themselves, but they could not. George then went to the neighboring Treeces for help—it took two more men and two Treece sons—six in all—to raise the cabin.

(This is the only time George mentions contradicting Simon.) Later, when they still had no bedcovers, Simon sent back a fine bearskin gift from their neighbor, Henry Treece. Simon's relentless work ethic is a secular Calvinism; Simon's name suggests Simon Legree and the children's game of "Simon Says," where the other children must obey Simon's commands. Orphan George's name suggests "Let George do it," and St. George the dragon slayer.

A few months after the marriage, according to George's then-accepted version, Simon was killed by a falling tree branch, while he and George were chopping a tree. George and Annie had to bury him by the cabin, as a blinding snowstorm had begun. George later got a cemetery marker, but never moved the bones. Fourteen-year-old George joined the kind Treece family; eventually, he married their daughter and saw his sons inherit their land along with his. In short, a pioneer success story.

As we learn from part III, a sequence of letters between the wilderness minister, Walter McBain, and the clerk of the peace, James Mullen, who ran the Walley Gaol (jail), the widowed Annie refused to join the Treeces and hid out in the bush all summer. According to McBain, the stubborn, unsubmissive Annie showed a particular aversion to himself and George (Munro, *Open Secrets* 198). When nights grew colder, she walked to Walley Gaol and confessed that she had murdered Simon by throwing a stone or smashing him with it, while the brothers were chopping in the snowy woods. Mullen disbelieved Annie's unconvincing stories, gave her his Gaol's shelter and food, and found her sewing jobs—as Annie suggested he might do (Munro, *Open Secrets* 201–02; see Howells 127).

Munro's Mullen-McBain correspondence reveals the assessments of the three authorities—secular, religious, and medical men—who assess the female prisoner, kindly or punitively, through humane beliefs or through harsh assumptions and doctrines about women, insanity, and prisons. The good-hearted Church of England Gaoler Mullen represents liberal Christianity and reform, in contrast to the harsh Calvinist Presbyterianism of the young Scots minister, Walter McBain, whose Lord gives blows that "we are bound to receive . . . as signs of his care and goodness" and sends us, as

---

McBain's hero, the great Presbyterian divine Thomas Boston, had preached, only from "'*one wilderness station unto another*'" (Munro, *Open Secrets* 198, 204 [ital. sic]; cf. Munro, *View* 14–19).

McBain, whose help the widowed Annie rejected, admits he cannot overcome women's stubbornness. He feels that Annie had incompletely submitted to her husband, as "her sex is prone to" do, was therefore overcome by harrowing remorse after his death and thus, like "many folk," was driven mad, perhaps first in play, then trapped by the Devil (Munro, *Open Secrets* 203). Poor McBain, whose name suggests the baneful (bane means poison) doctrines that hold him captive, is unable to trust men or women, or to admit his own desperate need for help; friendless, he sickens and perishes in the icy, imprisoning wilderness. McBain's epitaph is his landlord's reply to Mullen's unanswered letters: "he died here at the inn February 25. There is some books here, nobody wants them."[1]

Munro's third authority, the unnamed doctor examining Annie's sanity, claims she suffers from female delusions caused by reading escapist female romances of ghosts, demons, and noble "love escapades" that she forgot or slyly conceals. Annie then voices another delusion: they won't hang her because she is with child. The doctor finds that she has "deceived herself," having gone "so long underfed" and also from probable "hysteria" (Munro, *Open Secrets*, 205–06)—but Annie may be playing dumb with him. Mullen, writing to McBain, tactfully distances himself from the doctor's unkind and unseeing theories; but Munro's story shows such romances as both true and false: we will learn in part III that Simon Herron did prove a demonic ghost for Annie.

* * *

In Munro's "Wilderness," the compelling, arguably most true story is hidden inside the head of a woman who may be insane, or a liar, and whose earlier, implausible stories have not been believed. Annie's name suggests the enterprising Orphan Annie—and is very close to Munro's own middle name, Ann. Munro's enterprising mother was Anne, née Annie (Thacker 33). Annie Herron's secret, isolating story parallels aspects of Anne Laidlaw's initially secret, isolating post-encephalitic Parkinson's disease (S. Munro 157–61).

In part III, Annie Herron tells her story in a letter she tries to send secretly to her only friend, a consumptive girl from the orphanage—a letter perhaps lost; perhaps never received; perhaps known only to us readers; or, more likely, intercepted and hidden by the charitable Gaoler Mullen, who might well want to shield Annie, or George, or both.

Annie's letter tells us the murder story that she has been mentally telling her one friend for months. Annie had first seen George dragging "a log" across the snow; when she helps George drag Simon's body inside, she pretends it is "still the log" (Munro, *Open Secrets* 208). She and George show no grief or love for Simon, only fear, shock, and hatred. When Annie asks the turned-away George how he knows if his brother is dead, George says, "touch him if you want to know" (Munro, *Open Secrets* 208). But Annie avoids touch by keeping the wash rag between her skin and Simon's. When she and George turn the body, she sees: "I saw, I saw where the axe had cut. Neither of us said anything. I washed it out, blood and what not" (Munro, *Open Secrets* 209). In the frenzied burial scene, they kick and beat down the dirt over the husband/brother who had commanded and beaten them both.

Eighteen-year-old widowed Annie took charge of the dazed, staring young George, directed him in the burial and afterwards offered him a ritual of repentance and Bible-divining absolution: "You didn't mean to do it. It was in anger. . . . I saw he would knock you down for a little thing and you just get up and never say a word. The same way he did to me." (Munro, *Open Secrets* 210). But if George owns up, he'll be hanged, his land will go back to the Crown, and what will become of her? (Munro, *Open Secrets* 210–11). God "does not want a good lad like you to be hanged. . . . [Just] say you are sorry" (Munro, *Open Secrets* 211). The Bible says—Annie cheated and invented to get verses—you are to get old, get married, have a son; and *"Neither can they prove the things of which they now accuse me"* (Munro, *Open Secrets* 211–12; quoted Acts 24:13, ital. sic).

Fearing that the shocked, shuddering George had "a chill or the fever," Annie spoon-fed him hot catnip tea (Munro, *Open Secrets* 212). (George's confusion and apathy are symptoms of hypothermia, which could kill him.) Then she brought him into the bigger bed—the marriage bed—placed warm flat-irons and clothes about him, checked her own "black and blue marks"; then laid beside George all night, checking his warmth, perhaps maternally. In the morning, a more coherent George left to tell the falling-branch story to the neighboring Treeces; but when he returned, he looked at her in "the same bad way" that Simon had (Munro, *Open Secrets* 213).

Young George ended up living with the Treeces, but Annie could not, for fear they would see the bruises Simon had made, or her lack of tears. (Annie's fears and withdrawal are typical battered-woman symptoms.) Alone in the shanty, Annie had nightmares of George or Simon chasing her with the axe and of George telling her the lie that she had killed his brother. Hiding in the bush, unsheltered and semi-starving, Annie seems partly mad—only partly, because she still seems to know what is dream or lie, and what is real (Munro, *Open Secrets* 214). Her God protected her from feeling the stings of insects and "from any badness" in the red and black berries she ate until the colder nights impelled her to seek refuge in Mullen's Walley Gaol (Munro, *Open Secrets* 214). Unlike McBain, who in his last bodily sickness believed both man and nature were set against him by his unforgiving Calvinist God, Annie survives her isolation, walks out for shelter, finds a home.

Although Annie's letter is the only explicit witness to the axe wound in the back of Simon's head, numerous details strongly suggest the truth of her account. George's 1907 reminiscence (part II) hesitates only twice and only in the place where he would have to lie: "in some way" and "I cannot say how," a tree branch fell and killed Simon (Munro, *Open Secrets* 195). The minister ostensibly accepts George's account, but the crucial sentence of McBain's part III letter to Gaoler Mullen equivocates with a passive voice and a highly uncharacteristic dangling-modifier error that let slip McBain's inner doubts: "A branch was loosed while chopping down a tree and fell upon the elder brother so as to cause instant death" (Munro, *Open Secrets* 198).

George says he later set up Simon's cemetery stone, but never moved the bones because that would be foolish uselessness "when his soul has gone on to Judgment" (Munro, *Open Secrets* 196). Could George risk anyone seeing a telltale axe cut in Simon's skull?

George's reminiscence perhaps understandably forgets his sister-in-law's birth name—but curiously omits her months of living wild. McBain's letter to Mullen, however, says that neighbors left bannock and salt fish for Annie—and that George told McBain her unfriendliness to him justified George's not going after her when she left for Walley (Munro, *Open Secrets* 199). George's 1907 reminiscence, published in the ironically named *Argus*, says only, "My brother's wife did not continue in this place, but went her own way to Walley" (Munro, *Open Secrets* 197).

If Simon's death seems at all suspicious, should we consider possible motives? Certainly George benefited from Simon's death: young George escaped his demanding, Calvinistic brother; got the cooperative, nurturing home and family he wanted; wed the Treece's daughter; and saw his sons inherit their land.

Part IV is the 1959 reply of Mullen's granddaughter, Christena, to a historian researching Treece Herron, George's grandson. The now-elderly Christena has memory troubles and heart scares. Much of her letter is her own baggage: herself as a lively, independent young woman of twenty-five, driving her own Stanley Steamer, rising above her "love-troubles" to flirt with young Treece Herron (224).

Munro's truly charitable, Good Samaritan Gaoler Mullen eventually—we learn from Christena—took Annie into his three-generation home as a live-in sewing woman. There the reclusive "Old Annie" became a sort of tame madwoman in the attic,[2] sometimes cross or addled, but treated with tolerance and kindness by Mullen's widowed daughter-in-law and curious granddaughters (Munro, *Open Secrets* 216). One day, the elderly Annie suddenly had the twenty-five-year-old Christena take her to visit George—who had suffered a stroke shortly after writing the 1907 reminiscence that presumably prompted Annie's visit. Should we read George's stroke ironically? As a kind of retribution?

On the way home, Old Annie seemed "glad" and "gloating," presumably because she told the stroke-silenced George, when they were alone, how right she was to persuade him to conceal the murder so he would live and prosper (Munro, *Open Secrets* 225).[3]

After the visit, the image that follows Annie's glad gloating suggests Munro's quest for hidden truth: Walley's lake, seen from a distance, is just a series of "glimpses" and "shots of light, held wide apart in the trees and hills," that we can nonetheless gestalt into "all the same" lake. The very end of the story, however, lets us follow the unknowing granddaughter to dismiss what we have been told as only Christena's "ragbag" reminiscences and Annie's "'terriblest dreams'" (Munro, *Open Secrets* 225). Or, alternatively, we can see through the irony of those muddled disclaimers to Annie's true story.

"There were a lot of old people going around then with ideas in their heads that didn't add up," Christena concludes, instancing Annie's story of another orphanage girl who had a lifeless, rat-size baby burst from a big boil on her stomach. Put in the oven, it puffed up to life-size and color, and kicked its legs (Munro, *Open Secrets* 225). This garbled version of "The Gingerbread Man" sounds like George walking away—but it can also be read as a veiled version of miscarriage, or abortion. Did Annie lose a baby, after Simon's beatings, or during her solitary, hungry, nightmare months? Did her earlier claim to be with child (Munro, *Open Secrets* 205) convey some slanted truth?

Of all the *Open Secrets* stories, Munro's "Wilderness Station" develops most intricately what Hurlbert called her "especially large theme, [of] the disorienting power of time" (Thacker 458). Of time, of human perception, of memory. And of our human story-making, slanted and unreliable and unsettling; yet compelling and enduring.

* * *

Two real-life stories, from Annie's time and place, stand behind Munro's "Wilderness Station"—an 1853 [sic] family history and a celebrated 1843 murderess. Munro's 1852 tree-felling death of young Simon Herron comes partly part from Munro's family history, from Big Rob's 1907 pioneer reminiscence (Munro, *View from Castle Rock* 111–17).

On April 5, 1853, Big Rob and his cousins James and John Laidlaw (Munro's great-uncles), were felling a tree. A "'branch was broken in the falling, and thrown backwards,'" falling on James' head, "'killing him instantly.'" They carried the body back; Big Rob "'had to convey the sad news to his wife, mother, [youngest] brother [Munro's great-great-grandfather], and sister'" (qtd.in Munro, *View* 116). Apparently James was buried on family land and later moved to Blyth Cemetery (Munro, *View* 117). A convincingly real account of accident and close family ties—but not a great, compelling story.

Toronto's 1843 "celebrated murderess," the young maid-of-all-work Grace Marks, also stands behind Munro's "self-style murderess" (Moodie 157; Munro, "Wilderness" 206). The infamous double murders, of Grace's employer and his pregnant housekeeper-mistress, took place in an isolated dwelling. There was a murdered man, an axe-bloodied murdered woman, a second man who was hung for the murderers, and the imprisoned "murderess" whose conflicting stories and sanity were widely debated, never proved. Like Moodie's Grace Marks and like the protagonist of Atwood's 1972 *Surfacing*, Munro's Annie is an unreliable narrator who may be either crazy or right—or both crazy *and* right—we readers are invited to choose (cf. Gibson 23).

*   *   *

So far back as we can trace, stories have been made from other stories. And, as the great critic Northrop Frye has said, "In myth, folk and fairy tales may be found the blueprints for all stories coming after them" (18).

The Biblical Cain and Abel form the most powerful brother-slaying story in our literature. As Hamlet's guilty stepfather, the usurping King, says of his own fratricide, "'It hath the primal eldest curse upon't / A brother's murder'" (Shakespeare, *Hamlet* III: iii, li. 37–38). The Bible version is a triangle of three males: Cain, the firstborn son of Adam and Eve; Abel, their second-born; and their judging God, who, in accepting Abel's offering and refusing Cain's, moves Cain to slay his younger brother.

In "Wilderness" the younger brother, George, slays his older brother, Simon, who refused what George tried to offer: neighborly cooperation with the Treeces. The role of judgmental omnipotence is grounded and shared in two humans, Simon and the Presbyterian minister, McBain. Simon is a self-driven, remorseless, *secular* Calvinist, who rules his brother and wife in absolute Old Testament fashion. Simon's harsh patriarchal powers are sanctioned by law, custom, and by the young Calvinist Presbyterian minister, McBain (who seems to be an orphan, or as cut off as one.)

McBain's and Annie's stories are also versions of another story, found in early Canadian history and literature, of isolated Europeans—usually men—going bushed, wild, mad, often fatally, in the strange (to them) and dangerous North American wilderness. Earle Birney's classic poem, "Bushed," shows a northern trapper who cannot withstand the moon-carved, "unknown totems" that surround and deride him and, in the end, "could only / bar himself in and wait / for the great flint [of the mountain] to come singing into his heart" (115). Munro's Calvinist-driven, isolated, wilderness rejecting McBain also parallels Margaret Atwood's "Progressive Insanities of a Pioneer," who "fished for a great vision" and in the end disintegrated (V: 2, 38). Friendless, McBain sickens and dies in the "foul and noisy" inn, while outside there is, for him, "nothing but trees to choke off every exit and icy bog to swallow man and horse" (Munro, *Open Secrets* 205).

Annie Herron's solitary months, which seem outwardly like months of madness, are also months of escape and healing in her captivity narrative (cf. Baltaz on Mary Sitts). Nineteenth-century captivity narratives, particularly of European women seized by natives, were very popular—perhaps because they dramatized the plight of women carried off into the wilderness by their husbands. Though Annie is ragged, filthy, semi-starving, hiding from people, and pursued by nightmare dreams, she slowly heals, aided by the protecting God she believes in. When the nights grow colder, Annie has the sense and strength to walk out through the woods, wade the shallow river, and find safe winter shelter in the Walley Gaol, as others may have done (Munro, *Open Secrets* 202). Howells points out that Annie's murderess stories do "achieve her aim" of finding in Mullen's Gaol a home where she is "a kind of permanent lodger" (Munro, *Open Secrets* 127).

"A Wilderness Station," like much of Munro's work, is a prime example of Southern Ontario Gothic and involves both Gothic romance and female Gothic, with Simon as hero-villain, George as victim-villain, and Annie as victim-hero. Geoff Hancock's 1982/1986 interview with Munro characterizes Southern Ontario Gothic as Calvinistic, Bible-imaged, gothic and grotesque; Munro adds strongly Scots-Irish, "with a big sense of righteousness. But with big bustings-out and grotesque crime. And ferocious sexual humour and . . . killing each other off on the roads. There's always this sort of boiling life going on" ("Alice Munro" 204).

When Christena, the uncomprehending 1959 granddaughter, says "People always wondered about that—about explosions" (Munro, *Open Secrets* 223), she means only her steam-driven Stanley Steamer auto. But Old Annie, too, was all steamed-up on her mission to talk to George about how right her advice was, after their 1852 explosions.

George's pioneer reminiscence revealed his reasons to boil over that April day in 1852: he had been ruled and sorely driven, silenced and cut off from the helpful neighboring family, by his patriarchal brother Simon, who like a fairy-tale ogre imposed hardships—even the impossible task of raising the cabin by themselves (193).

*   *   *

Munro's historic "Wilderness" is also a transformation of the two Grimm Bluebeard tales, "Fitcher's Bird" and "The Robber Bridegroom," which have long inhabited her work. Munro's transformations go back to one of her earliest stories, the 1968 "Images," where the child narrator begins to apprehend something of the adult mysteries of sex and death; of her pregnancy-bedridden mother and muskrat-killing father; of the frightening home nurse and the dangerous, but welcomed axe-man, and she learns in the end that "our [terrifying, fairy-tale] fears are based on nothing but the truth" (Munro, *Dance* 43).

In the first Grimm Bluebeard tale an evil fitcher (wizard) carries off one sister, then another, then a third to his lonely house in the dark forest, where he gives each in turn her heart's desire of riches, an egg that must be kept spotless, and a key to a forbidden chamber. The wizard drags the first two sisters by the hair and hews them into pieces when their bloody eggs reveal that they have entered his forbidden chamber. But the third clever sister keeps her egg clean while she explores the bloody chamber and puts in order the pieces of her sisters, restoring them to life; together they deceive and rob the wizard. At the end, the clever bride tricks him and his friends into a marriage feast where they all are burned to death by her kinsmen.

Grimm's "Robber Bridegroom" is a similar tale of a maiden-devouring robber who is outwitted by a clever maiden and a brave old servant woman, then tricked with his men into a marriage feast, where she tells the story that sends all the robbers to execution. In "Robber" the cannibalism is overt and realism replaces the supernatural elements. When the robber bridegroom persuades his mistrustful bride to visit his home in the dark forest, she finds there a caged bird who warns her away and, in the cellar, a very old woman who hides her behind a great cask, where she soon sees another maiden dragged in, slain, and cut to pieces by the robbers. A severed finger with a gold ring lands in the bosom of the hidden maiden. The old woman distracts and drugs the robbers, and when they sleep the two women escape. At the marriage feast, the bride tells her story as if it were a terrifying dream and, at the tale's climax, flourishes the axe-cut finger with its gold ring. Her father's guests send the cannibal robbers to execution.

In Munro's "Wilderness Station" the Bluebeard's chamber becomes the imprisoning wilderness, the lonely cabin, and Annie's tormented memory, filled with her "'terriblest dreams'" (225). Here the three essential Bluebeard roles of killer, victim, and survivor are shared and multiplied among Munro's three main characters. Simon, who brought his orphan brother and orphan bride to the harsh and snowbound wilderness to better their fortunes, then drove them and himself unsparingly, is both a brutal, unmourned Bluebeard and an unloved victim, axed to death.

As Simon's slayer, George resembles a fairy-tale hero. As Simon's trapped and beaten victim, fourteen-year-old George is a gender-reversed, male bride from both Grimm's Bluebeard tales: shocked and incoherent after the murder, George goes to pieces and, like a fitcher's victim bride, needs his stronger sister and old-woman helper Annie to put him back together. Abandoning Annie to her fate, George is a reversal of the good woodsman who, in a similar Grimm tale with an animal Bluebeard figure, axes the wolf to save Little Red-Cap (Little Red Riding Hood) and her grandmother: instead George becomes, in Annie's "'terriblest dreams,'" an axe-wielding Bluebeard.

Annie's roles are the most multiple: she is a victim-bride, carried off into the wilderness and beaten "black and blue" by Simon, then abandoned by George and pursued by him and Simon in her "'terriblest dreams'" (A. Munro, "Wilderness" 213–14, 225). She is a healing fitcher's bride, who rescues young George and puts his life back together; but like the old woman helper in "Robber Bridegroom" and like many helpers in fairy tales, the rescuing Annie vanishes from hero George's reminiscence.

Putting the dead in order, Annie is a non-healing bride who sews up her hated husband's body, hobbling him with her petticoat and kicking the dirt into his grave, to keep him dead. Annie may be a tempting female Bluebeard, as well as a healing fitcher's bride, when she puts the incoherent, dangerously chilled young George into the marriage bed and keeps "touching him to see if he was warmed up," "though [n]othing bad happened" (A. Munro, "Wilderness" 213).

And finally Munro's Annie is the triumphantly surviving storyteller bride, discarding the false tree-felling tale that she had hoped would bind George to her, surviving terrors and privation to create the true, secret Bluebeard tale she sends to her friend: the tale that likely never reached her orphan friend, but may well have reached Gaoler Mullen—and may even have prompted him to give Annie her third-floor "domain" in his home (A. Munro, "Wilderness" 216; cf. Howells 127).

Notes

1. "Wilderness" 207–08; the landlord's curt reply evokes the stark epitaph for the would-be civilizer in Conrad's "Heart of Darkness": "'Mistah Kurtz, he dead'" (591). In title, plot, and subplot, Munro's "Wilderness Station" is a Canadian version of Conrad's "Outpost of Progress." Munro's landlord's note also echoes the brief "'Your father is gone, nobody can't find him'" of Atwood's 1972 *Surfacing* (24).

2. The reference is to Sandra M. Gilbert and Susan Gubar's analysis of *Jane Eyre*, in their groundbreaking 1979 book *The Madwoman in the Attic: The Woman Writer and the Nineteenth-Century Literary Imagination.*

3. Carrington, however, argues cogently that Annie is deluded by the "classic . . . Freudian projection" of her "guilty conscience" into seeing an axe cut that does not exist (82). Gittings, who sees subverted versions and multiple truths, quotes Munro on inventing "'a dreadful macabre incident'" for the family history behind "Wilderness" (29). Howells, who compares Annie to Atwood's 1996 *Alias Grace* hero as a secret-keeping, storytelling survivor, follows a Woodcock review that finds Simon's death an elusive mystery—was it George's axe, or Annie's rock, or a falling tree branch (127–28)? While neither the truth nor falsity of Annie's perception can be absolutely proved, I would argue that Munro's detective-quest structure is overkill if Annie is merely deluded. In Munro's kindred, later Grimm and Gothic Bluebeard story, the 1996/1998 "Love of a Good Woman," Mr. Willens' death is revealed/obscured through various persons, each one limited and in some way unreliable. Critics have disputed whether Willens died by murder or accident; I have argued that, with close consideration of Munro's clues, murder can be proved (McCombs).

Works Cited

Atwood, Margaret. *Alias Grace*. Toronto: McClelland & Stewart, 1996.

_____. "Progressive Insanities of a Pioneer." *The Animals in That Country*. Boston: Atlantic Monthly–Little, Brown, 1968. 36–39.

_____. *Surfacing*. Toronto: McClelland & Stewart, 1972.

Baltaz, Diane P. *Mary Sitts: More Than a Captivity Tale*. RR 1 Ayr, Ontario: Sand Plains, 1995.

Birney, Earle. "Bushed." 1952. *The New Oxford Book of Canadian Verse in English*. Ed. Margaret Atwood. Toronto: Oxford UP, 1952. 115.

Carrington, Ildikó de Papp. "Double-Talking Devils: Alice Munro's 'A Wilderness Station.'" *Essays on Canadian Writing* 58 (Spring 1996): 71–92.

The Complete Grimm's Fairy Tales. Trans. Margaret Hunt. New York: Pantheon, 1944.

Conrad, Joseph. "Heart of Darkness." 1902. *The Portable Conrad*. Ed. Morton Dauwen Zabel. New York: Viking, 1947. 490–603.

_____. "An Outpost of Progress." 1898. *Portable Conrad*. Ed. Morton Dauwen Zabel. New York: Viking, 1947. 459–89.

"Fitcher's Bird." *The Complete Grimm's Fairy Tales*. Trans. Margaret Hunt. New York: Pantheon, 1944. 216–20.

Frye, Northrop. *The Educated Imagination*. Bloomington, Ind.: Indiana UP, 1964.

Gibson, Graeme. "Margaret Atwood." *Eleven Canadian Novelists*. Toronto: Anansi, [1973]. 1–31.

Gilbert, Sandra M., & Susan Gubar. *The Madwoman in the Attic: The Woman Writer and the_Nineteenth-Century Literary Imagination*. New Haven: Yale UP, 1979.

"The Gingerbread Boy [Man]." *The Three Little Pigs and Other Favorite Nursery Stories*. Illus. Charlotte Voake. Cambridge, MA: Candlewick, 1991. 8–15.

Gittings, Christopher E. "Constructing a Scots-Canadian Ground: Family History and Cultural Translation in Alice Munro." *Studies in Short Fiction* 34.1 (Winter 1997): 27–37.

Hancock, Geoff. *Canadian Writers at Work: Interviews with Geoff Hancock*. Toronto: Oxford UP, 1987.

_____. "Alice Munro: an Interview." 1982. *Canadian Writers at Work: Interviews with Geoff Hancock*. Toronto: Oxford UP, 1987. 187–224.

The Holy Bible. King James Version. Cleveland: World Publishing, 1945.

Howells, Coral Ann. *Alice Munro*. Manchester, England: Manchester UP, 1998.

"Little Red Cap [Little Red Riding Hood]." *The Complete Grimm's Fairy Tales*. Trans. Margaret Hunt. New York: Pantheon, 1944. 139–43.

McCombs, Judith. "Searching Bluebeard's Chambers: Grimm, Gothic, and Bible Mysteries in Alice Munro's 'The Love of a Good Woman.'" *American Review of Canadian Studies* 30:3 (Autumn 2000): 327–348.

Moodie, Susanna. *Life in the Clearings*. 1853. Ed. Robert L. McDougall. Toronto: Macmillan of Canada, 1959. 152–71, 224–50.

Munro, Alice. "Images." *Dance of the Happy Shades and Other Stories*. Harmondsworth, Middlesex, Eng.: Penguin, 1968. 30–43.

_____. "The Love of a Good Woman." *New Yorker* (23–30 December 1996): 102+.

_____. "The Love of a Good Woman." *The Love of a Good Woman*. New York: Knopf, 1998. 3–78.

_____. *Open Secrets*. Toronto: Douglas Gibson-McClelland and Stewart, 1994.

_____. *The View from Castle Rock*. New York: Knopf, 2006.

_____. "A Wilderness Station." *Open Secrets: Stories*. New York: Vintage, 1995. 190–225.

_____. "A Wilderness Station." *New Yorker* (27 April 1992): 35+.

Munro, Sheila. *Lives of Mothers and Daughters: Growing Up with Alice Munro*. New York: Union Square/Sterling Publishing, 2008.

"The Robber Bridegroom." *The Complete Grimm's Fairy Tales*. Trans. Margaret Hunt. New York: Pantheon, 1944. 200–04.

Ross, Catherine Sheldrick. *Alice Munro: A Double Life*. Toronto: ECW, 1992.

Shakespeare, William. "The Tragedy of Hamlet, Prince of Denmark." *Shakespeare: Major Plays and the Sonnets*. Ed. G. B. Harrison. New York: Harcourt, Brace, & Co., 1948.

Thacker, Robert. *Alice Munro: Writing Her Lives*. Toronto: McClelland & Stewart, 2005.

Analogical Structure in the Novels of Jane Urquhart

Patricia Linton

Jane Urquhart is the author of seven novels, three volumes of poetry, and a collection of short stories, as well as a biography of L. M. Montgomery. Critical analysis of Urquhart's fiction has focused on the historical component of her work and on her distinctive use of geography as metaphor. Urquhart's treatment of history ranges from narratives in which national and international events figure prominently to narratives in which the influence of the past on the present is explored in narrower, more personal ways. For example, two of her novels, *The Underpainter* (1997) and *The Stone Carvers* (2001), deal with the Canadian experience in World War I as a defining element of Canadian national identity. *Away* (1993) focuses on the struggles of Irish immigrants to survive and prosper in Canada after escaping the great famine of the mid-nineteenth century, a chapter of Canadian history that has both national and familial significance for Urquhart. While other works focus less directly on critical events in public history, each of Urquhart's novels addresses the relationship between past and present, in the context of a particular time and place.

In an interview with Herb Wyile published in *Speaking in the Past Tense*, Urquhart comments, "I probably should have been a historical geographer" (100). Her narratives explore the mutual interactions of people and their physical environment. A characteristic component of narrative design in Urquhart's fiction is her use of a feature of the natural world as metaphor. For example, the governing metaphor in her 1986 novel *The Whirlpool* is the whirlpool at Niagara Falls; in *Changing Heaven* (1990), it is the wind and weather on the Yorkshire moors. In *Away* (1993), the excavation of a quarry by a multinational cement company represents the destruction of heritage by contemporary business interests. Each novel foregrounds either a natural phenomenon or human action upon the physical environment that serves as an analog for broader human experience.

This analysis focuses on related narrative strategies that span Urquhart's body of work. In the discussion that follows, this essay explores Urquhart's continuing attention to personal history, especially the influence of literature and reading on a person's worldview, and her sustained use of nature, particularly geography, as metaphor. A recurring pattern in Urquhart's fiction is a distinctive combination of story and narrative design: stories of vexed or doomed relationships, articulated by means of extended analogies with phenomena in nature. A less distinctive, but also pervasive, motif in Urquhart's work is the formative role of art—both high art and popular or folk art—in shaping values.

In this discussion, in addition to prior studies of Urquhart's own work, this essay draws upon Hilary Dannenberg's analysis of narrative design in *Coincidence and Counterfactuality: Plotting Time and Space in Narrative Fiction* to understand characteristic features of narrative structure in Urquhart's fiction. In her study, Dannenberg examines "plotting principles" typically deployed in narrative fiction—strategies that enable readers to make sense of fictional worlds. Chief among these are variations of three key principles: causation, kinship (genealogical lineage), and similarity (which is not entirely distinct from kinship, but broader). Dannenberg follows Ludwig Wittgenstein and Mark Turner in understanding these key principles as fundamental cognitive operations that structure language, but her study articulates their function more specifically in the context of historical and contemporary narrative fiction. In particular, Dannenberg explores the increasing use of "analogical plotting" in twentieth and twenty-first century fiction—a narrative strategy that connects characters or events conceptually, based upon abstract or figurative relationships. Further, as Dannenberg explains, the similarities that emerge in analogical plotting often involve links between different stories interwoven within a text rather than links within a single story (106–107).

Among the repertoire of plotting principles that enable readers to make sense of narrative texts, two that stand out, almost as a signature, in Urquhart's novels are distinctive articulations of causation and similarity. Urquhart demonstrates the shaping influence of cultural history, particularly individual exposure to reading and art, on her characters' thought, behavior, and understanding of the world. Personal/cultural history does not represent causation in the sense of direct force or manipulation, nor cause in the sense of a necessary or sufficient condition, but rather causation as a path by which one thing "springs from" another (Dannenberg 26). Urquhart's novels portray literature, art, and popular design as formative influences that subtly mold an individual's values and perspectives. A second strategy prominent in Urquhart's fiction is the development of narrative structures that establish similarities by analogy between the experience of a character and a phenomenon in the natural world, anchoring both in a particular time and place. To demonstrate the persistence of these plotting strategies across Urquhart's body of work, this essay will examine two novels published twenty years apart: *Changing Heaven* (1990) and *Sanctuary Line* (2010).

Reading as a Formative Influence

In Urquhart's fiction, early experiences of art shape both desire and expectation. This is true not only of formal art, but also of popular art and design; in different novels, character is developed and expressed in terms of painting, ceramics, and sculpture, as well as literature. But Urquhart most often traces a character's formative engagement with poetry or stories. Both *Changing Heaven* and *Sanctuary Line* are novels in which adult behavior is grounded upon literary models.

Changing Heaven is a complex narrative that intertwines the stories of four fraught relationships. In the present time of the novel (late twentieth century), Canadian literary scholar Ann Frear is facing the end of a tumultuous love affair with Arthur Woodruff, a professor of art history at the same university. She takes a sabbatical to Haworth Moor in Yorkshire, England, to research a book on wind and weather in Emily Brontë's *Wuthering Heights*. There she meets and is attracted to John Hartley, a Yorkshire moor-edger, displaced mill worker, and scholar manqué. Intercut with the account of Ann's relationship with Arthur and her developing connection with Hartley is a conversation between the ghost of Ariana Ether, a turn-of-the-century balloonist, and the ghost of Emily Brontë. From the dialogue of ghosts emerge stories of the failed love that destroyed Ariana Ether and her partner Jeremy Jacobs, as well as the anguished devotion of Emily Brontë to her brother Branwell. Within the story world of this novel, Ann, Arthur, and John exist on an earthly plane, while Ariana and Emily Brontë exist in an ethereal sphere that transcends time. The ethereal characters constitute an unseen "presence" in the corporeal world, at least until they fade at the conclusion of their stories, but they are not consciously perceived by the present-day characters.

Within the story world of *Changing Heaven*, all of these characters (corporeal and ethereal) are living, speaking subjects. However, beyond the unfolding action is the acknowledged fiction of Emily Brontë's *Wuthering Heights*. Readers of *Changing Heaven* enter a narrative world that makes some significant cognitive demands— parts of the story are "realistic" (they mimic ordinary experience), while other parts of the story require that readers "override" their consciousness of the text's anti-realistic elements (talking ghosts) in order to sustain readerly immersion (Dannenberg 24). The link between the corporeal and ethereal spheres in Urquhart's text, the connection that persuades a reader "to believe in the internal logic and autonomy of the narrative world" (Dannenberg 25), is belief in another story world altogether, the fictional world of *Wuthering Heights*. In other words, the plotting principle in *Changing Heaven* is similar to *Wuthering Heights*, in particular the similarity of various characters in Urquhart's story world to Brontë's Heathcliff.

Dannenberg begins her study of plotting principles by recognizing the importance of individual and cultural history. "The reader's historical-temporal location, identity within global and regional culture, and of course gender are key factors" that contribute to a reader's capacity for immersion in a particular text (Dannenberg 19). With respect to readership, *Changing Heaven* takes a considerable risk: it is not possible to take the measure of Urquhart's novel unless the reader also knows and believes in the world of *Wuthering Heights*; that is, "believes" in the sense of being capable of immersion in the story world Brontë creates. Unless readers not only know *Wuthering Heights*, but find the relationship between Brontë's Heathcliff and Catherine compelling, it is unlikely that they will find the characters and situations in Urquhart's novel absorbing. If Heathcliff is merely a boorish brute—if, at some level, readers do not recognize the intellectual and emotional force of a consuming passion—then Ann's desire to cast Arthur as Heathcliff and the question of whether she will choose instead the quieter, healthier relationship with John Hartley (the Edgar Linton analog) is not engaging. Similarly, unless the accounts of Jeremy Jacobs and Branwell Brontë that emerge from the dialogue of ghosts are read against the reader's perception of Heathcliff, the overall structure of Urquhart's novel is not coherent. As the novel observes of Ann's youthful efforts to explain Brontë's story to other children: "They have not read *Wuthering Heights*, and when Ann describes the book to them their eyes glaze" (Urquhart, *Changing Heaven* 21).

Urquhart develops, in detail, the sustained influence of *Wuthering Heights* upon Ann Frear's desires and expectations. Having read Brontë's novel for the first time during a hurricane as a child of eleven, Ann discovers in *Wuthering Heights* an alternate world where the orderliness and constraints of her Toronto milieu are supplanted by the "wonderful chaos" and passion of a different place and time (doubly fictional—invented by Brontë and reimagined by Ann). As Ann progresses through adolescence and into adulthood, the novel remains a touchstone for the sublime passion she seeks but doesn't find in mundane experience. There is no Heathcliff at dances for teenagers held in church basements, no Heathcliff at her university. Ann imagines or misperceives Arthur Woodruff and herself as Heathcliff and Catherine, but as Urquhart's story unfolds, the traits of Brontë's characters are redistributed between Arthur and Ann. In their final meeting, Arthur makes clear that he does not want the relationship Ann imagines for them:

> "I'm not what you think," Arthur's voice is practically inaudible, "and I never will be. I'm not desperate or passionate. We tumbled into each other, that's all. I'm fixed, Ann, stationary. Nothing like this should have ever happened to me. . . . the difference is that you want

to live the fiction or the life or whatever, and I . . . I simply don't" (*Changing Heaven* 236–237).

As Anne Compton notes in her analysis of romance in Urquhart's fiction, " . . . the consummation Ann Frear seeks is total possession, a fusing of lovers, such as exists in *Wuthering Heights* . . ." (130). It is ultimately Ann who is the Heathcliff figure, who experiences love as an all-consuming obsession, whereas Arthur chooses domesticity and a conventional marriage.

Although Ann's desire to live the relationship portrayed in Brontë's novel is placed in question as Urquhart's novel proceeds, the status of Heathcliff and Catherine as models of a consuming passion is reinforced by the dialogue of ghosts in the ethereal sphere of Urquhart's narrative. In the context of the contemporary world of Ann and Arthur and John Hartley, Heathcliff is unrealistic, unhealthy, and entirely fictional. On the other hand, the dialogue of ghosts offers other iterations of Heathcliff figures, one existent within the context of the story world (Jeremy Jacobs) and the other existent not only within the story world, but also historically, as a living person (Branwell Brontë). Both Ariana Ether and Emily Brontë have nurtured relationships with men whose attributes and behavior parallel those ascribed to Heathcliff. Jeremy, Branwell, Arthur, and Ann herself are knit together in Urquhart's text through the plotting principle of similarity to Heathcliff.

Twenty years after publication of *Changing Heaven*, Urquhart uses a similar technique in a more diffuse and nuanced way in *Sanctuary Line*. The novel is the extended first-person narrative of a Canadian research biologist, Liz Crane, who attempts to come to terms with the loss of her cousin Mandy, one year after Mandy's death in Afghanistan. Mandy—idealistic, intelligent, sensitive—had surprised the family by embarking on what was expected to be a brilliant career as a military strategist. The two cousins had been life-long friends and confidantes; Liz's narrative is both a family history and an effort to expiate the pain of Mandy's absence. The novel is structured as a sustained address to an unnamed "you,"

---

followed by a brief retrospective commentary on that conversation. The long first part of the novel begins with the following sentences:

> Look out the window.
> The cultivated landscape of this farm has decayed so completely now, it is difficult to believe that the fields and orchards ever existed outside of my own memories, my own imagination.
>
> (Urquhart, *Sanctuary Line* 3)

The brief second section of the novel, comprised of two short chapters, functions as a coda, in which the unnamed "you" is identified as Vahil, Mandy's Kurdish-Canadian lover and superior officer in the Canadian military, who visits the family home on the one-year anniversary of Mandy's burial. At first disinclined to be drawn into any sympathetic engagement with Vahil, whom she has regarded as an abusive lover, Liz ultimately provides an oral memoir of Mandy, with Vahil as listener. Although the two sections of the novel are sequential, the second part essentially frames and provides context for the first. Liz's account of Vahil's visit introduces their night-long conversation with the same language we have already read on the novel's opening page: "'Look out the window, Vahil,' I said. 'The cultivated landscape of this farm has decayed so completely now . . .'" (216).

Liz Crane's memoir of Mandy is laced with references to Mandy's reading, particularly her devotion to poetry. From their youth and into adulthood, Liz and Mandy had differed in the intellectual strategies they used to make sense of the world. Liz, the scientist, always mapped the human world in terms of her understanding of the natural environment, specifically her research on the life cycle of the monarch butterfly. Mandy, on the other hand, characteristically attempted to understand her challenges in terms of the language of poetry. In mourning for her cousin, Liz has traced Mandy's literary history, reading the books Mandy left behind in the family home, in an effort to reconnect with her, if only vicariously. Liz's account of Mandy, unfolding during the long conversation with Vahil, focuses on two issues that define Mandy's adult experience: the change in her professional role as the mission of the Canadian military has evolved from peacekeeping to combat in Afghanistan and her passionate affair with a superior officer. Liz provides no indication that Mandy intended to withdraw from either situation. Neither is resolved, but simply ended with Mandy's death, and Liz attempts to understand them from the perspective of someone who has experienced neither.

The recognition that commitment, devotion, and fidelity are also, viewed from another angle, constraint and imprisonment—a theme expressed in *Changing Heaven* in terms of romantic love—is more nuanced in *Sanctuary Line* and extended to both public and private contexts. Liz perceives both Mandy's profession and her love as a kind of bondage: "heavy links of iron but that she must have—at times—envisaged as golden" (Urquhart, *Sanctuary Line* 184). On the other hand, she portrays Mandy as someone "drawn to the beauty of difficulty":

> Mandy once said that if she let the difficulty go, her belief in poetry would disappear, along with her belief that her presence—and the presence of the others—in that faraway country might finally cause something good to happen. She said that the belief was a kind of poetry in itself, How could I argue with that? I have never been moved to participate in impossible situations. I have never fully understood poetry. I have never been a soldier. I have never been a butterfly. I have never loved in the difficult way Mandy loved. (Urquhart, *Sanctuary Line* 184)

The poetry that is meaningful to Mandy at different stages of her life serves as an index of her intellectual and emotional state. The long narrative that forms the first section of the novel chronicles Liz's retracing of Mandy's progress from the direct, uncomplicated language of Robert Louis Stevenson in *A Child's Garden of Verses*, to Edna St. Vincent Millay and Carl Sandberg, to Robert Frost and Emily Dickinson, to Pablo Neruda, Wallace Stevens, and Sylvia Plath. But the progression is more than an account of increasing sophistication in literary taste. Mandy's reading provides a reservoir of insights and alternatives upon which she draws as an adult.

The brief second section of the novel begins with an analysis of Mandy's college thesis, which focuses not on her most complex or sophisticated reading, but on Stevenson's poems for children. Liz comments:

> The poignancy of a young officer-in-training at a military college— one who would later die in active service—doing her honors thesis, after all her reading of contemporary poetry, on *A Child's Garden of Verses* was almost too much for me to bear. She would have chosen this subject as a refuge, I expect, a revisitation of the time before everything changed and shattered. (Urquhart, *Sanctuary Line* 209– 210)

Liz summarizes the argument of Mandy's thesis as a comparison of Stevenson's sensibility with that of Emily Dickinson, paralleling their shared focus on "smaller more fractional images" but articulating their difference as "a question of a light or a dark palette" (Urquhart, *Sanctuary Line* 210). In the face of war, Mandy chooses Stevenson's lighter palette as more affirmative, more capable of sustaining hope, and it is that affirmation with which Urquhart ends the novel. At the close of her narrative, Liz describes a walk along the shore of the lake with "these two nineteenth-century voices . . . side by side, debating in [her] mind" (Urquhart, *Sanctuary Line* 220). She quotes the first four-line stanza of Stevenson's "Where Go the Boats?" which cheerily describes a river that flows along forever, and then juxtaposes four lines from Dickinson describing a boat adrift, with no one to guide it to a town. But she imagines Mandy reciting Stevenson's closing lines: "Other little children/Shall bring my boats ashore" (Urquhart, *Sanctuary Line* 226). The requiem for Mandy that has comprised the novel ends with an affirmation of confidence in the future, based upon the formative influence of Stevenson's *Verses*.

Analogies Anchored in the Natural World

The second narrative strategy that recurs throughout Urquhart's body of work is development of analogical relationships between the natural world and human experience. In particular, Urquhart deploys these extended analogies to understand vexed relationships. In *Changing Heaven*, the relationship of Heathcliff and Catherine in *Wuthering Heights* is explicitly positioned as the archetype against which the other relationships in *Changing Heaven* must be read. The wind on the moors is the vehicle Urquhart uses to represent the passion between Heathcliff and Catherine: "Not a subtle wind, but one that is icy, fierce, and constant" (Urquhart, *Changing Heaven* 2). The attribute that links Ann in the corporeal world of the novel with Emily Brontë in the ethereal world and the Heathcliff/Catherine story in Brontë's fictional world is the desire to be overwhelmed and annihilated by passion. While wind may be a factor in all kinds of weather, gentle as well as tempestuous, the variety of weather Ann and Emily prefer is stormy. At one point, the novel describes Ann's opening a window to experience a blizzard:

> She sees the curtain dance into life, shaken by the teeth of tempest. The fabric snaps, then billows, then snaps again, straining outward from its valance, a celebrant of pure energy . . . This is what Ann wants, what she will get from him, what she will become in his presence . . . A curtain responding to storm. (Urquhart, *Changing Heaven* 90–91)

Fierceness, ruthlessness, and distance are particularly associated with Heathcliff and his avatars, all of whom are described as beautiful, dark, and destructive. When Ariana Ether protests that Jeremy's heart is open to her, Emily comments, "Black hair? Perfect profile? I have my doubts" (Urquhart, *Changing Heaven* 41). Brontë describes Heathcliff as a character made out of black stone: ". . . obdurate, unyielding, fixed, unchanging . . . . Practically unkillable" (Urquhart, *Changing Heaven* 180). When Ariana asserts that she wouldn't have liked Heathcliff, Emily implies that in loving Jeremy Jacobs, Ariana has already chosen such a man: "Really? Not interested in fierce men, nasty ones . . . is that it?" (Urquhart, *Changing Heaven* 180).

It is hardly surprising that the most insightful analysis of passion as storm is articulated by Emily's ghost, drawn from her own experience in the Brontë household: "I love a room that is full of wind," said Emily, "a room that *moves*. . . . I was never happier than when the wind was in the house—unless it was when I was out of the house myself, in the wind" (Urquhart, *Changing Heaven* 82). Her appetite for wind (echoed in the corporeal world by Ann) expresses metaphorically her chaotic emotional relationship with her brother Branwell, whose bad behavior was supported by the indulgence of his sisters, particularly Emily:

> We argued on and on . . . and the wind got into it of course, tossing words around as it does, and all the while this voice inside me kept saying, *I love him*, *I love him*. And I did, you know, he always touched some bright fuse in me. He ignited me like a torch and the world became clear in the eye of anger. I loved the way he left the house, a whistling boy, and then I loved the way he crashed drunkenly back into it. I cherished and protected the tormented side of him, the side that angered me, and I called it out of him too so that I could watch this side of myself reel clumsily through life meeting all the brutality head on. (Urquhart, *Changing Heaven* 168)

Although she claims never to have experienced or wanted to experience romantic love, Emily asserts that she died soon after Branwell's death because she was unable to bear his absence: "I died for love of him: that furious, catastrophic side of myself that was buried with him" (Urquhart, *Changing Heaven* 169). Emily's explanation of her novel to Ariana subtly aligns the relationship between Heathcliff and Catherine with her own feelings for her brother, including the constraints she maintains on the physical relationship between the lovers: "Their whole love affair was an hallucination! I never really let them touch—except once. One desperate embrace. But by then she was dying. And on purpose! To make him want her! Her death swallowed him whole. The new form she took—that of absence—obsessed him" (Urquhart, *Changing Heaven* 83).

Both Ann Frear and Emily Brontë's ghost present their desire for wind as exhilarating, exciting, and fulfilling in a way that renders everything else insufficient. But Ann's effort to pull Arthur Woodruff into a sustained passion as chaotic as her own is clearly destructive to him. He desperately wants to be settled, stationary, ordinary; he wants to end the affair and return emotionally to his family. Similarly, Jeremy Jacobs' obsessive passion for Ariana is portrayed as literally annihilating—unable to tolerate any change in Ariana, he rigs her parachute so that she will fall to her death. The novel raises the possibility, but does not confirm, that after Arthur rejects her, Ann may accept the quieter, healthier, more nuanced relationship offered by John Hartley. Nonetheless, the governing metaphor of the novel, the image that structures each of the relationships in the different levels of story is love as storm. At the novel's end, as Ariana and Emily fade and the weather softens, the value of tempest is reasserted: "[The ghosts] see that storms are really acts of love and that the earth demands this passion, this tantrum of response to its simply being there" (Urquhart, *Changing Heaven* 246).

In *Sanctuary Line,* Urquhart employs a similar strategy for understanding human experience by means of analogy with natural events. Liz Crane's professional career involves research on the complex life cycle of the monarch butterfly. In her effort to make sense of the human world, Liz analyzes experience in terms of the ecology of these butterflies. Indeed, one aspect of the parallel she draws between people and butterflies is her own relationship to them: "Even now I can only understand [Mandy's relationship to her lover] in the way that I understand butterflies; I know what they do, but I am at a loss to explain why they do it" (Urquhart, *Sanctuary Line* 184).

Throughout *Sanctuary Line,* the ecology of the monarch serves as the principle that knits together disparate strands of plot: the story of Liz's Uncle Stanley, Mandy's father, who disappears when the two girls are teenagers, and the story of Mandy herself. These two absences, unforeseen and irreparable, represent for Liz the intervention of chance in what otherwise seems to be a well-ordered world. She struggles to understand human loss within a larger context, modeled on aspects of the natural world that are most familiar to her. As Liz's long conversation with Vahil unfolds, three themes emerge: the abruptness of change, the interdependence of strength and weakness, and the privileging of the cohort over the individual.

Abrupt change characterizes Liz's most powerful relationships. In her long account of her Uncle Stanley and of Mandy, she struggles to communicate the glow of their presence and the shock of their absence. Her narrative associates sudden discovery and sudden loss—the disappearance of her Uncle Stanley, as well as the deaths of Mandy and of Teo, Mandy's half-brother and Liz's first love—with the arrivals and departures of the monarch butterflies each summer. The transcontinental migration of the monarchs and their annual congregation on particular trees at opposite ends of their route is regarded by Liz and her cousins, in childhood, as uncanny and magical. They do not question where the butterflies went or where they came from. The butterflies appear overnight, turning an entire tree orange like flowering foliage or a "burning bush," and disappear just as suddenly a short time later. As an adult and a scientist, "old enough to require explanations . . . suspicious of unpredictability and impressions," Liz imagines her uncle's disappearance as a long and arduous migration: "I picture him sometimes, standing on a mountain in Mexico surrounded by exhausted, tattered butterflies" (Urquhart, *Sanctuary Line* 10–12).

The ecology of the monarchs serves as an analog for the interplay of strength and weakness in human character. From the milkweed on which they feed, monarch butterflies absorb a chemical toxin that renders them largely invulnerable to predators. The capacity of monarchs to fulfill their destinies—migrations across half a world that require four generations to complete—depends upon this "gift of toxicity." Potential predators recognize the monarchs' coloration and markings and leave them alone. In Urquhart's fiction, the intensity and self-possession of charismatic people are always potentially toxic. While the metaphor of the chemical toxin is specific to this novel, the concept is not—the avatars of Heathcliff that recur in Urquhart's work are both enthralling and dangerous.

Before they meet, Liz regards Mandy's lover as a man with the gift of toxicity. She knows very little about him other than the pain Mandy has experienced in the relationship. Although the affair is intense and sustained over a period of years, he withholds emotional intimacy. Mandy and Vahil, her superior officer in the Canadian military, are rarely together except for stolen meetings in rented rooms; they do not have meals together; he doesn't believe in tokens of love; he never acknowledges that he loves her; she is never sure he will return. Nonetheless, Vahil is a man of extraordinary charisma: "... in spite of all this, in spite of the uncertainty, Mandy clearly believed he was a saint. Both men and women were mesmerized by him ... and obeyed his orders without question or complaint ... . They talked about him all the time while she stood in their midst" (Urquhart, *Sanctuary Line* 152). Mandy believes there is integrity in Vahil's refusal to privilege their personal relationship over his professional responsibilities as a soldier and commanding officer. But the discipline to withhold intimacy is also an exercise of power. Mandy is both wounded by her lover's aloofness and charmed by it. "In the face of this, of him," Mandy tells her cousin, "I am utterly powerless" (Urquhart, *Sanctuary Line* 181). Liz believes that, in order to win the affirmation of her lover, Mandy took increasing military risks; she holds Vahil indirectly responsible for Mandy's death because seeking his approval made her reckless. Liz imagines him as a ruthless and exploitive lover, the consummate professional, impervious to emotion. She remembers Mandy at a point of near-despair: "[A]ren't people like him, the smart, powerful ones, the ones everyone is drawn to, aren't they always almost monsters? They are an exaggeration, and everything around them becomes an exaggeration" (Urquhart, *Sanctuary Line* 181).

The complex ecology of the monarch provides a further analog for the interdependence of strength and weakness. Liz perceives both Vahil and her Uncle Stanley as beautiful, dangerous men— handsome, charismatic, naturally gifted, immune to harm and careless of the harm they do to others. But it is difficult to know with certainty whether someone actually has the gift of toxicity or whether, like the viceroy butterfly or the rare monarchs who lack the toxin, an individual has learned to mimic the attributes of the monarch in order to take advantage of its invulnerability.

My uncle was like one of those few vulnerable monarchs, or perhaps more specifically like its mimic, the viceroy. Most of us sailing in his midst saw only his color and his grace, and we assumed, therefore, his indestructibility. . . . Only someone very, very close to him would have been able to sense his defenselessness, his helplessness in the face of attack. . . .There may very well have been—part of me still wants to believe this—no latent poison in him. There may have been nothing manipulative associated with his charm. (Urquhart, *Sanctuary Line* 52)

Throughout the long narrative that forms the first part of *Sanctuary Line*, Liz maintains her judgment of Vahil as a ruthless and brutal lover. Only in the brief second section, the coda, is that perception of arrogant self-containment modified. The coda suggests that Vahil's unbending refusal of emotional intimacy was motivated not by selfishness or ambition, but by commitment to a larger cultural mission, in which his responsibilities as a Muslim cleric took priority over personal fulfillment. The "turn" in the positioning of Vahil that occurs in the final section of the novel develops the third element of the complex analogy that structures the narrative: privileging the cohort over the individual. When Vahil visits the Butler farm on the one-year anniversary of Mandy's burial, Liz learns that he is a second-generation Kurdish-Canadian Muslim. During his military deployment to predominantly Muslim countries, his sense of cultural identity was irrevocably altered. Recognizing himself as "a displaced Muslim" (Urquhart, *Sanctuary Line* 215), Vahil was "cracked open spiritually . . . . [I]n the midst of that displacement, there was this music of communion. The call to prayer" (Urquhart, *Sanctuary Line* 215–216). Vahil has become an imam, a commitment that would make a lasting relationship with Mandy impossible. "Of course I loved her" [he] said, "but we were never going to be able to enter each other's lives once our tours of duty were over" (Urquhart, *Sanctuary Line* 216).

The shift in emphasis from the loss of a treasured individual— the perspective that has dominated Liz's narrative for most of the novel—to a future-oriented focus on the destiny of the cohort is reconciled in terms of the analogy that has structured the entire novel. The generations of monarch butterflies succeed one another in four stages, across a year-long cycle. The four generations are different in their physical capacities and in their contributions to the survival of the species. Every year, the flight of monarchs migrates across the continent, Mexico to Canada and back, but no individual butterfly makes that migration:

> Not a single monarch ever returns . . . . The ones who come back to us may look exactly the same as those who departed, but it is their great-grandchildren who make the return flight, the two previous generations having mated and died at six-week intervals in springtime Texas and Illinois. The third generation we welcome in June mates and dies six weeks later in our very own Ontario fields, engendering the hardy fourth Methuselah generation, which amazes us on trees like the one at the end of the lane and lives an astonishing nine months in order to be able to make the long journey back. (Urquhart, *Sanctuary Line* 12)

The motif of an ecology that encompasses, but supersedes, the fate of the individual—derived from the novel's governing system of analogical relationships—alters the context for the failed relationship of Mandy and Vahil.

This motif also knits together the implications of the two narrative strategies that structure the novel. The migration of the monarch butterflies is longer, harder, more dangerous, and more remarkable than the achievement of any single generation, let along any single butterfly. In the closing pages of the novel, Liz says,

> I thought of all this . . . All the tough evolutions, the shedding of various skins, followed by those difficult migrations, over great stretches of open water, and across vast tracts of land, to and from Mexico, or America, or Kandahar. That longing we have to bring it all together into one well-organized cellular structure, and then the heartbreaking suspicion that, with the best of intentions, we never really can. (Urquhart, *Sanctuary Line* 225)

Her musings bring her to the novel's closure and Mandy's imagined recitation: "Other little children/Shall bring my boats ashore." In other words, on a technical level, the two structural devices that organize the text come together at its close in a doubled expression of faith that future generations will complete actions that seem cruelly fragmented in the present.

Hilary Dannenberg argues that the prominence of analogical plotting is a distinctive feature of contemporary literary narrative. That is, contemporary narrative fiction establishes relationships among characters and events "constructed through an indirect or figurative system of connection: relationships . . . cognitively constructed through the perception of correspondences" (Dannenberg 105, original emphasis omitted). Urquhart's body of fiction provides multiple examples of this principle of narrative design. *Changing Heaven* develops a network of parallels among characters who exist in different story worlds. In *Sanctuary Line,* characters who never meet are positioned in Liz Crane's narrative as "figures in an interlocking constellation of correspondences" (Dannenberg 107). Moreover, *Sanctuary Line* demonstrates the increasing complexity of Urquhart's analogical structures and the elegance of the insights they provide.

Works Cited

Compton, Anne. "Romancing the Landscape: Jane Urquehart's Fiction." *Jane Urquhart: Essays on Her Works.* Ed. Laura Ferri. Toronto: Guernica, 2005.

Dannenberg, Hilary. *Coincidence and Counterfactuality: Plotting Time and Space in Narrative Fiction.* Lincoln: U of Nebraska P, 2008.

Urquhart, Jane. *Changing Heaven.* Toronto: McClelland & Stewart, 1990.

_____. *Sanctuary Line.* New York: MacLehose, 2010.

Wyile, Herb. *Speaking in the Past Tense: Canadian Novelists on Writing Historical Fiction.* Waterloo, ON: Wilfred Laurier UP, 2007.

"By Mistake": Larry Weller as 'The Stone Guest' in Carol Shields' Novel *Larry's Party*___

Nora Foster Stovel

Larry's Party opens with the words "By mistake."[1] Larry takes another man's jacket by mistake, and his borrowed robes, a handsome Harris tweed jacket with leather buttons, offer Larry a new sense of possibility, transforming him into "the Big Guy" (4). After he discards it, his shirtsleeves fill with wind, transmuting him into a "Superman" (13), suggesting protean identities. *"Wait a minute, it's all a mistake"* (12), Larry thinks. But a "mistake can work both ways" (9–10), leading to good or bad luck.

Larry finds himself in "Floral Arts" by mistake: his mother meant to enroll him in the "Furnace Repair" course, but someone sent him the wrong brochure—"an accident," a "fluke" (7). Larry hesitates to tell his friend Sally "that it had been his mother's idea, and that this decision, like almost everything in his life, had presented itself without any easily available alternatives" (129). Dot Weller is, of course, the queen of mistakes: "One ancient mistake" (45), accidentally poisoning her mother-in-law, determined her life.

Even his marriage is a mistake. Larry and his first wife got together by accident: "It was sort of a mistake the way they got together" (10). Larry, in clown costume, had taken another girl to a costume party, but repelled by the painted moustache on his pirate-costumed date, he was attracted to the Martian-costumed girl—"Dorrie Shaw Weller, a policeman's daughter" (235). Later, Larry and Dorrie get married by mistake: that is, they get pregnant by accident. Eventually, Larry realizes, "He'd made mistakes in his life, one big mistake anyway, his marriage to Dorrie" (104). Even his friends realize, "He'd made a mistake. He'd married someone he had nothing in common with" (105).

Of course, *"we all make mistakes"* (252), but Larry Weller's whole life is one big mistake. How, then, does Larry succeed in life? Because his mistakes usually turn into "good fortune" (205).

Larry knew "he was going to be lucky" (331), and he was right: "Larry's good luck" is manifest (206). As Warren Cariou observes in *Larry's Party: Man in the Maze,* "Larry has always been a lucky man. He makes all the right mistakes" (93). Larry recognizes his "good luck, his dangerous history, his mistakes and promises" (201). Recalling the epiphany triggered by his initial mistake, Larry comprehends his realization of possibility: "Love was waiting for him. Transformation. Goodness. Work. Understanding. . . . And children, too, if he were lucky, and he was going to be lucky, that question was no longer in doubt" (331).

What is responsible for his Midas touch? Lucky Larry is just an ordinary guy, after all; Larry rhymes with "ordinary" (253): he's "a man condemned, no matter what his accomplishments, to be ordinary, and to pass slowly, painfully, through each of life's orderly prescriptive stages. . . . he knows himself doomed to live inside the hackneyed parentheses of predictability, a walking, head-scratching cliché" (165). When, amid the "enchantment and liberation of words" (331), he discovers the word "banal," he realizes it describes himself (85): "he's Larry Weller, an ordinary man who's been touched by ordinary good and bad luck" (249), but he is favored by *extra*-ordinary good luck. Things just "happen" to Larry, but they happen for the best, making him a "happy," or "lucky," man. "Happy" relates to *happenstance,* the title of Shields' first novel written about a male hero,[2] meaning the occurrence of things by chance. Chance favors Larry.

Larry's confidence in his good luck allows him to remain passive because he has learned that even his mistakes turn out well. Shields emphasizes Larry's passive nature: "He fell into the right line of work: flowers, plants" (73). Like the flowers he tends, *"[he] toils not, neither does [he] spin"* (76). He has a habit of "just letting his life happen to him" (83): "The wind that blew against his exposed body informed him of his good fortune. All he had to do was stand still and allow it to happen" (331). Like other men named Larry, "the nicknamed population possess greater adaptability, turning toward the world their sunny freckledness and their willingness to 'go along'" (250). So Larry just continues "doing what everyone tells him to do" (245). He lives at home with his parents, Dot and Stu Weller, until the age of twenty-six, in a prolonged adolescence, until the accident of Dorrie's pregnancy impels them to marry. Flying home from their honeymoon, Larry and Dorrie return to "the life they'd chosen or which had chosen them" (37), the second clause suggesting their joint passivity in the face of fate.

Why is such a passive guy so lucky? Because his helplessness attracts women who protect him. Passive to a fault, lucky Larry is directed by a succession of capable women: first Dot, his mother, responsible for Larry's enrolment in Floral Arts, leading to his success in landscape architecture; then Dorrie, his first wife, who bulldozes half his hedge maze, spurring him to become a "master maze maker" (127); then Beth Prior, his second wife, who encourages his "mazing" career; then Charlotte, his lady friend, who plans Larry's party, reuniting him with Dorrie and Beth; and finally Dorrie again.

Larry's boyhood dream was "to be cast into the wilderness [and] to be released, to be exalted" (114) by his friends. As boys, he and his friend Bill Hershel, equipped with map and compass, "willed themselves to become lost, so that they could arrive, heroically, at a state of being found" (112). At Hampton Court, on his honeymoon, he explores "the oldest surviving hedge maze in England" (34). Larry discovers a love of mazes because he enjoys the experience of being lost and then found: "getting lost, and then found, seemed the whole point" (35). Referring to his Hampton Court adventure, "I was lost," he later admits to Dorrie, "but I wanted to be lost" (335). Larry loves "the essential lost-and-found odyssey of a conventional maze" (289). He can enjoy the *frisson* of being lost in a maze, *a/ mazed* perhaps because he knows some woman will find him.

Hampton Court inspires an epiphanic experience: "He hadn't anticipated the sensation of feeling unplugged from the world or the heightened state of panicked awareness that was, nevertheless, repairable"—"the moment of willed abandonment, the unexpected rapture of being blindly led" (35–6). Mazes trigger that magic moment of transcendence that Shields treasures: "I'm interested in the transcendent moment, that 'moment of grace'" that realizes the extraordinary in the ordinary, which she refers to as "numinous moments," "moments of transcendence" or "random illuminations"[3]: "I believe in these moments when we feel or sense the order of the universe beneath the daily chaos. They're like a great gift of happiness that comes unexpectedly" (Wachtel 17). This "gift of happiness" is given to Larry by labyrinths: "It's really when entering a previously unknown maze, especially a hedge maze, that Larry is brought to a condition which he thinks of as spiritual excitement," the narrator explains: "All this ignites Larry's sense of equilibrium and sends him soaring" (171–2). In "Larry's A/Mazing Spaces" Coral Ann Howells argues that Shields "relocates the romantic experience of the sublime, with all its rapture and self-transcendence . . . from nature to culture as . . . it is miniaturized within the artificial space of the maze" (132). The maze allows Larry to escape the quotidian for the sublime, to intuit a richer grasp of possibility than his borrowed robes afforded: "Someone older than himself paced inside his body, someone stronger too, cut loose from the common bonds of sex, of responsibility. Looking back he would remember a brief moment when time felt mute and motionless. This hour of solitary wandering seemed a gift, and part of the gift was an old greedy grammar flapping in his ears: lost, more lost, utterly lost" (36). "In a maze you had to feel doubly lost," he realizes, leaving only "the teasing sense of willful abandonment" (153).

Repeating "the Hampton Court pilgrimage" years later with Beth, Larry recalls his earlier "transformative experience": "he remembers he felt a joyous rising of spirit that was related in some way to the self's dimpled plasticity. He could move beyond what he was, the puzzling hedges seemed to announce; he could become someone other than Larry Weller, shockingly new husband of Dorrie Shaw, non-speculative citizen of a former colony, a man of limited imagination and few choices" (217). Like the jacket, the maze offers Larry an expanded sense of possibility, an escape from "the lies, theatre, and staged manipulation of marriage" (279). After Dorrie bulldozes his hedge, he leaves her: "Departures and arrivals: he didn't know it then, but these two forces would form the twin bolts of his existence—as would the brief moments of clarity that rose up in between, offering stillness. A suspension of breath. His life held in his own hands" (37). Those precious interludes are precisely the phenomenon that Larry discovers in mazes. The maze is the template for Larry's life, even his sexuality. *Celtic Mazes and Labyrinths* (91) and the *Hedges of England and Scotland* become his bibles.[4] By being "lost in a shrug of ecstatic ease" (131) in his first sexual experience with Sally, he finds his place in life and assurance that "he's a man like any other" (152): "Love was waiting for him. . . . The discovery of his own clumsy body and how it yearned to connect" (331).

The maze, of course, is a metaphor for the self. As Garth McCord says, "at the centre of the maze there's an encounter with one's self. Center demands a reversal, a new beginning, a sense of . . . rebirth. In the turns of the maze, one is isolated and then comes alive again. . . .Which speaks to the contemporary human torment of being alternately lost and then found" (313). Garth and Marcia McCord, who commission Larry to build the McCord Maze in Toronto, are enchanted by "the mystery of [mazes], all they stood for, symbolically, transcendentally" (312) because "Mazes are like [. . .] thumbprints on the planet" (312). Garth compares the maze to human life: "The thing about a maze, there can be one route or many. If you think of that symbolically, it means that our lives are open" (313). This comparison recalls Shields' epigraph to *Larry's Party* from "Reflections on Walking in the Maze at Hampton Court" from *British Magazine*, 1747: "What is this mighty labyrinth–the earth, / But a wild maze the moment of our birth?" The Hollywood stone Christian maze, "the oldest dateable labyrinth in the British Isles, 550 AD" (214), that Larry later visits with Beth suggests "a more profound reading of the maze related to the difficulty of life and life's tortuous spiritual journey" (215)—a clear metaphor for Larry's mistake-laden life and Shields' complex narrative structure.

Larry and Beth consider "the modern inhabitants of the world were wanderers, pilgrims, and the labyrinth was their natural habitat" (221). Beth, a specialist in Christian female martyrs and portraits of the Annunciation, inquires, "what will happen to a world that's lost its connection with the sacred? We long for ecstasy, to stand outside of the self in order to transcend that self" (179). Beth articulates that mazes are our connection to the miraculous, our umbilical cord to the spiritual: there is a "theory that the medieval garden maze constituted a holy pilgrimage in microcosm, a place where a pilgrim might wend his way to the maze's secret heart and therein find sanctuary and salvation" (138). This spiritual theory relates to Beth's obsession with Christian subjects: "An avowed agnostic, believing the sacred has been taken over by psychology, she nevertheless was someone who melted toward the vision of God's grace, seeing it as a storm of sunlight, the most powerful force in history" (215). Beth's interest in Christianity complicates "mazing."

At the Leeds Castle maze, Larry and Beth have an important conversation about the cosmic or spiritual aspect of mazes. Larry explains to Beth, "The whole thing about mazes . . . is that they make perfect sense only when you look down on them from above." Beth replies, "Like God in his heaven," and asks, "what kind of a God wants us to get confused and keep us in a state of confusion?" Larry responds, "Isn't that what we've always had? Chaos from the first day of creation? But mazes are refuges from confusion, really. An orderly path for the persevering. Procession without congestion" (219). Dorrie, who later surprises Larry by informing him that she has read Spellman's book on mazes, quotes, "Controlled chaos and contrived panic" (313). Larry suggests that mazes provide an exit. "Salvation or death?" Beth asks. Larry designs a maze with four exits, "a maze in which there is not the slightest possibly of getting seriously lost" (181) because Death is a "maze without an exit" (273), recalling existentialist philosopher Jean-Paul Sartre's 1944 play *No Exit*.

Shields' use of maze patterns to signal each chapter emphasizes the importance of the metaphor because Shields "wanted to design each chapter as a little maze in itself" (Goertz 253).[5] Critics agree that the maze symbolizes the important issues of the novel. As Dee Goertz explains in "Treading the Maze of *Larry's Party*," "the maze functions not only as a symbol in the novel, but also as image, metaphor, and structural device," adding, "it underscores the main theme of the novel—that the human quest for meaning and pattern in the universe is a quest for connectedness" (231). In "Pioneering Interlaced Spaces: Shifting Perspectives and Self-Representation in *Larry's Party*," Patricia-Lea Paillot argues:

> The maze motif [. . .] constitutes the recurrent frame of reference and the central architecture in which each chapter is stamped with geometrical or labyrinthine figures. [. . .] Using the maze as a structuring principle, *Larry's Party* merges the material and human constituents of the world into a sensuous blend. (158)

And Howells argues:

> The novel offers a spatial figuring of Larry's life inside the a/mazing space of the text, where Shields refashions two conventional life-writing metaphors, the journey and the maze, to take into account the vagaries of the subjective life, registered through a narrative combination of surface reportage and changing perspectives. (132)

And this is significant because, Howells explains, "the maze may be appreciated as a spatial design which will accommodate multiple symbolic meanings, varying from spiritual or sexual to psychological, all within an aesthetic frame" (115–6). Nina Van Gessel argues in "'A Man's Journey': Masculinity, Maze, and Biography in Carol Shields' *Larry's Party*" that the "postmodern instability and the 'unmasculine' confusion of Larry's progress are imaged in a radically new form of biographical text: one whose narrative fluidity and indeterminacy Shields models—with a nod to the ancient association between labyrinth and life—on the maze" (154).

Shields employs the maze as both macrocosmic and microcosmic metaphor. Larry's "body is an upright walking labyrinth, and he feels the miracle of it" (269). His psyche, too, is a complex labyrinth. No wonder the citizens of Winnipeg created a memorial hedge maze in Shields' honor after the "Festival of Voices," the inaugural Carol Shields Symposium on Women's Writing, held in Winnipeg in 2009. "Can't you just imagine it—a real live maze in Winnipeg!" (106). She would have appreciated the irony of the fact that the delegates traced the path of the maze, even though the hedges were still only a few inches high, and so the possibility of getting lost was nonexistent.

Larry is in search of his self, "the sovereign self inside him" (284). Shields employs mirror imagery to convey Larry's sense of self, "seeing himself in his self's silver mirror" (11) or "snagged in a bevelled mirror" (241). Searching for his new self, following the shearing of his shoulder-length hair, he stands in front of the bathroom mirror experimenting with various expressions (17). Flying to England on his honeymoon, he tries to "outstare the image in the floating black glass of the window, that shorn, bewildered, fresh-faced stranger whose profile, for all its raw boyishness, reminded him, alarmingly, of [. . . his] father" (21). From then on, each morning he meets this ghostly presence in the shaving mirror (22): "Larry, shaving, washing, attempted to avoid his father's eyes in the mirror, that ghostly presence floating beneath the steamed-over surface" (25). The fact that his father, Stu Weller, never called him Larry, but only addressed him as "*you*" (55), emphasizing "his no-name status" (55), does not inspire a confident sense of selfhood.[6] "Larry Weller stars in his own life movie but no one else's" (258). Remembering that he is a *husband* and about to become a *father*, Larry "had to remind himself, announcing the fact to the mirror every morning as he blinked away the ghost of his father's face" (31).

Haunted, like Hamlet, by his father's ghost, Larry must reassure himself of his identity: "My name is Larry Weller. I'm a floral designer, twenty-six years old, and I'm walking down Notre Dame Avenue, in the city of Winnipeg, in the country of Canada, in the month of April, in the year 1977" (6). Viewing himself from within and without, like the poet's persona in Shields' poem "I/Myself," he realizes "Winnipeg was still his here and now, the black sphere that enclosed the pellet of his self" (154). But Larry does not feel like the star of his own story: "Larry's sense of touring in his own life adventure: The Larry Weller Story" (245) gives him not star status, but a minor role in some woman's drama. "His life, he feels, is not so much a story as a sequence of soundings" (267).

Larry recalls a photo taken of himself as a baby in a high chair. This photo, which Shields found in a bin and used as the original cover of *Larry's Party*, is a poignant representation of a powerless child's anxiety, "his infant face full of hurt and knowing" (331). Recalling it, Larry wonders, "Is it his future as a man he's seeing? That stumbling being who knows now that every single day something will be taken from him, and that one day it will be too much?" (331).

Larry has to grow into his "ongoing Larry self" (273); "the problem is, he doesn't know how to be the person he's become" (269). To his amazement, he's become "Mr. Maze" (147), "a monarch in his chosen sphere" (67). His expertise as a "garden maestro" (255) translates him to Oak Park, Illinois, birthplace of Carol Shields, where he has an office suite and a card reading "A/ MAZING SPACE INC." (145), a play on the 1779 hymn "Amazing Grace" by John Newton and perhaps on the collection of feminist essays, *A Mazing Space: Writing Canadian Women Writing*. Despite Dorrie's dismissal of his "Goddamn fucking bushes" (33), Larry becomes "Maze King of the Universe."

Initially, Larry builds his own maze in the front yard of his first, modest home on Lipton Street. Then Big Bruce Sztuwark commissions Larry to build a hedge maze on his riverside property— "a real live maze in Winnipeg!" (106). Aware that "every classical maze contains at its heart a 'goal'" (149), Larry hopes one day to install a small stone fountain, that phallic symbol, at the heart of the maze (92). Later, he plans to place a fountain at the centre of the Barnes maze in River Forest, Illinois, until he realizes the fountain's noise would reveal the secret of the maze (153). Later, he installs a mirrored wishing well, a vaginal symbol, at the centre of his Milwaukee maze (181). The shift from phallic fountain to vaginal well suggests a shift from masculine to feminine, gesturing towards Shields' investigation of gender roles.

Dr. Eric Eisner rejects the theory of a spiritual interpretation of mazes in favor of the idea that "the underlying rationale of the maze is sexual": "A labyrinth [. . .] twists through the mystery of desire and frustration. It doubles back on itself, relishing its tricks and turns.

It's aroused by its own withholding structure. In the centre, hidden, but finally with a burst, revealed—lies sexual fulfilment, heaven" (138–9). In Barcelona's Laberint d'Horta, Larry recalls "how Beth had reached out and stroked with her hand the smooth marble skin of Eros, turning toward him then with a look of perfect wonder in her eye" (227). Clearly, the maze relates to Larry and Beth's sexual relationship *and* their spiritual impulse, suggesting the connection between the two spheres.

"This maze foolishness he'd accidentally tumbled into" (152) symbolizes Larry's life: he realizes that "one wrong step would throw him off-course, and that what he would lose would be [. . .] his own self" (164). Even his marriage parallels his maze-making. Dorrie loathes "Larry's maze craze" (71), but, despite her contempt for his "shrub mania" (42), his "maze madness" (41), lucky Larry becomes "Shrub king of the universe" (42), sought by wealthy landowners to build mazes on their property on both sides of the forty-ninth parallel. "I'm married to a maze nut" (91), Dorrie complains, but she is the one driven mad: "She swore she was going nuts living in Larry's crazy bush pile" (159). Part of the appeal of the maze for Larry is a momentary escape from the quotidian reality of his marriage to Dorrie: just as he is lost and found in the maze, so his "deficient love for Dorrie" comes and goes as he keeps "finding it and losing it again" (35).

By bulldozing his hedge maze, Dorrie effectively ends their marriage: "She might as well have chopped his heart in two" (159), a friend remarks. Larry's heart is indeed cleft in twain: "He'd lost his son, his wife, his place on the planet" (110). Despite her desire to move to a new subdivision in Lindon Woods, however, Dorrie inexplicably remains in the Lipton Street house and keeps the other half of the maze going—a symbol of their broken marriage—a half-circle awaiting completion. Larry thinks, "this first maze may lack the enclosed secrets of the true form, but that its continued existence remains, so far at least, the most unexamined mystery of his life, a circling, exquisite puzzle of pain, and pain's consolation" (160)—a maze representing the mystery of marriage, for "Marriage was full of mysteries" (235), as Shields reminds us.

After he emerges from the "cramped crawlspace of his first marriage" (100) and meets his second wife, Beth inspires his continued exploration of mazes, and they enjoy "mazing every weekend in England" (221). Shields writes, "the modern inhabitants of the world were wanderers, pilgrims, and the labyrinth was their natural habitat" (221) because "A maze [. . .] is a kind of machine with people as its moving parts" (218), although "A man's journey is different than a woman's" (325). Enjoying the Bicton maze in Devon, Beth realizes, "You kept telling me they were about love or sex or death or God. But really they're just fun" (222). Finally, Beth gets the joke.

After Beth leaves him to teach Women's Studies in England, Larry "feels the undertow of something missing . . . he's tired—tired of his name, tired of being a man, tired of the ghostly self he's chained to" (178): "Here I am: a serious, likeable man scrolling through the flow of my life. A man—surely you can detect this—in a state of personal crisis" (178). Larry senses that he is approaching his "'midlife crisis' or 'male menopause'" (166). Larry feels lost within the maze of himself, cut off from others: "His two failed marriages, the distance he feels between himself and his dead parents, his inability to understand his son, or to will himself in love with Charlotte Angus—all these failings speak of the separateness of human beings, with every last person on earth withdrawing to the privacy of his own bones" (283). Is Larry's fabled luck failing him?

Larry is "persuaded that he's only been pretending to be lost at forty, a man on the verge of nothing at all," indulging in "sham despair" (181). Soon "he's back to being Larry Weller again, husband, father, home owner, tuxedo wearer. An okay guy with work to do. So far, so good" (181). Clothes make the man, and the switch from Harris tweed to tux baffles Larry,[7] for he has trouble negotiating his varied roles: "The fact is, he can never quite believe in his tuxedoed self, cousin to that phantom presence that lurks in his dreams, the guy watching the action, suffering, scared, and greedy in his borrowed, baggy clothes, but never actually stepping on stage and exposing his face" (165).

Larry encounters his life crisis—an attack of encephalitis triggering a three-week coma. This abrupt interruption in his life—

recalling similar transformative illnesses, not only in Shields' own novels *Small Ceremonies* and *Unless*, but also in D. H. Lawrence's *Sons and Lovers*, Doris Lessing's *The Summer Before the Dark*, and Gabrielle Roy's *Street of Riches*, to name but a few—proves a metamorphosis, a cocoon, from which he emerges "well, weller, wellest" (253). Shields' language—"He yearned to go back to the silent, unreachable place he couldn't remember, to cradle his consciousness in a nest of softness" (273) suggests an embryonic state. His "great day of awakening" (272) makes him realize that "he's spent his whole life in a state of recovery" (284). His critical coma helps him "recover" his son Ryan, who devotes every day to reading the newspaper aloud to him from cover to cover, and his friend Charlotte Angus, who sleeps in the chair by his bed every night so that, if and when he awakens, he will not find himself alone.

"But it isn't true" that he is lost: someone is bound to find him: "It is impossible to live a whole life sealed inside the constraints of a complex body. Sooner or later, and sometimes by accident, someone is going to reach out a hand or a tongue or a morsel of genital flesh and enter that valved darkness" (283). Larry has viewed himself as "a grown man who stumbled, fell into error, got lost, made a fool of himself, but was willing, at least, to be rescued. Something good was bound to come of this" (225). Larry is lost within himself during his coma, but he is found by Ryan and Charlotte, for Charlotte's vigil and Ryan's "ghostly benevolent presence" (271) help him recover.

But can he find himself, "that stranger Larry Weller" (112)? Larry may be experiencing an existentialist dilemma: he doesn't know what he's doing here; is he really "plugged into the planet" (77)? Essentially, Larry is "the stone guest," not only at his own party, but in his own life. Samuel Alvero, who identifies himself as "the stone guest" at Larry's dinner party—defines the term as "one who is invited to occupy a place at the table, to fill a slot. He is not expected to say much. Or do much. He is just—" there (329). Similarly, Larry "fill[s] a slot" in Dorrie's life, then Beth's, then Charlotte's, then Dorrie's again. Larry's party emphasizes the way Larry has been passed around from one woman to another: "These women are separate selves, but also part of Larry's self"

(330), Shields writes: "Where would his life be without women? A stone guest at his own party. That's the truth of the matter. Filling a slot" (330). Curiously, his attempts to explain the reason for the party—the coincidence that both his wives are in town at the same time—are continually frustrated.

Ultimately, Dorrie finds him. The reader is just as surprised as Larry when she declares in "*After the Party*," "I love you. I've always loved you," and he replies, "I love you too. I've been waiting. Only I didn't know I was waiting" (336). By telling him she "loves" the remaining "half a maze" (half a/mazed?) (313-4), she reignites their marriage. Midge says, "I had a hunch she was waiting for a second ride on the merry-go-round" (338). As Beth puts it in her goodbye letter—a letter that Larry attacks "with a surgical red pencil. C-minus" (297)—it's just a case of "taking the right corner at the right moment—like one of your beautiful mazes" (339). She concludes her letter, serendipitously, with a poetic passage that reflects Shields' epigraph to the novel:

> Some run the Shepherd's Race—a rut
> Within a grass-plot deeply cut
> And wide enough to tread—
> A maze of path, of old designed
> To tire the feet, perplex the mind,
> Yet pleasure heart and head;
> 'Tis not unlike this life we spend
> And where you start from, there you end. (339)

This does make a neat ending by echoing Shields' epigraph, creating a Möbius strip circularity, or a palimpsest, a structural configuration that Shields employs in poems, as well as the happy ending that she favors in novels. The problem, however, is that it is not really credible because it has not been prepared for.[8] Does the novel end, then, as it began, with a mistake? Shields confessed: "I regret concluding *Larry's Party* with the traditional 'happy ending' of marriage. I wish I had ended it differently. I was enchanted with the idea of coming back to the place where you started. But I think that the published ending doesn't work because it hasn't been led up to.

The logical ending for Larry is general misalignment with women and the contemporary world." Perhaps Shields was inspired by the famous lines from T. S. Eliot's poem *Little Gidding*:

We shall not cease from exploration
And the end of all our exploring
Will be to arrive where we started
And know the place for the first time. (222)

Many postmodernist novels, including Doris Lessing's *The Golden Notebook*, display that circular structure. But perhaps it is a mistake for *Larry's Party*. Shields suggests, through her phrase "a general misalignment with women and the contemporary world," that Larry has not really found himself. Perhaps he remains happily lost within the maze of his own life, waiting to be found by a woman. The answer to the question posed at Larry's party, "What's it like being a man these days?" (315), may be one that troubles traditional definitions of masculinity: perhaps it means being dependent on women. Men are the stone guests in their own lives. Indeed, Larry depends on a woman, his creator, Carol Shields, for the ultimate "mistake" of a happy ending.

Notes

1. Unless otherwise specified, all references will be to *Larry's Party*.

2. *Happenstance* (1980) is Shields' first novel written from the point of view of a male protagonist.

3. Shields' phrase "random illuminations" provides the title for Eleanor Wachtel's 2007 collection of interviews with Shields.

4. Larry's devotion to the book *Hedges of England and Scotland* parallels Morag Gunn's interest in *The Clans and Tartans of Scotland* in Margaret Laurence's *The Diviners*.

5. Just as Larry reads "*Mazes and Labyrinths: Their History and Development*" (82), so Shields' youngest daughter—as the Shields Archives at the National Library in Ottawa, Canada, reveal—researched mazes for *Larry's Party*.

6. Even on his deathbed, Stu greeted his son with the statement, *"So it's you"* (176).

7. Although it may be a coincidence that Shields employs the word "tuxedo," Tuxedo is a relatively affluent neighbourhood of Winnipeg.

8. I agree with Cariou, who writes, "I can't help feeling disappointed when Larry arrives at this goal" ["a reunification with Dorrie"] because "Larry's joyous return into the arms of his first wife feels contrived" (92–3).

Works Cited

Cariou, Warren. *"Larry's Party*: Man in the Maze." *Carol Shields: The Arts of a Writing Life*. Ed. Neil K. Besner. Winnipeg: Prairie Fire Press, 1995. 133–144.

Eliot, T. S. *Little Gidding*. *T. S. Eliot: Collected Poems, 1909–1962*. London: Faber, 1963. 214–23.

Goertz, Dee. "Treading the Maze of *Larry's Party.*" *Carol Shields, Narrative Hunger, and the Possibilities of Fiction*. Ed. Edward Eden & Dee Goertz. Toronto: U of Toronto P, 2003. 230–254.

Howells, Coral Ann. "Larry's A/Mazing Spaces." *Carol Shields and the Extra-Ordinary*. Eds. Marta Dvorák & Manina Jones. Montreal, QC: McGill-Queen's UP, 2007. 115-135.

Paillot, Patricia-Léa. "Pioneering Interlaced Spaces: Shifting Perspectives and Self-Representation in *Larry's Party.*" *Carol Shields and the Extra-Ordinary*. Eds. Marta Dvorák & Manina Jones. Montreal, QC: McGill-Queen's UP, 2007. 151–171.

Neumann, Shirley, & Smaro Kamboureli, eds. *Amazing Space: Writing Canadian Women Writing*. *Canadian Woman Studies* 8.3 (1987).

Shields, Carol. "I/Myself." *Coming to Canada: Poems*. Ed. Christopher Levinson. Ottawa: Carleton UP, 1992. 6.

_____. *Happenstance*. Toronto/New York: McGraw-Hill Ryerson, 1980.

_____. *Larry's Party*. Toronto: Random House, 1997.

Van Gessel, Nina. "'A Man's Journey': Masculinity, Maze, and Biography in Carol Shields' *Larry's Party.*" *Studies in Canadian Literature/ Études en literature canadienne*. 32.1 (2007): 154–171.

Wachtel, Eleanor. *Conversations with Carol Shields: Random Illumination*. Fredericton, New Brunswick: Goose Lane Editions, 2007.

Listening and Loving: Reading Margaret Laurence's *The Diviners*

Carol L. Beran

- No matter how many times I read *The Diviners*, the final book in Margaret Laurence's series of five fictional works connected with the fictional Manitoba town of Manawaka, I cry when Jules dies.
- The first time I spoke about *The Diviners* at a conference, a person in the audience accused Laurence and me of cultural appropriation. Jules is a Métis.
- I'm very tempted to read *The Diviners* as a parable of how a writer loves Canada in all its diversity, with Morag's lovers representing key pieces in the Canadian mosaic.

A Parable

Reading *The Diviners* as a parable is attractive because the raw materials for such a reading are readily available in the story. It suggests a pleasing image of a potentially united country with compassion for all, no matter their race, class, or gender, and it excuses—sort of—Laurence for writing a book with a heroine who scandalously takes many lovers, and for shockingly writing out her love (or is it her character's love?) for specific parts of the Canadian mosaic in sensuous sex scenes that incited parental groups to try to ban the book in high schools.

Morag, a writer, has lived in or visited in Manawaka, Winnipeg, Vancouver, England, Scotland, and Ontario, locales that put the writer in significantly symbolic places with respect to Canada (heartland, west, east), its colonial past (England), and the past of Morag's immigrant ancestors (Scotland). In marrying Brooke, a university professor, Morag embraces Canada's British heritage through the literature he teaches, and Canada's connection to the British Commonwealth through his upbringing in India. Her sexual encounters with Jules show her love for the indigenous peoples of

Canada. A man she has sex with in Vancouver is a radio broadcaster who doesn't read books, and another (who batters her) is apparently from the lower classes; these lovers join the writer with less educated Canadians. Dan, her lover in London, connects her with her Scots heritage as well as linking her to artists. The parabolic reading works fairly well with the facts of this novel, and makes Morag's moving around and taking various lovers seem part of a grand scheme by the author that reaches beyond her character's own desires. Linda Hutcheon sees "in the physical and passionate attraction of the sexes (and in its possible result) a model for the energy of creation, with a strong emphasis on maternal images of birth, of potential generation" (205); this idea connects Morag's sex life with her creativity, linking both to the parabolic reading.

Furthermore, a parabolic reading tempts because this theme is worthy of a national epic, placing *The Diviners* on the route to becoming the great Canadian novel. Here is a book about the two founding peoples of the heartland—the Métis and the Scots, a variation on the eastern mythos of the French and English as the founders of Canada. Pique, the daughter of Morag and Jules, symbolizes in her DNA (or "in her veins" [A Bird 179], to use Laurence's image) the union of the two peoples.

In addition, *The Diviners* uses both as a theme and as a structure one often cited as the theme that contributes to the greatness of many famous works of fiction: time. In the first section of the novel, "The River of Now and Then," Pique leaves Morag, who now resides in Ontario, to seek her identity among her Métis relatives in Manitoba, which triggers Morag's memories of the past. The river by her cabin mysteriously flows both ways, but the mystery is soon explained by the forces of the current moving one way, while the wind ruffles the surface in the opposite direction. Like the river, time moves both ways for Morag, as her daughter's present abandoning of her triggers memories of her initial abandonment, her parents' death. "And then" are the final words of *The Stone Angel*, the first of Laurence's Manawaka books, read variously to suggest Hagar's death, her possible placement in Heaven or Hell, and the fact that life goes on, not just for the creator, but for her characters too (see

Beran 170–71). Because the ending of the first novel flows into the beginning of the last, and many of the characters and actions from the four earlier books appear briefly in *The Diviners*, the final book ties together all Laurence's Manawaka fiction, capping the series. Although some critics assert that the book is made to carry too much weight (Howells affirmed in Keith), another has entitled his work on Laurence *Margaret Laurence's Epic Imagination* (Comeau). Most importantly for the parabolic interpretation, the time element unites Canada's past and present, its European roots and its indigenous history juxtaposed with the present, giving the book the scope of a nationalistic epic.

Apologues and Actions

Much as I like reading *The Diviners* as a parable, I question the attraction, remembering Sheldon Sacks' distinctions between prose fictions organized as represented actions and those organized as apologues. In an action, Sacks says, "characters about whose fates we are made to care are introduced in unstable relationships which are then further complicated until the complications are finally resolved by the complete removal of the represented instability" (15); the story makes readers desire the characters' fate to be commensurate with their desert in some way. In apologues, on the other hand, all elements work towards presenting a message to readers: "The informing principle of all such works is that each is organized as a fictional example of a formulable statement or closely related set of such statements" (Sacks 8). Hans Hauge writes of Laurence, "it is my contention that her novels can be regarded as 'typical' and that her characters are 'types'" (129). Similarly, Helen Buss speaks as though this novel were an apologue when she writes, "Morag is not really a character in the traditional sense, but a feminine mode of questing, one which involves the articulation through language of the mutable self as it forms and reforms through a lifetime, creating the prismatic reality of the creative woman" (164). For Buss, Christie and Jules both stand for concepts: "Although, in many ways, Christie represents in his character and his language the ways in which the creative female writer incorporates that part of the patriarchy which has been excluded and demeaned, it is in Jules that we see how the female writer's need for a libidinal but unrepressive connection with masculinity is achieved" (161). W. J. Keith asserts that Pique Gunn Tonnerre "is a symbolic figure uniting native peoples and immigrants, a new Canadian woman emerging out of the ancestral past to represent a revivified, more democratic Canada" (*Sense* ch. 7). Laurence herself prompts readings like this when she insists that Morag mispronounces Jules' name as "Jewels" (*Diviners* 153), or has Jules explain the meanings of his nickname "Skinner" (*Diviners* 84), or names Morag's husband Brooke, seemingly shallow in a novel that begins and ends with a river. Sacks would use the term "walking concepts" for characters that "appear in a variety of situations, possess a sizeable number of concrete traits, and are successfully infused with animation," but function to convey an idea (165). However, while the ideas represented by walking concepts help readers evaluate other characters (see Sacks 166), such characters usually do not evoke our deep sympathy for themselves the way Morag and Jules do.

When I cry at Jules' death, I am reading an action: the presentation has made me care deeply about the characters and want them to come to an ending commensurate with their desert, although within the realistic framework that *The Diviners* presents. In contrast, I don't cry for the beaten man in the biblical parable of the Good Samaritan (Luke 10:30–37), though intellectually I pity the victim in this apologue, despise the passersby who fail to assist him, and affirm the actions of the Samaritan who helps the man of another cultural group. By telling the parable, Jesus gives a vivid answer to the question posed to him about who is one's neighbor, but the purpose of the telling clearly is to teach rather than to arouse emotions. I do not cry for Brooke when Morag leaves him; I experience him as a walking concept. I cry for Jules because I care for him, because I respect his difficulties, and because I know that marrying Morag and living happily ever after with their daughter is not something that can happen within the probabilities of the world Laurence invites readers to imagine in this book. However, I am not crying for the loss of a symbolic marriage that would imply a symbolic resolution of tensions between two parts of the Canadian mosaic. The ending for Morag, in fact, is happy, at least as an ending of a modern novel: she is alone, growing older, but reconciled enough to these factors to be able to write her novel. And I am happy for her, satisfied that her difficulties have come to a realistic, if limited, resolution. I'm reading the novel as an action, not an apologue.

Recent scientific studies suggest that "individuals who often read fiction appear to be better able to understand other people, empathize with them, and view the world from their perspective" (Paul). Annie Murphy Paul reports that psychologist Victor Nell found that "when readers are enjoying the experience the most, the pace of their reading actually slows," which "gives deep readers time to enrich their reading with reflection, analysis, and their own memories and opinions. It gives them time to establish an intimate relationship with the author, the two of them engaged in an extended and ardent conversation like people falling in love" (Paul). In another study reported in *Science* and summarized in *The Guardian*, psychologist David Comer Kidd is quoted as saying that "fiction is not just a simulator of a social experience, it is a social experience"; he and his associate concluded that reading "literary fiction improves social empathy" ("Reading Literary Fiction"). In other words, when I cry at Jules' death, I am learning and practicing social empathy, a scientifically observable response to fiction:

> That immersion [in the narrative] is supported by the way the brain handles language rich in detail, allusion, and metaphor: by creating a mental representation that draws on the same brain regions that would be active if the scene were unfolding in real life. The emotional situations and moral dilemmas that are the stuff of literature are also vigorous exercise for the brain, propelling us inside the heads of fictional characters and even, studies suggest, increasing real-life capacity for empathy. (Paul)

Readers have long known what these studies confirm. Martha Nussbaum writes that a novel "is a cultural construct that itself helps to constitute its readers as social beings. It uses the language of community, and joins readers with both characters and author (and with one another) in bonds of community" (166). In addition, Nussbaum asserts that:

> literature is an extension of life not only horizontally, bringing the reader into contact with events or locations or persons or problems he or she has not otherwise met, but also, so to speak, vertically, giving the reader experience that is deeper, sharper, and more precise than much of what takes place in life. (48)

But don't novels often have messages? And don't the greatest novels have profound messages? Laurence herself wrote to Gabrielle Roy when fundamentalists were trying to ban *The Diviners* use in high schools, "at its deepest level, it is a novel about God's grace" (Socken 8). If other critics and I have found the "writer as unifier of the Canadian mosaic" message in the novel, isn't it there? Well, of course. But is it primary or secondary? I'm voting for the latter. Does that matter? Yes, because of two factors: the problem of cultural appropriation and the question of whether there are important aspects of the book that have been overlooked because of the emphasis on its great epic themes or its myriad of other themes, such as divining and the community of diviners (Hjartarson 62), learning from experience (Stratford),[1] escaping/changing/accepting the past (Hjartarson 44), identity (Buss 166), and the making of a woman writer (Brydon 186, Stovel 251ff). If we see the book as contributing to Canadian nationalism, we are reading thematically, following the pattern Frank Davey criticizes as leading readers to focus on the theme rather than on what makes this a unique literary work with unique literary effects: "the literary work comes to have little significance outside the body of the national literature. It can be valued not for its unique or idiosyncratic qualities but only for what it shares with the larger body" (Davey 4; see also "Perceiving Recent Canadian Fiction" in this volume).

Cultural Appropriation

When I cry at Jules' death, am I affirming that Laurence is guilty of blatant cultural appropriation? Is she, like a colonial official, using a culture presumed inferior for her own purposes, without regard for its own needs, its own betterment defined in its own terms, chosen to support its own values? Does the idea of Jules being part of a victimized group, the Métis, make his death more poignant? Is his race used to evoke pathos? Laurence has Morag face the cultural disjunction problem directly with respect to Jules when she visits him just before his death: "Or was she interpreting him, as usual, only through her own eyes? How else could you interpret anyone? The thing now was not to interfere, not to enter fear" (*Diviners* 469). Novels, in fact, would be incredibly limited—as would histories, biographies, anthropological studies, and sociological reports—if their authors were limited to writing or studying about only their own race, class, and gender. Laurence, in creating characters to whom readers become attached, takes into account the importance of interpreting the Other, even if only through our own eyes. The characters may be fictional and seen through Laurence's appropriating eyes, but because my tears are real for me, Laurence has aroused my compassion for a Métis man and his relatives.[2]

Storytelling and Listening

One of Laurence's responses to the perplexity of cross-cultural understanding is storytelling, which happens constantly in *The Diviners*. Nora Foster Stovel, having studied Laurence's manuscripts of the book and read letters from her editor, Judith Jones, tells us that among other edits, stories about Piper Gunn were cut and stories told by Morag were excised or shortened at Jones' suggestion for the published version (253–54). The book as we have it, then, includes only some of the stories Laurence originally wanted it to contain. In current editions, after the ending of Morag's story, a section called "Album" presents four ballads purportedly written by characters in the book, suggesting one partial compromise between editor and author as a way to present more stories and reinforce the imagined reality of the characters. Reading the novel as an action rather than an apologue frees us to listen to the storytelling.

In *The Diviners*, storytelling is not just important to Laurence, it is important to us as readers, too, both because of the way it illuminates the characters and their cultural heritages and because the scenes in which these stories are told generally involve listeners. As alter egos for readers, these listeners show us how to respond: with silence, with skepticism, and with creativity.[3]

Near the end of the novel, Pique sings her own song for Morag: "Then silence. Pique could not speak until Morag did, and Morag could not speak for a while" (Laurence, *Diviners* 465). Morag takes Pique's hand and requests a copy of the lyrics, which "was apparently all she could say" (465). One mode of listening, then, is awed silence. Another mode involves questioning, as when Morag listens to Christie's stories. She questions values inherent in the tales: "Were they bad, the breeds and them?" (Laurence, *Diviners* 97). She questions the veracity of the tales: "They walked? A *thousand* miles? They couldn't, Christie" (Laurence, *Diviners* 96), or "Oh Christie! They didn't. We took it in History" (Laurence, *Diviners* 145). Morag asks of the stories she hears of battles in World War II, "What is a true story? Is there any such thing?" (Laurence, *Diviners* 159). When Morag identifies Riel as the hero of one of the stories Jules has heard from his father, Jules replies, "Sure. But the books, they lie about him. I don't say Lazarus told the story the way it happened, but neither did the books" (Laurence, *Diviners* 161–62). Jules questions received histories, but that doesn't exempt his stories from questioning. When the tale Jules recounts suggests the Scots fighters were mercenaries, Morag interrupts, "Hired guns? I bet they weren't!" (Laurence, *Diviners* 160), letting cross-cultural values interplay.

Morag's other response to the tales that she hears is to create. Hearing Christie's tale of Piper Gunn, in which the Piper's woman is named Morag, Morag tells herself a story: "MORAG'S FIRST TALE OF PIPER GUNN'S WOMAN" (Laurence, *Diviners* 61). When Morag learns the stories of Scotland and the Scots pioneers to Manitoba from Christie, the tales seem to give her heritage and "a place to stand on," to borrow Laurence's phrase ("A Place"). Paul Hjartarson asserts, "having listened to Christie's stories, having heard herself named, Morag can, in turn, name herself, insert herself in the story, become herself the teller" (51). Later, Morag goes eagerly to Scotland to see this heritage for herself, only to find that her ancestral land is not Scotland, but "Christie's real country. Where I was born" (Laurence, *Diviners* 415); this suggests that sharing stories from a culture, though powerful, may not be the whole impetus to creativity for Morag. Nevertheless, ultimately, all the tales she hears and divines become part of the imaginary out of which she creates her novels.

At the end of *The Diviners* the narrator states, "Morag returned to the house, to write the remaining private and fictional words, and to set down her title" (477). By writing, she becomes a creative non-victim in Margaret Atwood's terms, someone for whom "creative activity of all kinds becomes possible" because energy is no longer being used up dealing with victimization: "And you are able to accept your own experience for what it is rather than having to distort it to make it correspond with others' versions of it" (Atwood, *Survival* 38–39). Our hopes and fears for Morag find a pleasurable, if not final, conclusion in her renewed ability to write her story. Laurence's slant reference to the final pages of James Joyce's *A Portrait of the Artist as a Young Man* specifies the writer's creation as a form of divining: "I go to encounter for the millionth time the reality of experience and to forge in the smithy of my soul the uncreated conscience of my race" (Joyce 252–53).

The Diviners indicates a source of the materials in the soul's smithy: listening, divining. Morag listens to tales Christie tells, to those Jules tells (or retells of his father's tales) or sings to get beneath the surface, beyond the stereotype. One of the ways Morag—and Laurence—reach beyond stereotypes to enter another culture is by regarding listening as a process that includes hearing skeptically, questioning, taking what is heard and transforming it into new art. If compassion is at the heart of Laurence's art as some have argued,[4] it is not a compassion that blindly accepts, but one that approaches the Other by skeptical questions, which paradoxically allow a cultural interaction which transforms into new art—the future to which the river calls Morag.

The final pages of *The Diviners* pick up again key double-edged motifs in the book: surfaces/divining and listening/silence. Divining seems like a magic trick—or a miracle; just as Royland

---

finds underground water that cannot be seen on the surface of the ground, the "magic tricks" of the writer (Laurence, *Diviners* 477) allow her to see into people of many races, classes, and genders. The italicized sentence on the last page of the novel commands the writer to divining, conflating the river's paradoxical flow with the writer's double vision in time: "*Look ahead into the past, and back into the future, until the silence*" (Laurence, *Diviners* 477). It is also a command for the reader to join Morag and Laurence in creative listening and divining.

Conclusions

In Laurence's *A Bird in the House*, the narrator Vanessa describes herself as a "professional listener" (8). She writes her story based not only on what she sees, but on what she hears as she listens. In *The Diviners*, Laurence takes Morag and readers beyond Vanessa as Morag models a type of listening characterized by questioning, doubting, being perplexed, divining hidden rivers, and sometimes remaining silent.

The incredulity, disbelief, and doubt with which Morag greets the stories she hears is also what Morag points to when she says that, unlike Royland, she can never be sure her tricks work (Laurence, *Diviners* 477). Instead, as she questions Christie's tales, or skeptically identifies characters in the stories Jules tells as historical figures known by other names, she subverts an easy interpretation of an apologue imagining a more compassionate Canada, without barriers based on race, class, and gender. If we learn from Morag to be questioning listeners/readers of *The Diviners*, if we don't trust the themes other readers find in the book, but rather listen to the characters' stories with respectful skepticism, we have learned the first part of the process Morag models for us. The second challenge is to transform the received vision into a better imaginary through the use of our doubts.

The imaginary that readers of *The Diviners* face, then, is a more doubting, vexed, and perplexed one than critics usually point out.[5] If we read the novel as an action rather than as an apologue, cry at Jules' death, feel horror and compassion at what happens to Piquette and her children, perhaps even love Christie and Prin more than Morag seems to, and care that Morag is able to write her next novel, we may participate in an imaginative compassion described by the psychologists that carries over into the real world. The imagined community, to borrow Benedict Anderson's phrase, that we enter in this book is one of inclusivity rather than cultural appropriation, but one that is undercut by Laurence's realism and her indication that we must read/listen sometimes in silence, sometimes skeptically, and sometimes creatively—creating beyond the fiction. By avoiding politically correct adoration of the native, by showing gritty details respecting Jules and his family, by modeling how to listen questioningly in order to divine, Laurence offers a skeptical imaginary of the Canadian mosaic.

So how might I read the book if I have learned by participation in Morag's life that the listener/reader should be a doubting Thomas, unconvinced, incredulous, cynical about everything heard, questioning factuality, positing alternative stories, creating her/his own stories? First, I should doubt the easy themes. Compassion alone, no matter how deeply and sincerely felt, won't solve the problems of race, class, and gender that the novel depicts. A nationalism based on the compassionate society foregrounding multiculturalism may fail for the same reason colonialism did: it posits an Other in need of help from those in the dominant position. On the other hand, each reader who reads the book primarily as an action and only secondarily for themes can practice empathy, practice feeling for these characters from the inside. As Wayne Booth attests, "we discover the powers of any narrative only in an act of surrender. Reference to the depth, force, and quality of that surrender is our initial and indispensable resource as we then compare it with other invitations from other narratives" (32).

Notes

1. Stratford writes, "The thrust of the story is moral, its premise that one learns from experience; Morag's values are not just desired, but are pragmatically realized in action and displayed in time."

2. I note that Maria Campbell's autobiographical *Halfbreed* tells of the terrible victimization of a Métis woman, yet the book does not make me cry; like the Parable of the Good Samaritan, it evokes a more intellectual response than *The Diviners* does. Crying for Jules includes crying for a failure of social justice, but it includes empathy coming from experiencing with the characters.

3. Linda Hutcheon notes that in *The Diviners* Laurence makes clear the dichotomy between oral and written narratives: "she sets up the oral Scottish narratives and Métis songs against Morag's writing—and, implicitly, her own" (51). However, I suggest a commonality in the way we should approach both kinds of narratives.

4. Hauge writes of *The Stone Angel*, "The novel is not primarily about ethical acts. It is itself an ethical act. It literally says: Go and do thou likewise. Who is to do what? The reader. The novel succeeds if the reader begins to love Hagar. The act of reading becomes practicing spontaneously the social gospel. Reading becomes an act of *caritas*" (131).

5. Hauge says that "The epistemology of *The Diviners* can be characterized as skepticist" (131). Hauge sees Laurence's books as opportunities to be compassionate, whereas I emphasize the call to practice skepticism. When Morag points to the fictionality of the tales she hears and tells as well as that of her memories and the inadequacies of language itself, she is, in effect, saying, "don't trust what you read and hear."

Works Cited

Anderson, Benedict. *Imagined Communities: Reflections on the Origins and* Spread of *Nationalism*. 1983, Rev. ed. New York: Verso, 1991.

Atwood, Margaret. *Survival: A Thematic Guide to Canadian Literature.* Toronto: Anansi, 1972.

Beran, Carol L. "Hagar's Hymns: Echo and Allusion in Margaret Laurence's The Stone Angel." *American Review of Canadian Studies* 41.2 (June 2011): 165–176.

Booth, Wayne C. *The Company We Keep: An Ethics of Fiction.* Berkeley: U of California P, 1988.

Brydon, Diana. "Margaret Laurence and Women." *Crossing the River: Essays in Honour of Margaret Laurence.* Ed. Kristjana Gunnars. Winnipeg, Canada: Turnstone Press, 1993. 183–205.

Buss, Helen M. "Margaret Laurence and the Autobiographical Impulse." *Crossing the River: Essays in Honour of Margaret Laurence*. Ed. Kristjana Gunnars. Winnipeg, Canada: Turnstone Press, 1993. 147–68.

Campbell, Maria. *Halfbreed*. 1973. Lincoln: U Nebraska P, 1982.

Comeau, Paul. *Margaret Laurence's Epic Imagination*. Edmonton, Canada: U of Alberta P, 2005.

Davey, Frank. *Surviving the Paraphrase*. Winnipeg, Canada: Turnstone Press, 1983.

Gunnars, Kristjana, ed. *Crossing the River: Essays in Honour of Margaret Laurence*. Winnipeg, Canada: Turnstone Press, 1993.

Hauge, Hans. "The Novel Religion." *Crossing the River: Essays in Honour of Margaret Laurence*. Ed. Kristjana Gunnars. Winnipeg, Canada: Turnstone Press, 1993. 121–32.

Hjartarson, Paul. "Christie's Real Country." *Crossing the River: Essays in Honour of Margaret Laurence*. Ed. Kristjana Gunnars. Winnipeg, Canada: Turnstone Press, 1993. 43–64.

The Holy Bible. King James Version, 1611. New York: World, n.d.

Hutcheon, Linda. *The Canadian Postmodern: A Study of Contemporary English-Canadian Fiction*. Toronto: Oxford UP, 1988.

Joyce, James. *A Portrait of the Artist as a Young Man*. 1916. New York: Viking, 1965.

Keith, W.J. *Sense of Style: Studies In The Art Of Fiction In English-Speaking Canada* (1989): 116. *Canadian Literary Centre*. 23 June 2012.

Laurence, Margaret. *A Bird in the House*. 1970. Toronto: McClelland, 1981.

_____. *The Diviners*. 1974. Toronto: McClelland, 1993.

_____. "A Place to Stand On." *Heart of a Stranger*. 1976. Toronto: McClelland, 1986. 1–8.

_____. *The Stone Angel*. 1964. Toronto: McClelland, 1980.

Nussbaum, Martha. *Love's Knowledge: Essays on Philosophy and Literature*. New York: Oxford UP, 1990.

Paul, Annie Murphy. "Reading Literature Makes Us Smarter and Nicer." *Time.com*. Time, Inc., 3 June 2013. Web. 17 Apr. 2014. <http://ideas.time.com/2013/06/03/why we should read>.

"Reading literary fiction improves empathy, study finds." *The Guardian.* 8 Oct. 2013. Web. 17 Apr. 2014. <http://www.theguardian.com/books/ booksblog/2013/oct/08/literary-fiction-improves-empathy-study>.

Sacks, Sheldon. *Fiction and the Shape of Belief.* Berkeley: U of California P, 1967.

Socken, Paul G. *Intimate Strangers: The Letters of Margaret Laurence and Gabrielle Roy.* Winnipeg, Canada: U Manitoba P, 2004.

Stratford, Philip. *All the Polarities: Comparative Studies In Contemporary Canadian Novels in French and English* (1986): 45. *Canadian Literary Centre.* 23 June 2012.

Stovel, Nora Foster. *Divining Margaret Laurence: A Study of Her Complete Writings.* Montreal: McGill-Queen's UP, 2008.

Riding the Waves: Aritha van Herk's *Restlessness*

Mary K. Kirtz

Everyone wants to be a definable person. But clear edges, not
blurred or torn or smudged, that's impossible. (Aritha van Herk,
Restlessness 82)

Born in 1954 in Alberta, Aritha van Herk came of age during three
significant movements taking place in Canada: the emergence
among Canadians of a new, self-conscious sense of nationhood;
the rise of second-wave feminism; and, finally, a focus on the
multicultural makeup of Canada's citizenry. In all three cases, the
initial sense of optimism permeating the 1960s and 1970s had, by
the 1980s, given way to an acknowledgement that progress would
be neither swift nor sure. As the end of the century approached, an
even more negative *Zeitgeist* took over, with feminism becoming
ironized and even trivialized by the attitudes embodied in "post-
feminism." In the political sphere, Canada's sense of solidarity was
severely shaken during the 1990s by a separatist vote in Québec,
which barely defeated the call to separate from Canada. The razor-
thin margin left the nation still intact, but its integrity was constantly
questioned, not just by the issue of Québec, but by the centrifugal
push of multiculturalism. Enshrined into law in 1972 and intended
as a means to hold the nation together, the declaration of Canada
as "a multicultural nation within a bilingual framework," instead
had the perhaps unintended consequence of destabilizing and de-
centering its disparate parts even further.

These movements held extraordinary significance for Canadian
literature as well. Such a national body of literature was scarcely
acknowledged to exist before the 1960s, with even well-known
writers, like Mordecai Richler, moving outside the country in an
effort to make a literary mark, while others, like Sinclair Ross, toiled

in unfulfilling day jobs as their novels languished, unsung and unread. The post-World War II government, no longer fettered by a view of Canada as a colony of Great Britain, began conscious efforts to create a sense of unique Canadian identity through specific government programs targeting culture and the arts. This development provided a foundation upon which writers choosing to live and work in Canada could build a coherent body of work recognized as being not only literature, but specifically Canadian literature. Yet this effort to create such a foundation came during a period when writers in the rest of the developed world were questioning the very nature and possibility of such essentialism. Canadian writers of the period were thus caught between two opposing impulses: to create the kind of work that would be viewed as quintessentially Canadian, while simultaneously questioning the very validity of the enterprise.

In two published articles, I have used the term "intramodernism" to define this tug-of-war between the centripetal force of realism (the literary equivalent of national foundation building) and the centrifugal tendencies of postmodernism (the literary equivalent of globalism) in which Canadian writers of this period found themselves, suggesting that "intramodernism offers readers entry into a fictive world through realism's window only to point out how that window can be refracted or distorted by a blind acceptance of that vision" (Kirtz, "Facts" 351) and that:

> by using the formal structures of realism–but at the same time hinting at various ways that the nature of the constructed reality within these structures might be questioned–the writers of intramodernist fiction call attention to classical realism's unexamined belief in our own absolute reality. (Kirtz, "Inhabiting" 209)

Even a writer such as Robert Kroetsch, dubbed "Mr. Canadian Postmodern," exhibits this fluctuation in his work.[1]

The problem of creating a national literature in a "post-national" world was paralleled by the second-wave feminist movement, which led women to question their particular roles in society. Canadian women writers took an active role in drawing attention to the myriad ways in which women were portrayed as subservient, silent, and sexualized within the established social structures. Margaret Atwood's novels, *The Edible Woman* (1967) and *Surfacing* (1969), broke new literary ground with their critique of mid-century gender roles. Throughout the second half of the twentieth century, the work of Atwood, along with that of Margaret Laurence, Marian Engel, and Carol Shields, among others, represented a new strain in Canadian literature, focusing on women rather than men as the protagonists of their fiction, calling into question not only the denigrating ways in which women (and particularly in Laurence, ethnic groups) were often portrayed, but also the narrative structures within which these portrayals occurred. Works like Laurence's *The Fire-Dwellers* (1969) and *The Diviners* (1974); Atwood's *Lady Oracle* (1976), *The Handmaid's Tale* (1984), and *Alias Grace* (1996); and Shields' *Swann* (1987) and *The Stone Diaries* (1993), with their protagonists determinedly looking for a center that may not hold even as the narrative structure fractures, exemplify this trend. Each of these works begins in what we think of as traditional realism, but as the narratives progress, the reader sees the story being told fall apart into varying fragments of 'truth,' calling into question the nature of the particular reality being portrayed.[2]

Multiculturalism, in many ways, was an unintended consequence of Canada's conscious effort to develop a sense of its unique identity. After the violent events of October 1970 led to a reassessment of the relationship between Québec and the rest of Canada, other ethnicities demanded to be recognized as integral contributors to the Canadian 'mosaic' rather than as second-hand recipients of Anglo- and Franco-Canadian largesse. Throughout the 1970s and 1980s in particular, a concerted effort to celebrate various ethnicities in literature and the arts took hold, with immigrant groups exploring their relationship to the two dominant languages, the Francophone and Anglophone, and their concomitant cultural influence.[3] Van Herk herself has acknowledged the difficulty of knowing how to define oneself within the larger culture. Although born in Alberta, she has often talked about the impact of her parents' immigrant status upon her. Her parents, coming from Holland, speaking Dutch with their children, and never fully assimilating into the new land, left her both with a sense of her "Otherness" as a child and also with a desire to hide that sense from others. In an interview with Christl Verduyn, she noted that "you learned very quickly to disguise who you are and what you know and try to look much more like the Other. . . . But it has an effect, it takes a toll. Are you going to go with your own disguise? Are you going to fall into the trap of the disguise others invent for you? Or are you going to assert who and what you are?" ("Grace" 21)

Between 1978 and 1998, van Herk published four novels, works which both reflect and react against the ways in which these movements affected both the country as a whole and its literature as one part of the national enterprise. Her first novel, *Judith*, was given the Seal Books First Novel Award, an impressive start for a young writer of twenty-four. This book was followed by *The Tent Peg* (1981) and *No Fixed Address* (1986), nominee for the Governor-General's Award and winner of the Howard O'Hagan Award for Best Alberta Novel. Together, these three novels critiqued an evolving society and women's place within it: In *Judith*, the protagonist resigns from a typical, pre-feminist career—that of secretary—to take up the very male-centric job of pig farming. Among her chores is the castration of the males, a role she carries out with a certain amount of gusto, so much so that her lover worries she might do something similar to him. The protagonist of *The Tent Peg*, Jael, disguises herself as a man named J. L. so she can work as a cook at a mining camp, suggesting the interchangeability not just of gender roles, but of gender itself. In *No Fixed Address*, another role reversal is depicted, with a woman setting out on a typical male picaresque journey, one that begins in a tangible place (the Canadian west) and ends in mythological space (the mysterious Arctic north) into which the protagonist disappears, becoming a myth herself. We observe a trajectory from resolution to dissolution: moving from the affirmative portrayal of Judith as a feminist heroine, through that of Jael/J. L. straddling the feminine/masculine divide, to the disappearance of Arachne into the unknown.

Between these three novels and the publication of a fourth, *Restlessness*, in 1998, three other works were published: *Places Far from Ellesmere. A Geografictione: Explorations on Site* (1990), *In*

Visible Ink: crypto-frictions (1991), and *A Frozen Tongue* (1992). In these texts, van Herk attempts to move beyond the boundaries of various genres, incorporating fiction, memoir, and literary and social criticism into various configurations. Moving within these various existential states and through the social movements they embody, van Herk's writing oscillates between a desire to establish new definitions for ways of being and an acknowledgement that every definition can quickly be exploded and redefined indefinitely. Thematically, in both the experimental works and in her fiction, she grapples with what it means to be a woman in a world defined by men, to be an immigrant from one of the 'lesser' ethnic groups in Canada, to be a westerner in a country dominated by its eastern wing, and finally, to be a citizen of a prosperous country on the fringes of global power.[4] While the three experimental works can be seen as postmodern works of criticism, her novels, enclosed within traditional realistic structures, but asking questions of themselves throughout the text, fall into the space between classical realism and postmodernism, what I have called intramodernism.

In *Restlessness*, van Herk has returned to the form used in her first three novels. While the narrative structure remains well within the realist mode, with a first person narrator ruminating over the course of an evening on her past life and impending death, serious doubts are gradually raised about the nature of the reality she presents to the reader. To a certain extent, the novel can be considered as a mirror held up (albeit obliquely) to van Herk's picaresque novel, *No Fixed Address*. Dorcas, the protagonist of *Restlessness*, is a traveler, working as a global courier; Arachne, in the earlier book, is a traveling salesperson. Unlike Arachne, who lights out for territory beyond the borders of the 'real' Alberta into a northern realm that exists mostly in the imagination, Dorcas is forever leaving and coming home, this final time in order to arrange her own death in a landmark hotel in Calgary, Alberta. Death, of course, is an even more mysterious destination than the mystical/mythical north, and so this text moves towards an address that is not only not 'fixed,' but impossible to pin down in any earthly way.

Dorcas, using the present tense, describes her evening spent sharing stories with her hired assassin, contracted to kill her before dawn. Texts narrated in the first person posit an 'ideal reader,' to whom the tale is being told and with whom the actual reader invariably identifies. The reader of traditional realist fiction accepts, without question, the reality of such a fictive world; as van Herk herself has said about such novels in a discussion of *No Fixed Address*, "there is a sense that you are following the adventures of someone, but there's never a recognition that someone is doing the following" (van Herk, "Shifting" 88). Intramodernist texts retain this sense, but add to it a "layer of constructed meaning between the reader and the text, a layer focusing upon the nature of reality within the fictive world itself; [this is presented through] a fictive character within the text who is observed by the actual reader to be creating his or her own reality" (Kirtz, "Facts" 354). In *Restlessness*, that character is Dorcas, the teller of the tale and the person through whom the entire narrative is filtered. Unlike postmodern texts, there is no "self-reflexive acknowledgment within the confines of the text, of the fiction's own artificiality" (Kirtz, "Inhabiting" 209), and such writers "work within the [categorical] boundaries, merging levels of awareness within their texts as the ocean does its separate waves, rather than focusing self-reflexively on their differences" (Kirtz, "Facts" 353).

Dorcas immediately situates us in a hotel room in the very real Palliser Hotel, an E-shaped structure built during the period of railroad expansion in the Canadian west, one of many such bulwarks intended to establish dominion over this part of the country; ironically, it is now itself overshadowed by the glittering glass towers of a post-national age. Dorcas travels the world working as a courier, touching down briefly in other cities, both ancient and modern, looking "for a person I could be. I searched for—a, how Canadian of me—an identity" (van Herk, *Restlessness* 81). In addition to Dorcas and her hired assassin, two other characters feature prominently in the narrative: Tante Katje, Dorcas' aunt and guardian, and an unnamed red-headed woman renting a room directly opposite the one Dorcas occupies. In the shadows lurks her unnamed "dear one," her most recent lover, who has apparently refused to help Dorcas achieve her goal of oblivion and who "promised that if I left, he would erase me" (van Herk, *Restlessness* 80).

Dorcas tells us that the assassin, Derrick Atman, appears to be exactly the kind of person she wanted to be her murderer. On more than one occasion, she marvels at how well he "fills the bill," worrying that he's "too plausible, too convincing. . . . I asked for a man neither too large nor too small, clean, nicely proportioned, a man who enjoys the company of women, a man flexible and imaginative. How did they arrive at the characteristics that embody that?" (van Herk, *Restlessness* 72). Acknowledging how comfortable she feels with him, she notes that the agency "seems to have fulfilled my request with such exactness that I'm almost shocked. I nudge this thought curiously" (van Herk, *Restlessness* 85). The actual reader notes this nudge and becomes curious as well, recalling her earlier statement that he "fits the description I have invented for myself, a man who looks rather like Bruno Ganz in [the film] *Wings of Desire*" (van Herk, *Restlessness* 38). Coupled with her comments that "A hotel is not a home but a place to fantasize" (van Herk, *Restlessness* 168) and may also be "a theater, with the guest starring in her own drama" (van Herk, *Restlessness* 179), these statements suggest the possibility that not only this man, but also this narrated world, may indeed be too good to be "true." Alluding to the killer's resemblance to a fictive character within a fantasy celluloid world, one in which Ganz plays an angel guarding human beings, brings yet another level of fictionality into play, yet another "space between" the actual reader and Dorcas' narrative, and thus raises more questions in the reader's mind about the world she is describing.

Besides Atman, the other characters are also associated with angels and their guardianship of human beings. She recalls her "dear one's" hand on her neck as "light, tender with reassurance, as if to offer me angelic cognitions" (van Herk, *Restlessness* 58). Atman, spying the red-haired woman pacing in her hotel room, chuckles that she must "be your guardian angel" (van Herk, *Restlessness* 89). Tante Katje too is implicitly associated with angels, guiding women seeking abortions through gauntlets of protesters and also serving as Dorcas' guardian when her parents return to Holland. Although Dorcas claims that she doesn't "merit" (van Herk, *Restlessness* 89) a guardian angel, she has surrounded herself with versions of them nonetheless.

Further references to angels and angelic spaces appear in other forms as well. Images of and references to churches abound. In Egypt, she recounts entering a tomb and lying down on a sarcophagus. In Vienna, royal corpses rest "guarded by angels. . . . Cast iron angels pointing towards heaven [the dead] resting with their ancestors and their sculpted angels" (van Herk, *Restlessness* 120). Even Las Vegas, with its myriad ersatz landmarks, is populated by women "promising companionship in some version of the hereafter" (van Herk, *Restlessness* 136). The Palliser Hotel itself is full of "staircases that float towards heaven" (van Herk, *Restlessness* 176). The desire for wings, for escape from the earthly world, is palpable.

After a long evening of languid storytelling between Dorcas and Atman, the narrative pace quickens when they unexpectedly encounter, in turn, Tante Katje and the red-headed woman. Coming across the couple in the hotel lounge, Tante Katje recounts the history of the Calgary Stampede as only an immigrant can, sprinkles her sentences with Dutch words, and gaily compares modern hotels with *grande dames*, like the Metropole, before quickly taking her leave. Here, Tante Katje presents the antithesis to her niece's sense of rootlessness. Dorcas, a native Canadian, has wandered the world searching for home, feeling that every "country I travel to proves me visible—my clothes are wrong, my accent is wrong, the very cut of my hair is asymmetrical, out of culture . . . the flash in a stranger's eye that says foreigner, *vreemde*, is worst of all" (van Herk, *Restlessness* 91). Tante Katje, on the other hand, is comfortable in her own skin, proud of her European heritage, but feeling right at home in Calgary. Clearly, she has no need to wrestle with that existential crisis of identity bedeviling Dorcas, who has created this world of "restlessness" out of her own sense of belonging nowhere. Tante Katje also represents another contrast to Dorcas. As a woman who has had an abortion and braves protest lines to help other women obtain one, she is clearly a feminist, while Dorcas exemplifies the ennui of post-feminism, with her lack of career ambition, her desire for men to do what she can't/won't do for herself.

Dorcas meets the red-headed woman in the lounge's restroom and discovers that they have been simultaneously watching each other through their respective hotel windows. The woman, like Tante Katje before her, has a view of life that is an antithetical echo of our protagonist's. An "antiassassin" (van Herk, *Restlessness* 173), perhaps an inverse double, she wants Dorcas to learn to live with, not die from, restlessness; their encounter ends with a reciprocated kiss. Before leaving, she had told Dorcas about a note she had written and slipped under her hotel room door. The note proves to be pivotal to a reader's assessment of Dorcas' carefully constructed fictive world. Before Dorcas can retrieve the note, she and Atman encounter the woman once again as they enter the elevator on their way back to their room. At the end of what seems an interminable ride to the fifth floor while listening to the woman soliloquize about the nature of hotels, the narrative suddenly veers from the present to the future tense, at the very moment that Atman puts on his gloves.

Now focused on what "will happen" rather than on what "is happening now," Dorcas projects us into the moment when she will read the note from the red-headed woman: it will say *"When he reads this, he'll kill you. Be careful"* (van Herk, *Restlessness* 186), an echo of an earlier note Dorcas had sent to her dear one: *"When you read this, you'll kill me. Be careful not to hate me, please"* (van Herk, *Restlessness* 186). The juxtaposition of these two notes in the text triggers an obvious question in the reader's mind: If dear one's act of reading the note will kill her, is HE the assassin? He had, after all, threatened to "erase" her, a verb that applies equally to writing and murder. Or has Dorcas written both men, and even the woman, into existence? Early in the narrative, Dorcas had stated that "for the past twenty years I feel as if I have been waiting for my life to happen between the pages of a book"(van Herk, *Restlessness* 15). Is this then the life that she has written, has fantasized, into existence? Dorcas, of course, is herself a figment of another's imagination: Has the actual auburn-haired van Herk, in the guise of the red-headed woman, inserted her authorial presence within the fictional world?[5]

Was that reciprocal kiss meant to signal the author's complicity in creating Dorcas' world? The notes' uncanny similarity and the future tense used in this final section call into question everything that has gone before, including the authorial guiding hand so trusted in traditional realism.

The fate of the biblical Dorcas, raised from the dead by St. Peter, also casts doubts on the probability of the protagonist's death.[6] The ambiguity of the ending suggests that this Dorcas, too, may rise out of a textual death into a new life beyond the page. The final two sentences of the text revert to the present tense: "I am a traveler on my way to bed, to sleep, perchance to dream. Is death a happy ending?" (van Herk, *Restlessness* 193). The first sentence contains a fragment from Hamlet's soliloquy, perhaps the most famous suicide speech in literature and a path Hamlet rejects after delivering it. The final question, a sly allusion to a 1978 article titled, "Death is a Happy Ending," by Robert Kroetsch, Van Herk's frequent literary sparring partner, remains unanswered, but is clearly directed at the reader outside the text.[7] The fictive window of realism has been fractured and it is the actual reader who must decide who lives, who dies, and how the novel itself will end and then be 'killed' when the reader closes the book.[8]

Van Herk has asserted that "Realism can become its own prison, its own enclosure. Fiction's mandate is to explore the possibilities of the imagination, the possibilities of the world beyond its closure. I see my characters as representing possibility rather than probability" (Jones, "Interview" 7). *Restlessness*, in its use of a realist framework that nevertheless hints at possibilities beyond those expressed on the page, brilliantly exemplifies this approach.

Notes

1. As I noted in an earlier article, the formulation of "Mr. Canadian Postmodern" itself mirrors this dichotomy: "'Canadian' suggests Kroetsch's search for some fundamental basis for differentiating Canadian writing from British and American, and 'Postmodern' foregrounds his questioning of the validity of such fundamental categories" (Kirtz, "Inhabiting" 207).

2. Heidi Slettedahl Macpherson in her book, *Women's Movement*, suggests that intramodernism can apply not only to Canadian writing, but also more generally to contemporary fiction, including that of feminist writers, noting that the "formulation of intramodernism can be extended beyond national boundaries to incorporate fiction such as [Ann] Tyler's contemporary fiction which, by failing to embrace postmodernism wholeheartedly, is thus almost automatically seen as realist, despite obvious problems with that designation" (214).

3. A more detailed exploration of this topic can be found in my article in *Canadian Ethnic Studies*, "Old World Traditions, New World Inventions: Bilingualism, Multiculturalism, and the Transformation of Ethnicity."

4. As Coral Ann Howells similarly noted in an essay on *No Fixed Address*, van Herk has a "distinctive sense of otherness: as a woman she feels herself to be "other" than man, as an immigrant child whose first language was Dutch she feels "other" than Anglo-Canadian, just as the West sees itself and has always seen itself different from centres of power in the East, like Ottawa and Toronto, and as Canada itself is "other" than traditional centres of culture in Europe"("Space" 7).

5. I am grateful to Carol L. Beran for calling my attention to the similarities in hair color between the novel's author and the fictional character within the novel.

6. In fact, van Herk herself has asserted in an interview, "I didn't kill her. I haven't killed anyone yet" (Sellery, "Robert" 47).

7. That the allusions are to men (one fictive, one real) rather than to women may be another example of post-feminist irony.

8. As Robert Budde has stated, "the reader as assassin must work hard to keep up and anticipate what the text is asking. The reader, like the assassin, must analyze and judge how the text should be handled . . . and finally, how to complete the act and close the covers over" (47).

Works Cited

Beeler, Karin. "Shifting Form: An Interview with Aritha van Herk." *Canadian Literature* 157 (1998): 80–96.

Budde, Robert. "The Aesthetics of Annihilation: The Restless Text and the Reader as Assassin in Aritha Van Herk's *Restlessness*." Ed. Christl Verduyn. *Aritha van Herk: Essays on Her Works*. Toronto: Guernica, 2001: 45–59.

Howells, Coral Ann. "Aritha van Herk's *No Fixed Address*: An Exploration of Prairie Space as Fictional Space." *The London Journal of Canadian Studies* 1 (1996): 6–19.

Jones, Dorothy. "Interview with Aritha van Herk.: *Span* 25 (1987): 1–15.

Kirtz, Mary K. "'Facts Become Art Through Love:' Narrative Structure in Marian Engel's *Bear*." *The American Review of Canadian Studies.* 22.3 (1992): 351–362.

_____. "Inhabiting the Dangerous Middle of the Space Between: An Intramodernist Reading of Robert Kroestsch's *Gone Indian*." *The Great Plains Quarterly* 14.3 (1994): 207–217.

_____. "Old World Traditions, New World Inventions: Bilingualism, Multiculturalism, and the Transformation of Ethnicity." *Canadian Ethnic Studies* 28:1 (1996): 8–21.

Kroetsch, Robert, & Diane Bessai. "Death Is a Happy Ending: A Dialogue in Thirteen Parts." *Figures in a Ground.* Ed. Diane Bessai & David Jackel. Saskatoon: Western Producer Prairie Books, 1978. 206–15.

Sellery, J'nan Morse, Robert Kroetsch, and Aritha van Herk. "Robert Kroetsch and Aritha van Herk on Writing & Reading, Gender and Genres: An Interview." *Canadian Literature* 170–171 (2001): 21–55.

Macpherson, Heidi Slettedahl. *Women's Movement: Escape as Trangression in North American Feminist Fiction.* Amsterdam-Atlanta, GA: Rodopi, 2000.

van Herk, Aritha. *Judith.* Toronto: McClelland & Stewart, 1978.

_____. *The Tent Peg.* Toronto: McClelland & Stewart, 1981.

_____. *No Fixed Address: an amorous journey.* Toronto: McClelland & Stewart, 1986.

_____. *Places Far From Ellesmere. A Geografictione: Explorations on Site.* Red Deer, AB: Red Deer College Press, 1990.

_____. *In Visible Ink: crypto-frictions.* Edmonton: NeWest Press, 1991.

_____. *A Frozen Tongue.* Sydney, Australia: Dangaroo Press, 1992.

_____. *Restlessness.* Red Deer, AB: Red Deer College Press, 1998.

Verduyn, Christl. "The Grace of Living and Writing. An Interview with Aritha van Herk." *Aritha van Herk: Essays on Her Works.* Toronto: Guernica, 2001: 15–30.

_____, ed. *Aritha Van Herk: Essays on Her Works.* Toronto: Guernica, 2001.

Naming and Becoming: Finding Love in the Klondike

Aritha van Herk

Published in tandem with the one hundredth anniversary of the Klondike Gold Rush (1896–1899), *The Man From the Creeks* by Robert Kroetsch, is a novel celebrating that epoch extravagance with a tongue-in-cheek response to the event's haunting of our collective consciousness. The Klondike, or the Yukon Gold Rush, also known as the "last great gold rush in history" (Gray 43), flared with a sudden bold intensity, and before most of the would-be prospectors had reached the site, it was over, the creeks solidly staked and just as firmly enshrined in the historic imagination of North America.

The background to this unique stampede, inspired by greed, hope, and the financial panics of 1893 and 1896, is essential to an understanding of the picaresque adventures of the novel's three main characters. In 1896, when gold was discovered at Bonanza Creek in the Yukon, the area was quickly staked, but news of the find did not reach the outside world until the following summer. Then, according to Kroetsch's narrator,

> a ship had sailed into Seattle's harbour out of the north . . . , a ship loaded with sixty-eight prospectors and two tonnes of placer gold. And that did it. After that the gold rush was on, and the devil himself couldn't stop thousands of people from throwing down their newspapers and rushing out to buy mining pans.
>
> Thousands and then tens of thousands of ordinary folk became gold-hungry lunatics. Half of them couldn't find Dawson City or Bonanza Creek or Eldorado Creek on a map. (Kroetsch 8)

Exaggerated stories in the press fuelled the rush, and some one-hundred-thousand people set out for the Klondike without the faintest idea of where they were going or how to get there. Only thirty- to forty-thousand people actually made it to Dawson City

(Berton 396), and of that number, only a small percentage grew rich, even fewer on gold. Most of the wealth was generated by those providing food and services, for in that remote region, with supply routes challenged by distance and weather, prices on everything from clothing to transportation skyrocketed. Seattle was the preferred embarkation port, and sixty to eighty percent of the Stampeders were Americans (Fetherling 125), gamblers, and dreamers eager for adventure and in their trek physically and temperamentally extending Frederick Jackson Turner's frontier from the west to the north. This great migration became a legend of no small magnitude, enlarged by Charlie Chaplin's *The Gold Rush* and Robert Service's *Songs of a Sourdough,* where "The Shooting of Dan McGrew" first appeared.

It is that "barrack-room balladry" (MacMechan 220) that inspires *The Man from the Creeks.* The title is taken from Robert Service's "The Shooting of Dan McGrew," one of the well-worn rhymed narratives embedding the Klondike in the popular mythology. Simply enough, a miner who has been digging for gold in miserable circumstances stumbles into the Malamute saloon on a cold winter night, and after playing the piano so hauntingly that the entire place is mesmerized, denounces Dangerous Dan McGrew as "a hound of hell." A gunfight ensues, and in the dark, both Dan McGrew and the stranger are killed. Service's poem claims that when the lights go up again, the man from the creeks is "clutched to the breast of the lady that's known as Lou" (Service 62) and that she both kisses him and pinches his poke, or his gold, rendering her a version of fickle thief.

Robert Kroetsch picks up his tale from the narrative embedded in Service's famous doggerel, but makes the subject of *The Man from the Creeks* not Dangerous Dan and his Malamute saloon, but the unrecorded backstory of Lou, her teenage son, Peek, and her partner, Ben, "the man from the creeks." While the romance of the Klondike would tempt most writers to reiterate Service's "yarn" (Grace 336), Kroetsch explodes this archetypal set piece of betrayed man and unfaithful woman and transforms it into a critique of the gold rush and its continuing depictions, fictionally mining the odyssey that so many foolish and desperate folks undertook. The novel can be read as a virtual documentary of the Klondike's extravagant history, how thousands of men, determined to make their fortunes, walked and floated and rode to the Yukon in a mad scramble for both real and imaginary wealth. But beyond its employment of actual facts, it is more effectively both an elegy on that dramatic quest and an elaboration of the poetic calumny of a moment frozen in metaphor. In that performance, *The Man from the Creeks* unfolds a wry exegesis of both invented and historical referents.

Theorist Hayden White reminds us that, "there is a certain necessity in the relationship between the narrative, conceived as a symbolic or symbolizing discursive structure, and the representation of specifically historical events" (30). Still, the historical novel, as Georg Lukács early outlined, is prone to seduction by its own content. Too often historical fiction turns toward costume drama or stinks to high heaven of background research. But a novel that captures the fractures and contradictions of both an intense historical phenomenon *and* its representation performs an unusual sleight of hand, a writerly "spread misère" (the game that Dan McGrew plays in the poem), where the bidder plays with all his cards exposed. The embedded risk in *The Man from the Creeks* is Kroetsch's ferocious deployment of transparency, a transparency in direct contravention to the many lies and prevarications that characterized the gold rush.

Kroetsch accomplishes this effect partly through his chosen narrator, Lou's son, who is fourteen in 1897 and, in the novel's present time, an improbable one-hundred-fourteen years old. The unguarded perspective of an adolescent Peek enables Kroetsch to capture the sheer exuberance of the gold rush, its crazy intensity, and its hyperbolic excess. Without the mitigation of adult skepticism and measurement, the Klondike becomes a kaleidoscope of experience intensified by Peek's innocence. Concomitantly, present-day Peek, one-hundred-fourteen years old and having never left Dawson, acquits his cameo as a living icon of the past. He exacerbates his own doubled vision and knowledge when he tells contemporary visitors "the fib they're dying to hear," that he plays his "sad songs in memory of Dan McGrew" (Kroetsch 333). Peek performs as witness and record, survivor and victim. His occupation of the cabin originally built by Dan McGrew for Gussie Meadows, his ownership of the Malamute Saloon, and his secret burial of Ben's gold nugget with his mother's body obtain for him a redemptive version of the Yukon's mythology. He has lived the "real" story, and it is nothing like the tourist lore coloring the gold rush now.

Kroetsch does not let mythologizers and prevaricators off the hook. Owen D. Percy claims that, as a character, Peek evidences a desire to "prevent or reverse the freezing" of human particularity into the "fact" of history (Percy 226). Certainly, although he is a "fabrication of a fabrication" (226), Peek has it in for the poet who invented him. He has every right to call Service into question, since Service didn't show up in the Yukon as a bank clerk until 1904 and didn't set foot in Dawson City until 1908. Peek declares early in the novel: "What I want to get straight before I kick the bucket is the matter of Mr Robert Service and his saying that Lou pinched the stranger's poke—the corpse's poke—and all the gold that was in it. Poets are liars. We know that. They'll say just about anything to make themselves sound good" (Kroetsch 18). Frustrated by what he insists is a misrepresentation of his mother, Peek sets out to amend Service's dismissal of "the lady that's known as Lou" by detailing the story of their adventures together as stowaways, *cheechakos* and ultimately sourdoughs, from their initial discovery on board the *Delta Queen* to the end of their journey in Dawson City.

As narrator, Peek exhibits a shy reserve, inverse to a story fuelled by gossip and journalism, the wonderful outrageousness of exaggeration and rumor and gamble and hot air. Orality, the story of storytelling, is as much the subject of *The Man from the Creeks* as misery and sanity and madness and failure and gold-fever and luck. The novel abounds with talk and argument, with feasts and drunk-ups, wingdings and parties and wakes, crowd scenes noisy as bragging. "Their own bragging couldn't keep up with what was actually happening," and these embellishments are observed by Peek, a solitary and inevitably voyeuristic narrator at the edge of the action. At the end of the novel, just before the shooting occurs (as it must), Peek's rhetorical *cri de coeur* is wrenched from him at the moment when "the stranger" steps into the Malamute, just before the penultimate scene in Service's poem. "'A miner fresh from the creeks,' the poet says. He wasn't there at the time and didn't show up in the Yukon as a bank clerk for another six years. No, indeed, the poet wasn't there. He, not the miner, was the stranger of whom he goes on to speak. Why are poets such bluffers and prevaricators, such dotards in the face of the bald truth? Why do poets fail, ever, to look at the facts themselves?" (Kroetsch 302). The answer to that question is provided by Peek's version of events within Kroetsch's novel, where the fictional facts stand outside of the invention of a tall tale worthy of one of history's extraordinary legends.

The novel repeatedly comments on the slippery texture of history, how facts are inevitably contradicted by their human engagement, how the statistics that are all that remain of the gold rush conceal incredible stories. And while the narrator is certainly unreliable, we hunger as readers to believe him, now that he is an old man in a wheelchair, and the last remaining witness to a period of time when logic fled and good sense was abandoned. As that of a man determined to brave history's lies, Peek's almost intimate perspective compels the reader to follow the pilgrimage undertaken by Peek and his mother and Ben Redd with the same avid attention that those earlier pilgrims paid to the stories of the Klondike and the promise they held out. Sherrill Grace observes, "Peek performs another way of mining for gold, albeit one less destructive than the moiling that killed or disillusioned thousands during the great Klondike Gold Rush" (336). His "dredging" counters the individual story dominating Yukon lore with a story of family.

The first half of the novel focuses on their journey to Dawson, since it was the difficulty of getting to the Klondike that stymied most Stampeders, and the reason most gave up. Lured by the siren call of wealth, Lou and Peek abandon their meager life working in a Seattle pawn shop and stow away on an overloaded boat bound for Skagway. Somewhere on the Inside Passage, they are discovered, and the paying passengers on the boat, frustrated at the length of the trip and their own desperation, insist that the stowaways should be dropped overboard, into the frigid water. The two are saved by an altruistic cooper named Ben Redd, who exchanges their—and his—safe conduct to shore for two kegs of whiskey. He has secreted, inside his sacks and barrels of compulsory supplies, fifteen kegs of whiskey, which he intends to barter for a stake in Dan McGrew's gold holdings. Given the remote location, Canadian authorities had introduced rules that anyone entering the Yukon had to bring a year's worth of food (Berton 154) and Ben's whiskey repeatedly semaphores a chief concern in the novel: what is wanted versus what is required. By replacing his survival supplies with whiskey, Ben actually enables their survival, his gesture initiating the intricate partnership between Ben and Lou. The ongoing tension between necessity and luxury speaks to the conundrum of the gold rush: gold itself can sustain no life, but the quest for gold fuels actions that lead to terrible hardship and deprivation, and most especially, hunger.

In exchange for further kegs of whiskey, four powerful Tlingit canoeists transport the unlikely trio from the remote shore where they were stranded to Skagway, and they begin the now-famous trek, over the Chilkoot Pass into Canada, and on to Lake Bennett before floating down the Yukon to Dawson City. Despite the haste that fuelled the rush itself, the novel progresses by degrees of delay. At Sheep Camp, Peek falls ill, and they have to wait for him to recover before they begin the ascent of the Golden Steps (Berton 244), that hellish climb to the top of the summit. At Bennett City, while Ben tries to build a boat, Peek works for Gussie Meadows, a "'crackerjack businesswoman'" (Kroetsch 126), who has set up a hardware tent supplying that camp of would-be shipwrights with "axe handles and saw blades and kegs of nails and coils of rope" (Kroetsch 134). Gussie is identified as Dan McGrew's lover, but she makes no bones about her disaffection with his gambling and cheating. Instead, having "traded her gold jewelry for a hardware business that was going broke" (Kroetsch 138), she makes a killing selling supplies to those waiting for breakup so they can resume their journey. When the ice does go out, she hosts an incredible party (with one of Ben's kegs of whiskey) before taking her personal effects and her bags of money and heading back to San Francisco, one of the few gold rush successes.

Ben's lack of skill in boat-building puts the trio three days behind the bulk of the Stampeders, and when they finally get through Miles Canyon and the White Horse Rapids and across Lake Labarge to Dawson, they are almost dawdling, as if arrival at their destination will constitute a disappointment. Peek claims they are the very last of the rush. "The Mounted Police reported that 7,124 vessels of one sort or another set out within one week to go downriver from the headwaters of the Yukon to Dawson City. We must have been number seven thousand and one" (Kroetsch 178). While for Peek and Lou, Dawson is configured as "'the beginning,'" the destination that will enable them to "'do something with [their] lives'" (Kroetsch 196), it is of course the place that will rupture the relative happiness of their difficult journey together. Dawson City is destined to be disappointing, for like all boom towns, it is a collaboration of dream with trickery and deception. While four thousand miners toil at digging gravel out of the permafrost, thirty thousand people in Dawson scheme to get their hands on gold without picking up a shovel. The disproportion in that equation signals the imbalance that *Man from the Creeks* depicts, through a Kroetschian awareness of how competing mythologies "destabilize . . . unity" (Brown 119). While the historical mythology accruing to the Yukon seeks to find a retrospective equilibrium, the novel successfully demonstrates how any attempt at balance is illusory.

This effect is accomplished not only by the crazy fluctuations of supply and demand, but the material conditions that afflicted the gold rush. Adding to the extremities of weather and geography (and they were extreme) are the appetites and incompatibilities of the wayfarers and itinerants who found their way to Klondike and who contributed to its monstrous exchanges and trade-offs. The miners— the real miners who worked the claims, burrowing through dirt to reach an imaginary streamed that might contain a few flecks of gold—were as much in the minority as fresh eggs ($1 apiece) and green vegetables. Their toil fed dozens of hangers-on, exemplified by the deal between Dangerous Dan and Ben: Dangerous Dan plays cards in the Malamute Saloon, while Ben digs deeper and deeper in the black pit on their claim. The heedless quest for that fool's errand, gold itself, confuses time and meaning, calling into question every notion of profit. And scarcity in the face of flagrant "wealth," if gold can be classified as wealth, establishes a conundrum that makes for richly mineable fiction.

The backgrounds of those who make the Klondike their destination illustrate a carnivalesque discarding of personal history. Because it is no longer possible to go west, this gold rush is perceived as the LAST frontier, the last chance to alter life's trajectory. Ben Redd is a wet cooper, a maker of barrels, and Lou worked in a pawn shop in downtown Seattle. They are completely unprepared for their adventure. "Ben had read a guidebook. One that came out a month after the gold was discovered. Lou had read the Seattle papers" (Kroetsch 48). The miners working downstream from Ben are "a former tram driver from San Francisco, an escaped convict from a New York pen, two ex-lawyers, and a minister who had given up the cloth" (Kroetsch 259). Other characters have reinvented themselves from earlier occupations. Soapy Smith's enforcer in Skagway "'was something of an accountant'" (Kroetsch 80) before; when Peek gets sick at Sheep Camp, Lou finds "two men who had been doctors before they became stampeders" (Kroetsch 103). Before their little vessel hits the Whitehorse Rapids, they consult with two men in a rowboat who "were printers by trade" (Kroetsch 182). Everyone has had other occupations: "Gussie knew a group of stampeders who, until four months earlier, had been musicians" (Kroetsch 168). The urgencies of the rush impel the actions of its players, enabling people to disguise themselves. Gussie Meadows says, "'in Dawson City, if you dress like a dancer, then you're a dancer'" (Kroetsch 149). By dressing as a woman, Whipsaw becomes a woman (Kroetsch 202), eventually ending up working as a prostitute in the cribs, where there are more miners than out in the creeks (Kroetsch 288). The transformation of these various characters gestures toward the metamorphosis offered by the Klondike: it is possible for every person to become what they are not.

Such transformation is further measured by the naming of different characters; the announcement of their names tracks the extent to which the Klondike encourages changes of identity. This potential is introduced early in the novel, when Peek's mother names herself. The cook, when he catches her stealing cinnamon buns, asks,

> "Just who do you think you are, lady?"
> "Don't lady me," my mother said. "The name is Lou."
> Just like that. That was the name she gave herself, as if she'd picked it up with the pan that was warming her forearm.
> That's what the poet called her, later, when he wrote his famous poem. (5)

Peek's naming is a result of Lou's inability to spell rather than because he is a boy who peeks, although he does serve as the novel's constant voyeur. "My mother was no great speller, although she got through grade eight before her parents sent her out to work. She thought she was naming me after Mount Baker, the peak that glowed white and beautiful up there in the sky above her childhood . . . Anyway, somewhere in a government office, she wrote down my name as Peek, and that was that" (66). Ben's name is marked on the kegs of whiskey that he transports. "BENJAMIN REDD SALT HERRING" (16). The lie of the contents readily matches the potential lie in the name. "Dangerous Dan" is first labeled in the note Gussie Meadows leaves for Ben at Chilkoot summit.

> "'Dangerous Dan is worried about my travelling alone. He says I should try to partner up with you.'" . . .
> That was the first time ever that Ben heard McGrew referred to as Dangerous Dan. He read the name again and chuckled. "Dan McGrew," he said, hardly able to contain himself, "must be known as Dangerous Dan up there in Dawson City." He shook his head. "Well I'll be danged." (121)

Gussie Meadows' own name serves up a combination of pragmatism and dream, but it is likely that Kroetsch bases it on showgirl Mae McKamish Melbourne Meadows (Morgan 38), who travelled up to the Yukon with supplies for a bar and casino, and lost them in a landslide. And tied to baptisms are character summaries, Gussie's pronouncement that Peek is "'a good man'" (176) in that mass of

---

ne'er do wells. Ben's last words in the Malamute Saloon, condemn Dangerous Dan: "'One of you here is a hound of hell'" (319), "'And that one is Dan McGrew'" (320), a naming that leads to the shoot-out and the deaths of Ben and Lou and Dangerous Dan.

Names are an essential part of historical record, and designations in *Man from the Creeks,* while derived from the Service poem, echo the orality of the story. Just as the geographical names of the Klondike haunt the novel (Sheep Camp, Lake Bennett, the Chilkoot Pass, Miles Canyon, Lake Labarge, Dawson City, Bonanza Creek, Eldorado Creek), so do the names of "real" characters, the Mountie Sam Steele, and the photographer Eric Hegg, who documented the gold rush and who in this novel, wins the Malamute Saloon on the last losing bet that Dan McGrew makes. Of course, Service himself is named and re-named, "the poet" (5) first, and then "Mr. Robert Service" (18) with all the scorn that Peek can muster when he declares that he wants to set the record straight. In a powerful turn at the end of the novel, Peek suddenly declares that the poet's rendition of the final scene is accurate. "Robert Service says he was wearing a buckskin shirt that was glazed with dirt. Ben was wearing a parka. But then the poet says that he clutched the keys with his talon hands. And I want to tell you, that's how it looked. The poet hit it smack on (311). Peek's depiction of Ben's piano playing as an autobiography so powerful that it unhinges everyone listening becomes the final unmeasurable gesture in that world overturned in name and deed, raucous and miserable and without comfort or value. "It sounded as if he was trying to come back from the dead" (320). When all that is left is darkness and drudgery, a terrible aloneness is all that meets the silence.

In *The Man from the Creeks,* fidelity is as illusory as gold. The novel takes up that scarcity and relates it directly to Lou and Ben and Peek, who separately embody constancy, the rarest of commodities in Dawson. Although Lou works for Dan McGrew in the Malamute, she knows he is a cheat and refuses to partner with him. As the woman in charge of the scales, she is trusted; "she would never cheat [the miners] when weighing their gold, whether they were sober or drunk" (271). "She was so honest she was a legend. Men trusted her with their fortunes" (308). On balance, Ben is relentlessly faithful to Lou. Peek is first faithful to his grail of becoming a sourdough in the north, and then to his own lost love and his mother's memory.

Kroetsch does not succumb to the redolence of nostalgia in his re-creation and extension of "The Shooting of Dan McGrew." And while the historical traces of the last great gold rush are inescapable, *The Man from the Creeks* does not stink of a dusty or recovered past. It does smell, however, and smells in the novel articulate the intensity of sensation that such an excursion evokes. There is the undercurrent of the smell of money, "'the stink of ill-gotten gains'" (138) in contrast the honest sweat of those working their claims. The stampeders on their way to the goldfields reek of desperation, Peek remembers: "I didn't mean a sweat and smoke and tar smell. I mean the smell of their wanting to get to Dawson City and the Klondike River and dig deep holes in the frozen gravel and muck" (Kroetsch 140). By contrast, nature has its own olfactory lure. When they are stranded on shore, before Peek sees the bear, he smells the bear who gifts him the salmon (30); to him it is a smell both frightening and pleasurable, a foreshadowing of the bearskin that he later receives as a birthday gift and a further foreshadowing that he will become a sourdough and stay in the Yukon. As the object of Peek's adolescent affection, Gussie Meadows comes with a cornucopia of smells, first the smell of roses, and then the smell of commerce. When he puts his head under her skirts, "I could smell oakum and canvas. I could smell the boxes of cartridges we had for sale and the oilskins that came folded into neat squares" (151). The combined smell of men in close quarters, the smell of desire, and the smell of the Klondike itself becomes an olfactory cassoulet relentless as greed.

Hunger and the smell of hunger accompany one another: it is the smell of "freshly baked cinnamon rolls" competing with "the fire bucket at our feet that was our toilet" (3) that lures Lou out of the lifeboat where she and Peek have stowed away. Peek almost hallucinates about food when they hit the wharf at Skagway.

We could smell the wharves before we saw them. We couldn't see them at first, because of the falling snow. The wind had let up. But we could smell the new lumber and the tarred ropes. And the dried apricots. I swear, dried apricots, I could smell them. I was hungry. Then I began to think I could smell dried apples and black pepper. And then I thought of cured hams and great slabs of smoked bacon and sacks of split peas. I thought of bags of onions and gunnysacks full of potatoes that still smelled of soil from home. (61)

Living as they must on canned and dried goods, a yearning for food is constant throughout the novel, and the aroma of food is almost better than an aphrodisiac. Certainly, it competes with the hunger for gold that fuels the rush and exacts its terrible cost. And hunger amplifies the horrific loneliness that comes along with adventure and risk, the gamble (a spread misère) that every stampeder took. The metaphor of hunger persuades Peek to applaud Service's rendition of Ben's piano playing that dark cold night when he becomes "the stranger" from the creeks who has stumbled into the saloon.

The poet talks about hunger. He talks about some kind of gnawing hunger that bacon and beans won't satisfy, and, believe you me, every man and woman in that saloon had tried enough bacon and beans to know what that was. A hunger not of the belly kind. Another kind entirely. Something about love. That's what Ben's playing was all about. (311)

Ben's playing evokes hunger and food and comfort and loss, all human elements that a gold rush plays havoc with. And it is that evocative and terrible and beautiful yearning for love and for home that precedes the shooting and deaths of Ben Redd, and Dangerous Dan, and in Kroetsch's rendition, Lou as well.

In *The Man from the Creeks,* Lou is transformed not by disguise or trickery, but love. She is no percentage girl, but the mother of a mooning teenage son, not a fancy woman but a character to be reckoned with. She does not steal Ben's poke, but dies with him, "at once protecting him and holding him close" (Kroetsch 326). The bags of gold fall to Peek, who gets rich (Kroetsch 235), but who knows wealth is a useless weight on the scales of happiness. He is condemned to live a long and lonely life, remembering the fragrance of Gussie Meadows and playing the piano in the Malamute for gawking and ill-informed tourists, parvenu stampeders looking for the gold of legend. What Peek comes to understand, at the end of his picaresque *Bildungsroman,* is that only love matters. "We must learn to hold each other. I play to join two partners who, once they were together, were never really apart again" (Kroetsch 334). In a place as mythic as the Klondike, such love has value beyond value.

As a writer, Robert Kroetsch surveys mythology and history the way a grizzled veteran regards a now-commemorative battlefield, with a good deal of experiential suspicion and a keen awareness of the dirty details underneath the neatly laid-out paths designed for tourists. He combines, in *The Man from the Creeks,* the craziness and cruelty of this last extravagant gold rush, its relentless allure, its ardent failures, and its legendary excess. The immoderation and exaggeration that enabled this phenomenon are made in this novel both beautiful and ghastly, truly a legendary meta-revision.

Works Cited

Berton, Pierre. *Klondike: The Last Great Gold Rush, 1896–1899.* Toronto: Doubleday, 2001.

Brown, Russell Morton. "Robert Kroetsch, Marshall McLuhan, and Canada's Prairie Postmodernism: The Aberhart Effect." *History, Literature and the Writing of the Canadian Prairies.* Eds. Alison Calder & Robert Wardhaugh. Winnipeg: U of Manitoba P, 1995. 101–140.

Fetherling, George. *The Gold Crusades: A Social History of Gold Rushes, 1849–1929.* Toronto: U of Toronto P, 1997.

Grace, Sherrill. "Afterword." *The Man from the Creeks.* By Robert Kroetsch. Toronto: McClelland & Stewart, 2008. 335–341.

Gray, Charlotte. *Gold Diggers: Striking It Rich in the Klondike.* Toronto: HarperCollins, 2011.

Kroetsch, Robert. *The Man from the Creeks.* Toronto: McClelland and Stewart, 2011.

Lukács, Georg. *The Historical Novel.* Lincoln, NE: U of Nebraska P, 1983.

MacMechan, Archibald. *Headwaters of Canadian Literature.* Toronto: New Canadian Library, 1924.

Morgan, Lael. *Good Time Girls of the Alaska-Yukon Gold Rush.* Kenmore, WA: Epicenter Press, 1998.

Percy, Owen D. "Melting History: Defrosting Moments in Novels by Wayne Johnston, Michael Winter, and Robert Kroetsch." *Studies in Canadian Literature/Études en littérature canadienne.* 32.1 (2007): 212–30.

Service, Robert W. *Songs of a Sourdough.* Toronto: The Ryerson Press, 1957.

_____. *The Spell of the Yukon and Other Verses.* New York: Barse & Hopkins, 1907.

Turner, Frederick Jackson. *The Frontier in American History.* 1920. Web. 24 June 2014. <http://xroads.virginia.edu/~HYPER/TURNER/>.

White, Hayden. "The Question of Narrative in Contemporary Historical Theory." *History and Theory* 23.1 (Feb 1984): 1–33.

Understanding a Father's Pain in Madeleine Thien's "Simple Recipes"

Janice Fiamengo

"Somewhere in my memory, a fish in the sink is dying slowly" (Thien 19). So reads the penultimate sentence of Madeleine Thien's "Simple Recipes," the first story in her award-winning collection by the same name.[1] We have encountered the image of the dying fish earlier in the story, but the phrase *somewhere in my memory* is new. It draws the reader's attention to the disorderliness of the narrator's recollections. Rather than a sharp linear sequence of past images, memory in this formulation—and, indeed, in the story—is murky, uncertain, its potent, but perilous depths best plumbed gingerly. The phrase suggests that, even as the narrator concludes her assembling of moments from her past, her personal history remains unresolved. "Simple Recipes" is about the failure of memory to provide consolation or certainty. A poignant tale of a daughter's love for her troubled father, the story juxtaposes wistful remembrance of lost intimacy with reflections on the father's violence. With resonant symbols of an ethnic inheritance at once comforting and alien, the story addresses the generational and cultural tensions that have shattered the narrator's family.

Unhappy families are a dominant theme in Thien's collection as a whole. Many stories are about absent or inadequate parents, divorce, and abandonment, highlighting the "tacit understandings" (Thien 165) and accepted betrayals that bind people together. Some family members "bypass love" (Thien 157) altogether, some are stricken by it, and some "fail each other in so many unintended ways" (Thien 166). No family is safe. Characters invariably learn that their evasions and attempts to protect themselves from heartbreak are unavailing, as the narrator realizes in "A Map of the City": "Walking away had not saved me as I had hoped it would" (Thien 163). A paradigmatic moment in that story occurs when the young narrator sees herself as having changed places with her parents, recognizing with dread a needy love she cannot return: "My parents seemed so childlike to me, so in need of love. I thought they only had themselves to blame that I didn't know how to give it to them" (Thien 195).

Similarly, in "Four Days from Oregon," three sisters have come to perceive their mother's emotional volatility in terms of role reversal: "We were just kids then—Helen was nine, Joanne was seven, and I was six—but we thought of our mother as a young girl. She cried so much and had a temper" (Thien 24). In "Home," two daughters, trying to convince themselves that their unstable mother has not abandoned them for good, spend her birthday waiting in front of their former house in hopes of a family reunion that does not materialize. In "Alchemy," the narrator's parents "hardly noticed whether I was home or not" (Thien 60). She stays over frequently at her friend Paula's, but discovers that Paula's family offers no refuge either. In every case, recognition of parental failure is devastating.

"Simple Recipes" is one of only two of the stories in the collection—the other being "A Map of the City," the concluding novella, discussed in more detail below—in which immigration and ethnicity are explicitly at issue; fathers in both these stories suffer not only the ordinary pains of disappointed or failed love, but also what the narrator of "A Map" calls "the tragedy of place" (Thien 201), of living in a country that does not feel like home. In "Simple Recipes," all the father's culinary "tricks" (Thien 6) and techniques of mastery cannot assuage his wrenching displacement and confusion. Even in the kitchen, site of his greatest ease, he seems, in the narrator's memory, always to have been "out of place" (Thien 4).

Thien has mentioned that while writing the collection she was thinking about her own parents, ethnic Chinese who emigrated from Malaysia to Vancouver in the early 1970s. Thien was born in the year they immigrated, and her father left the family home when she was a teenager. Though we should be wary of drawing too-direct parallels between Thien's fiction, on the one hand, and her real-life family experience, on the other, the autobiographical dimension of the story is one, among other elements, that offers a potential interpretative entry-point. As Thien has observed, personal experience often plays an explicit role in a writer's story, though not always in an expected or conscious manner.[2] Reflecting in a 2009 interview on the meaning of immigration for her parents' generation, Thien has noted its differential impact on men and women: "For women—at least in the case of my mother—the women found a lot of strength," she observes:

> Being in North America gave them opportunities that weren't available to them in their home countries. They kind of blossomed, whereas for the men, they lost a lot of control over circumstances; there was a loss of dignity from not being able to provide for your family that was humiliating. They didn't know how to connect with their families differently than as providers, because that was the model they grew up knowing. ("Interview")

"Simple Recipes" pursues this theme of a father's humiliation and attendant rage. It is structured as a narration in a present time, during which the narrator is alienated from her family and heritage, and looks back upon a past in which she and her father together "cast a spell" (Thien 16) in the kitchen, broken by her father's violence. The build-up to and aftermath of that violence form the story's primary memory, told over a number of narrative segments, interspersed with other, more benign, recollections. For the second-generation daughter of immigrant parents, the process of growing up involves recognizing the impossibility of reconciling her father's contradictions.

Much of the symbolic richness of the story comes from its adroitly deployed images of food and cooking, including the recipes that evoke the parents' homeland, which their children can only partially appreciate, and the family bonds both enacted and strained through shared meals. The narrator remembers how she and her parents and brother would gather around the table, "leaning hungrily forward while my father, the magician, unveiled plate after plate" (Thien 9). Initially, father and daughter work together harmoniously to prepare meals; the father shares techniques of food preparation with his daughter, who is awed by his skill, watching with pleasure "how he sifted the grains in his hands, sure and quick" (Thien 3). His way of measuring the amount of water needed for the rice figures him as a kind of diviner, a possessor of a near-mystical culinary art: "My father did not need instructions or measuring cups. He closed his eyes and felt for the water line."

But when the son refuses the father's food, choking on it and expressing repugnance at the fish the father has set before him—"I don't like the eyeball there," he says, "It looks sick" (Thien 11)—the father loses all self-control as he castigates the son for ingratitude. He beats his son brutally and excessively with a bamboo pole, and the daughter observes the scene. The next morning, as the mother attempts to coax the wounded boy back into the family with the offering of a breakfast meal (significantly, a non-Asian meal of French toast), the narrator ponders her divided loyalties and the difficulty of loving her father's "unbearable" pain (Thien 19).

In the story's present, the extent of the narrator's estrangement from her family is indicated by the rarely used rice cooker, a gift from her father when she first moved out on her own and tucked in the back of her cupboard, "the cord wrapped neatly around its belly" (Thien 9). She keeps the walls of her apartment scrubbed clean, devoid of the "dense," oily air redolent of "countless meals cooked in a tiny kitchen, all those good smells jostling for space" (Thien 8), that she remembers from her childhood with such longing. The final image of the fish dying while she and her father watch suggests that her sadness and guilt have not faded.

* * *

The art of making rice dominates the opening scene of the story, highlighting both the precious ritual that binds father and daughter in memory, and suggesting the cultural tensions that will ultimately separate them. Everything was fine when the daughter could simply watch her father's deft movements, an entranced spectator. But when he passes the job of rice-making to her, she worries over her inability to do "so simple a task right" (Thien 4). She knows she should be more conscientious, but she rushes the job, going "through the motions, splashing the water around, jabbing my finger down to measure the water level" (Thien 4). Her worry seems excessive, especially given that her father doesn't mind how the rice turns out, and eats heartily, "pushing the rice into his mouth [. . .] as if he noticed no difference between what he did so well and I so poorly" (Thien 4).

The cultural implications of her embarrassment and concern are clarified a few pages later when the narrator mentions a similar inability—and her brother's overt refusal—to learn her parents' native language. The language "never came easily to [her]" and although her brother was born in Malaysia, "the language left him. Or he forgot it, or he refused it, which is also common, and this made my father angry" (Thien 7). Both children's difficulty with the language seems a refusal of their Asian inheritance, a tacit rejection of affiliation and family identity. The narrator's guilt-tinged emphasis on her poor rice is thus linked in her memory with her failure generally to be the kind of daughter she thinks her father expects. When she hears her father and mother speaking in their native tongue, she feels "as if they are words I should know; as if maybe I did know them once but then I forgot them" (Thien 12).

The fact that the title of the story is "Simple Recipes" and that the first sentence of the story tells of the father's recipe for rice alerts us to the likely thematic and symbolic implications of the phrase. A recipe refers, of course, to a cooking method, but it can also refer to any guaranteed formula: a recipe for happiness, we say, or a recipe for success. The fact that it is a "simple" recipe has a double irony. There is no simple recipe for happiness in a family, and furthermore, the supposedly simple recipe for making rice actually requires a good deal of experience and finesse, as the narrator finds when her attempts at rice-making turn out "mushy gruel" (Thien 4). At the end of the story, the narrator recognizes that she is still gripped by a longing for a simple resolution, "a smoothing out, finding the impurities, then removing them piece by piece" (Thien 19) that is not to be had.

At first, a reader may be inclined to think that the father's comfort in the kitchen and his refusal to criticize his daughter's rice is evidence of his easy-going nature, his security in the family. A man who does the cooking at home may be a maternal sort, we think, someone who is happy to take over some of his wife's duties while she is at work (but we wonder: why *isn't* he working? Is it choice or necessity? Temporary or permanent? Liberation or cage?). An early image of him, eating his daughter's rice as if there is nothing the matter with it, "eat[ing] every last mouthful, his chopsticks walking quickly across the plate" and rising while "whistling" to "clear the table, every motion so clean and sure," suggests that he is perfectly at home both in the domestic space and in a domestic role, a nurturing man who can convey through a few gestures to his daughter, through his easy movements and gentleness, that "all was well in the world" (Thien 5). Similarly, when the narrator cannot learn the language he tries to teach her, the father "ran his thumb gently over my mouth, as if trying to see what it was that made me different" (Thien 7). He seems easily to accept her linguistic difference, not bothered by it and capable of making his daughter feel safe.

The daughter also remembers happy memories with her father watching cooking shows on television, especially a popular Chinese-Canadian show called "Wok with Yan." The father claims to be at least as good a cook as Yan, and he demonstrates to his daughter his skill with a green onion, which he could make "bloom like a flower" (Thien 6). He loves Yan's cultural punning, especially "Take a wok on the wild side!" at which he "chuckled heartily" (Thien 6). Some readers will remember Stephen Yan's 1980s show, particularly the (now rather embarrassing, retrograde) verve with which Yan seemed to play up his Asian accent, crafting his role as a comically exotic purveyor of foreign food and self-denigrating jokes to the (mostly) non-Asian television viewer. Each week, he wore an apron with a different 'Wok' pun.[3] The father's enjoyment of the program—he even makes careful notes when Yan demonstrates Peking Duck—may again suggest his ease with cultural difference, his confidence in the possibility of cross-cultural adaptation. A postcolonial reader, attentive to power differentials inflected by race, might note that Yan's success was based not only on his material skill, but on his ability to represent Chinese culture in a way that appealed to white consumers. To the daughter, however, the show merely provides a framework for seeing her father as a "man of tricks, who sat for an hour mining a watermelon with a circular spoon, who carved the rind into a castle" (Thien 7). His genius with food is a gift of love to his wife and children.

Not all the memories involving the father's cooking are so happy and comfortable. Another memory segment involves the fish the father has brought home in a plastic bag to be cooked for the family's meal. The narrative dwells on the agony of the fish as the water is drained out of the sink in which it has been placed. "The fish is lying on its side, mouth open and its body heaving. It leaps sideways and hits the sink. Then up again. It curls and snaps, lunging for its own tail. The fish sails into the air, dropping hard. It twitches violently" (Thien 8). The emphasis on the fish's suffering adds a new, disquieting dimension to the images of father-daughter bonding, as does the narrator's fascinated awareness of its fear. She feels a desire to "prod it with both hands, its body tense against the pressure of my fingers. If I hold it tightly, I imagine I will be able to feel its fluttering heart" (Thien 8). Whether the description suggests the narrator's own fear is left unclear. The scene of the fish's slow dying, moreover, may also make us think of the associations of the phrase "a fish out of water," an expression indicating displacement, maladjustment, the kind of expression used about someone who does not belong—like the father, as we soon learn.

In "The flavors of multi-ethnic North American literatures," Astrid M. Fellner highlights the symbolic dimensions of food and cooking in contemporary ethnic literature. As Fellner phrases it, images of food "construct and reflect relationships to racialized subjectivity, addressing issues of belonging, authenticity, and nostalgia" (241). Cooking and eating are powerful "rituals of cultural belonging" (Fellner 242) for all peoples, not only for racialized individuals; but they signify with particular and ambivalent force for diasporic and immigrants subjects, for whom specific tastes, aromas, spices, national dishes, and methods of food preparation are intimately linked to the past, to former identities and experiences, and to the desire to maintain a connection to one's homeland or ancestry in changed circumstances. Often, such images are charged with nostalgia, recalling a past never to be regained. In "Simple Recipes," the narrator is clear that she has "no longing for the meals themselves," but rather for "the way we sat down together, our bodies leaning hungrily forward" (Thien 9). Her memories of mealtime are of a utopian unity, with her father as convener of family pleasure in his production of dish after dish: "We laughed and ate, white steam fogging my mother's glasses" (Thien 9).

Because of the way shared meals offer the comfort of the known in an unstable world, they may function as a bulwark against threatened dissolution, against the trauma of loss of meaning and identity. But they can do so only if each family member is willing to play his or her accustomed part in the production and sharing of dishes. To refuse to play the culturally mandated role—in particular to refuse food altogether—is to disavow one's ethnic and familial identity. The family dinner table, therefore, may be a site of continuity and renewal, or equally of disruption and fracture. In "Simple Recipes," the narrator's father at first responds with jocularity and conciliation to his son's expression of disgust at the fish. "You don't like it?" he asks him, coaxingly, picking up a piece of fish "gingerly" and offering it with a smile. "Try it," he says, relying on the ethnic humor he has imbibed from popular culture, "Take a wok on the wild side" (Thien 14). But when his gift of love is rejected, he "slams his chopsticks down on the table" and declares that he doesn't "know what kind of son you are," slapping him hard across the face. In turn, the narrator's brother smashes his plate, throws a fork at his father, and screams that he hates him, calling him "a fucking asshole chink!" and declaring "I wish you weren't my father! I wish you were dead" (Thien 14). Referring to this scene, Fellner notes that "The cultural significance of the chopstick and the fork cannot go unnoticed" (256). Wanting to be Canadian, the son does not want to be son to his "chink" father.

The scene of the beating that the daughter witnesses is disturbing not only because of its content—the agony of the son's body receiving the strikes of the bamboo pole—but because of the parallels between this scene and the earlier description of the fish dying in the kitchen sink. Where the fish was described as "lying on its side, mouth open and its body heaving" (Thien 8), in the charged moments before the beating, the narrator's brother's "mouth is open" (Thien 14) and, a little later, "his small chest heaving" (Thien 15). While the fish "folds its body, trying to turn or swim" (Thien 5), the narrator's brother has his "knees folded into his chest, the crown of his head burrowing down" (Thien 15–16). Why are the two scenes of suffering, in every other way quite different, described in such similar terms? Perhaps Thien here suggests something about the nature of traumatic memory, the manner in which pain inserts itself into other, seemingly innocent, remembrances. Because the father's contradictions cannot be reconciled, all family memories are shadowed by his violence. Trying to keep the two parts of him separate, attempting to hold on to the gentle father whose love filled her with confident pride, the narrator worries instead that all her "unadulterated" love will "turn [. . .] to shame and grief" (Thien 18).

In the second-to-last scene in the story, as the mother attempts to entice her son to eat French toast the next morning—it's not clear if the father has himself prepared it, but it seems likely that he has—we realize that the story is about the process through which the daughter comes to a partial understanding of her father, an understanding of the vulnerability and despair that underlie his violence. As the narrator's mother comforts her son, the father stands in the doorway, and his daughter sees that "Even my father, the magician, who can make something beautiful out of nothing, he just stands and watches" (Thien 18). We are also told that as he goes about preparing breakfast for the rest of the family on that morning, he occasionally stops "as if he has forgotten what he was doing mid-motion" (Thien 17). He appears to be in a daze, in the grip of a powerful disassociation.

Some of the interest of the story comes from its ambiguity about the source of the father's helpless rage. We know only that his face expresses to his daughter both "anger" and "so much pain that it is unbearable, his face so full of grief it might dissolve" (Thien 19). Some clues are given: his wife earns the family's living—we do not know why she has been able to find work more successfully than he— and he cannot communicate with, or demand obedience and respect from, his resentful teenaged son. Whether these issues are directly related to his immigrant experience cannot be determined: is this a story about an immigrant father's troubles in his adopted country, or is it a story about a father who has lost control of his life and his son? Is the son's choice of epithets all determining or is it merely an expression of the alienation felt by many teenagers, regardless of ethnic context? The story leaves room for both interpretations, inviting the reader to supply his or her own context.

The complexities of family unhappiness are suggested in the narrator's references to the guilt she feels: "I'm afraid that if I turn around and go to him," she comments of the morning after the beating, "I will be complicit, accepting a portion of guilt, no matter how small that piece" (Thien 18). She has done nothing to precipitate the violence. Is she guilty for needing to love her father? For thinking more of her own loss than of her brother's pain? Or merely for being a member of a family that has not been able to survive intact the transition to a new country? In a temporally unplaced memory, her mother suggests that her guilt, like the impurities in rice, might be isolated, compressed, and removed through an act of visualization, flecked away "like a speck of dirt" (Thien 12). We do not know if the narrator spoke of her guilt to her mother or if her mother intuited her daughter's feelings. Regardless, the narrator cannot summon a "magical" (Thien 12) acceptance of the fault-lines in her family. The story's conclusion returns to the image of removing impurities ("Warm water running over, the feel of the grains between my hands," Thien 19) to express the daughter's regretful longing for an easy way out.

Some of the missing details about the father in "Simple Recipes" are provided in "A Map of the City," the last story in the collection, also an elegiac retrospective about a daughter's damaged father. "A Map" is its own story, of course, and not merely an expanded version of "Simple Recipes," but it does take up many of the themes more obliquely addressed in the earlier story, in particular the melancholy of an immigrant father and his daughter's haunted sense of having failed him, and, therefore, it can productively be read as a parallel text whose emphases and perspectives corroborate interpretative hunches about "Simple Recipes." Christine Lorre reads the narrator's "meandering reflection" in the story as part of her route to "a better understanding of her feeling of guilt" (206). In "A Map," we learn about the father's failures in business (he ran a furniture store, which was forced to close, attempted numerous other ventures, and finally worked for a time as a real estate agent before abandoning that career), and his inability to feel at home in Canada after leaving Irian Jaya, now Indonesia, at age thirty.

The narrator's father is humiliated by his perceived inadequacies, believing that "his lack of luck, of ingenuity, had [. . .] forced us to struggle for what he failed to provide" (Thien 192). Unlike in "Simple Recipes," the reason for the daughter's guilt is explicit. She thinks "how things might have turned out differently. If I had been the kind of daughter I never was, faithful and capable, who could hold a family together through all its small tragedies" (Thien 161). A particularly painful moment occurs when the father comes into his daughter's room to speak to her and is refused: "'Listen.' My father's expression, as if on the brink of speech. He looks so soft, standing there. I could touch him and it would hurt. 'There's something I need to tell you.' 'Not now, please'" (Thien 195). The refusal of her father's appeal haunts the daughter forever. Sometime after this, the father moves to Indonesia and then returns to Vancouver, but lives separately. He has become someone "who took his own failures so much to heart, he could no longer see past them" (Thien 178). He attempts suicide, and the story ends with the narrator wondering if she can ever repair their life together, "redraw this map, make the distance from A to B a straight line [. . .] bypass those difficult years and bring my father up to this moment, healthy, unharmed" (Thien 188). She realizes, though, that to do so "would remove all we glimpsed in passing, heights and depths I never guessed at" (Thien 188). At the end of the story, she knows that all her old landmarks have disappeared, and whether she can find her way into the future remains an open question.[4]

"Simple Recipes" also ends in uncertainty, with the question of whether the daughter can find a way to love her father despite his betrayals; she knows that she cannot turn away. She begins to realize that she might be able to love him as an adult apart from her own needs, "because he was complicated, because he was human, because he needed me to" though, as a child, she did not know "how to love a person that way" (Thien 19). The challenge of learning how to love him may be a project for a lifetime.

It is not simple, and there is no recipe. She thinks of the process by which rice is purified, all the little dark stones and spots sifted out. "If there were some recourse," she thinks, "I would take it. A cupful of grains in my open hand, a smoothing out, finding the impurities, then removing them piece by piece. And then, to be satisfied with what remains" (Thien 19). But such resolutions are not found, and the story ends with the memory of the "fish in the sink" slowly dying as she and her father watch. It is an elegiac image linking her and her father in an over determined moment of intimate, but seemingly helpless, witnessing.

The story as a whole is also an act of witnessing—both an effectively realized and a deliberately ambiguous one. The narrator's painful story cannot heal the rupture in the family or in the daughter's psyche. All it can do, in its fragmented narrative segments, is approach and retreat from the father's violence, interweaving the intolerable memory with other, less toxic, images of the past and thus attempting to hold disparate realities in perilous balance. In doing so, the story seeks to acknowledge the family past in a way that neither represses nor resolves the heartbreak at its core.

Notes

1. The manuscript for the collection won the 1998 Asian Canadian Writer's Workshop's Emerging Writer Award. The published collection received the City of Vancouver Book Award, the VanCity Book Prize, and the Ethel Wilson Fiction Prize.

2. Speaking of the theme of lost fathers in her writing, she stated in interview that "The weird thing about writing fiction is you're not really aware of it [the role of personal experience, in this case the father's disappearance]—it takes other people to point it out to you" ("Interview").

3. "Wok with Yan," which was filmed in Vancouver, aired on the CBC and became internationally syndicated. While some critics were made uncomfortable by its tendency to play Asian ethnicity for laughs, many viewers loved the exuberant host, Stephen Yan.

4. The emphasis of my reading is slightly different from that offered by Christine Lorre, in "Ordinary Tragedies in Madeleine Thien's 'A Map of the City,'" who sees the story's ending as affirmative, arguing that the narrator is now "ready to confront what life holds in store" (11). Though "A Map" is more hopeful than "Simple Recipes," both stories deny resolution to their narrator's sad remembering.

Works Cited

Fellner, Astrid M. "The flavors of multi-ethnic North American literatures: Language, ethnicity and culinary nostalgia." *Culinary Linguistics: The Chef's Special*. Ed. Cornelia Gerhardt, Maximiliane Frobenius, & Susanne Ley. Amsterdam: John Benjamins, 2013. 241–60.

"An Interview with Madeleine Thien." *Mason Fiction: An Alternative Online Resource for Faculty, Alumni, Current Students, and Prospective Students, with a Slight Focus on Fiction*, 23 June 2009. Web. 16 Mar. 2014. <http://gmufictionmfa.blogspot.ca/2009/06/interview-with-madeleine-thien.html>.

Lorre, Christine. "Ordinary Tragedies in Madeleine Thien's 'A Map of the City.'" *Journal of the Short Story in English* 38 (Spring 2012): 1–12. Web. 16 Mar. 2014.

Thien, Madeleine. *Simple Recipes*. Toronto: McClelland & Stewart, 2001.

RESOURCES

Additional Works of Contemporary Canadian Fiction

Atwood, Margaret. *The Blind Assassin*. 2000.

_____. *Alias Grace*. 1996.

Bowering, George. *Harry's Fragments*. 1990.

Boyden, Joseph. *Three Day Road*. 2005.

Carrier, Roch. *The Hockey Sweater and Other Stories*. Trans. Sheila Fischman. 1979.

Davies, Robertson. *Murther and Walking Spirits*. 1991.

_____. *The Rebel Angels*. 1981.

Engel, Marian. *The Tattooed Woman*. 1985.

Findley, Timothy. *The Wars*. 1977.

Gallant, Mavis. *Home Truths: Selected Canadian Stories*. 1981.

Hebert, Anne. *Kamouraska*. 1970. Trans. Norman Shapiro, 1973.

Highway, Tomson. *Kiss of the Fur Queen*. 1998.

Johnson, Wayne. *The Colony of Unrequited Dreams*. 1998.

King, Thomas. *Green Grass, Running Water*. 1993.

Kogawa, Joy. *Obasan*. 1981.

Kroetsch, Robert. *Alibi*. 1983.

_____. *Badlands*. 1975.

Kulyk Keefer, Janice. *The Green Library*. 1996.

Laurence, Margaret. *A Bird in the House*. 1970.

Lee, Sky. *Disappearing Moon Cafe*. 1990.

Maracle, Lee. *Ravensong*. 1993.

Martel, Yann. *Life of Pi*. 2001.

Mistry, Rohinton. *Family Matters*. 2002.

Mosionier, Beatrice Culleton. *In Search of April Raintree*. 1983.

Munro, Alice. *The Love of a Good Woman*. 1998.

_____. *Too Much Happiness*. 2009.

Ondaatje, Michael. *Anil's Ghost*. 2000.

Proulx, Annie. *The Shipping News*. 1993.

Richler, Mordecai. *Solomon Gursky Was Here*. 1989.

Schoemperlen, Diane. *Our Lady of the Lost and Found*. 2001.

Shields, Carol. *The Stone Diaries*. 1993.

_____. *Unless*. 2002.

Thien, Madeleine. *Dogs at the Perimeter*. 2011.

Thomas, Audrey. *The Wild Blue Yonder*. 1990.

Urquhart, Jane. *A Map of Glass*. 2005.

_____. *The Whirlpool*. 1986.

Van Herk, Aritha. *No Fixed Address*. 1986.

_____. *The Tent Peg*. 1981.

Vassanji, M. G. *The In-Between World of Vikram Lall*. 2003.

Bibliography ───────────────────────────

Atwood, Margaret, ed. *The New Oxford Book of Canadian Verse in English.* Toronto: Oxford UP, 1952.

──────. *Survival: A Thematic Guide to Canadian Literature.* Toronto: Anansi, 1972.

Balibar, Étienne, & Immanuel Maurice Wallerstein. *Race, nation, classe: Les identités ambiguës.* Paris: Découverte, 1988.

Beran, Carol. "The Luxury of Excellence: Alice Munro and the *New Yorker.*" *The Rest of the Story: Essays on Alice Munro.* Ed. Robert Thacker. Toronto: ECW, 1999. 204–31.

──────. "The Pursuit of Happiness: A Study of Alice Munro's Fiction." *The Social Science Journal* 37.3 (July 2000). 329–45.

Besner, Neil K. *Carol Shields: The Arts of a Writing Life.* Winnipeg: Prairie Fire Press, 1995.

Bush, Catherine. "Michael Ondaatje: An Interview." *Essays on Canadian Writing* 53 (1994): 238–49.

Buss, Helen. *Mother and Daughter Relationships in the Manawaka Works of Margaret Laurence.* Victoria, BC: U of Victoria P, 1985. English Literary Studies Ser. 34.

Carscallen, James. *The Other Country: Patterns in the Writing of Alice Munro.* Toronto: ECW, 1993.

Coleman, Daniel. *Masculine Migrations: Reading the Postcolonial Male in "New Canadian" Narratives.* Toronto: U of Toronto P, 1998.

Comeau, Paul. *Margaret Laurence's Epic Imagination.* Edmonton: U of Alberta P, 2005.

Cox, Ailsa. *Alice Munro.* Tavistock: Northcote House, 2004.

Dannenberg, Hilary. *Coincidence and Counterfactuality: Plotting Time and Space in Narrative Fiction.* Lincoln: U of Nebraska P, 2008.

Davey, Frank. "Alternate Stories: The Short Fiction of Audrey Thomas and Margaret Atwood." *Canadian Literature* 109 (Summer 1986): 5–14.

──────. *Reading Canadian Reading: Essays by Frank Davey.* Winnipeg: Turnstone, 1988.

──────. *Surviving the Paraphrase.* Winnipeg: Turnstone, 1983.

_____. "Toward the Ends of Regionalism." *A Sense of Place: Re-Evaluating Regionalism in Canadian and American Writing*. Ed. Christian Riegel & Herb & Herb Wyile. Edmonton: U of Alberta P, 1997. 1–17.

Davis, Robert Con, & Ronald Schlefer, eds. *Contemporary Literary Criticism: Literary and Cultural Studies*. 2nd Ed. New York & London: Longman, 1989.

Dvořák, Marta. "Alice Munro's 'Lovely Tricks' from *Dance of the Happy Shades* to *Hateship, Friendship, Courtship, Loveship, Marriage*." *Open Letter* 9 and 10. (Fall–Winter 2003–2004): 55–77.

Fee, Margery. *The Fat Lady Dances: Margaret Atwood's* Lady Oracle. Toronto: ECW, 1993.

Ferri, Laura, ed. *Jane Urquhart: Essays on Her Works*. Toronto: Guernica, 2005.

Florby, Gunilla. *The Margin Speaks: A Study of Margaret Laurence and Robert Kroetsch from a Post-Colonial Point of View*. Lund, Sweden: Lund UP, 1997.

Frye, Northrop. *The Anatomy of Criticism: Four Essays by Northrop Frye*. New York: Atheneum, 1968.

Gammel, Irene, and Benjamin Lefebvre, eds. *Anne's World: A New Century of Anne of Green Gables*. Toronto: U of Toronto P, 2010.

Gammel, Irene, & Elizabeth Epperly, eds. *L.M. Montgomery and Canadian Culture*. Toronto: U of Toronto P, 1999.

Gammel, Irene, ed. *Making Avonlea: L.M. Montgomery and Popular Culture*. Toronto: U of Toronto P, 2002.

Godard, Barbara. "Tales within Tales: Margaret Atwood's Folk Narratives." *Canadian Literature* 109 (Summer 1986): 57–84.

Grace, Sherrill. *Violent Duality: A Study of Margaret Atwood*. Montreal: Vehicle P, 1980.

Gray, Charlotte. *Gold Diggers: Striking It Rich in the Klondike*. Toronto: HarperCollins, 2011.

Green, Mary Jean. "Accenting the French in Comparative American Studies." *Comparative Literature* 61.3 (2009): 327–334.

Griffiths, N.E.S. *The Acadian Deportation: Deliberate Perfidy or Cruel Necessity?* Toronto: Copp Clark, 1969.

_____. *The Acadians: Creation of a People*. Toronto: McGraw-Hill Ryerson, 1973.

Guilford, Irene, ed. *Alistair MacLeod: Essays on His Work*. Toronto: Guernica, 2001.

Hammill, Faye. *Canadian Literature*. Edinburgh: Edinburgh UP, 2007.

Heble, Ajay. *The Tumble of Reason: Alice Munro's Discourse of Absence*. Toronto: U of Toronto P, 1994.

Hengen, Shannon. *Margaret Atwood's Power: Mirrors, Reflections and Images in Select Fiction and Poetry*. Toronto: Second Story, 1993.

Hudson, Aïda, & Susan-Ann Cooper, eds. *Windows and Words: A Look at Canadian Children's Literature in English*. Ottawa: U of Ottawa P, 2003.

Hutcheon, Linda. *The Canadian Postmodern: A Study of Contemporary English-Canadian Fiction*. Toronto: Oxford UP, 1988.

Kertzer, Jon. *"That House in Manawaka": Margaret Laurence's A Bird in the House*. Toronto: ECW, 1992.

King, James. *The Life of Margaret Laurence*. Toronto: Knopf, 1997.

Kirtz, Mary K. "Old World Traditions, New World Inventions: Bilingualism, Multiculturalism, and the Transformation of Ethnicity." *Canadian Ethnic Studies* 28:1 (1996): 8–21.

Lecker, Robert, ed. *Canadian Canons: Essays in Literary Value*. Toronto: U of Toronto P, 1991.

_____. "The Canonization of Canadian Literature: An Inquiry into Values." *Critical Inquiry* 16.3 (Spring 1990): 656–71.

_____. *Making It Real: The Canonization of English-Canadian Literature*. Concord, Ontario: House of Anansi P, 1995.

_____. *Robert Kroetsch*. Boston: Twayne, 1986. Twayne World Author Ser. 768.

Ledwell, Jane, & Jean Mitchell, eds. *Anne Around the World: L.M. Montgomery and Her Classic*. Montreal: McGill-Queen's UP, 2013.

Lynch, Gerald. "No Honey, I'm Home: Place Over Love in Alice Munro's Short Story Cycle, *Who do You Think You Are?*" *Canadian Literature* 160 (Spring 1999): 73–98.

_____, & Angela Arnold Robbeson, eds. *Dominant Impressions: Essays on the Canadian Short Story*. Ottawa: Ottawa UP, 1999.

MacMechan, Archibald. *Headwaters of Canadian Literature.* Toronto: New Canadian Library, 1924.

Martin, W. R. *Alice Munro: Paradox and Parallel.* Edmonton: U of Alberta P, 1987.

May, Charles E. "About This Volume." *Critical Insights: Alice Munro.* Ed. Charles E. May. Ipswich, MA: Salem Press, 2013.

Metcalf, John. "A Conversation with Alice Munro." *Journal of Canadian Fiction* 1.4 (1976): 54–62.

Neumann, Shirley, & Smaro Kamboureli, eds. *Amazing Space: Writing Canadian Women Writing. Canadian Woman Studies* 8.3 (1987).

New, William. *Articulating West: Essays on Purpose and Form in Modern Canadian Literature.* Toronto: New P, 1972.

Osborne, Carol. "Compassion, imagination, and reverence for all living things: Margaret Atwood's spiritual vision in *The Year of the Flood.*" *Margaret Atwood Studies.* 3.2 (August 2010): 30–42.

Porter, John. *The Vertical Mosaic: An Analysis of Social Class and Power in Canada.* Toronto: U of Toronto P, 1965.

Pryse, Marjorie. "Writing Out of the Gap: Regionalism, Resistance, and Relational Reading." *A Sense of Place: Re-Evaluating Regionalism in Canadian and American Writing.* Ed. Christian Riegel & Herb Wyile. Edmonton: U of Alberta P & Textual Studies in Canada, 1998. 19–34.

Rasporich, Beverly J. *Dance of the Sexes: Art and Gender in the Fiction of Alice Munro.* Edmonton: U of Alberta P, 1990.

Redekop, Magdalene. *Mothers and Other Clowns: The Stories of Alice Munro.* New York: Routledge, 1992.

Ricou, Laurie. *Everyday Magic: Child Languages in Canadian Literature.* Vancouver: U of British Columbia P, 1987.

_____. "Regionalism in Literature." *The Canadian Encyclopedia,* 13 Dec. 2013. Web. 17 Sept. 2014.

Riegel, Christian. *Writing Grief: Margaret Laurence and the Work of Mourning.* Winnipeg: U of Manitoba P, 2003.

Rosello, Mireille. *Declining the Stereotype: Ethnicity and Representation in French Cultures.* Hanover, NH: Dartmouth, 1998.

Roth, Verena Bühler. *Wilderness and the Natural Environment: Margaret Atwood's Recycling of a Canadian Theme*. Tübingen: Francke Verlag, 1998.

Rubio, Mary Henley, & Elizabeth Waterston, eds. "L.M. Montgomery's Interior/Exterior Landscapes." *Anne of Green Gables: A Norton Critical Edition*. New York: Norton, 2007.

Rudin, Ronald. *Remembering and Forgetting in Acadie: A Historian's Journey through Public Memory*. Toronto: U of Toronto P, 2009.

Schweickart, Patrocinio. "Reading Ourselves: Toward a Feminist Theory of Reading." *Contemporary Literary Criticism: Literary and Cultural Studies*. Ed. Robert Con Davis & Ronald Schlefer. 2nd ed. New York and London: Longman, 1989. 118–41.

Simpson-Housley, Paul. *A Few Acres of Snow: Literary and Artistic Images of Canada*. Toronto: Dundern, 1992.

Stovel, Nora Foster. *Divining Margaret Laurence: A Study of Her Complete Writings*. Montreal: McGill-Queen's UP, 2008.

_____. "'Love and Death': Romance and Reality in Margaret Laurence's *A Bird in the House*." *Dominant Impressions: Essays on the Canadian Short Story*. Ed. Gerald Lynch & Angela Arnold Robbeson. Ottawa: U Ottawa P, 1999.

_____. "Reading Beyond Race in Margaret Laurence's 'The Loons' from *A Bird in the House*." *International Journal of Canadian Studies* 41 (2010): 213–30. *Erudite.org*. Web. 22 Aug. 2013.

_____. *Stacey's Choice: Margaret Laurence's* The Fire-Dwellers. Toronto: ECW, 1993.

_____. "Temples and Tabernacles: Alternative Religions in the Fictional Microcosms of Robertson Davies, Margaret Laurence, and Alice Munro." *International Fiction Review* 31.1–2 (Jan. 2004): 65 (13). *CPIQ Thomson Gale*. Web.

Thacker, Robert. *Alice Munro: Writing Her Lives*. Toronto: McClelland, 2005.

Thomas, Clara. *The Manawaka World of Margaret Laurence*. Toronto: McClelland, 1976.

Thomas, Peter. *Robert Kroetsch*. Vancouver: Douglas, 1980.

_____. "Robert Kroetsch and Silence." *Essays on Canadian Writing* 18/19 (Summer/Fall 1980): 33–53.

Tiefensee, Dianne. *Deconstructing Robert Kroetsch and His Critics.* Montreal: McGill-Queen's UP, 1994.

Vallee, Frank G. "Vertical Mosaic." *The Canadian Encyclopedia*, 16 Dec. 2013. Web.

Wilson, Sharon Rose. *Margaret Atwood's Fairy-Tale Sexual Politics.* Jackson: UP of Mississippi, 1993.

Woodcock, George, ed. *A Place to Stand on: Essays by and about Margaret Laurence.* Edmonton: NeWest P, 1983.

Wyile, Herb. "Introduction: Regionalism Revisited." *A Sense of Place: Re-Evaluating Regionalism in Canadian and American Writing.* Ed. Christian Riegel & Herb Wyile. Edmonton: U of Alberta P, 1997. ix–xiv.

_____. *Speaking in the Past Tense: Canadian Novelists on Writing Historical Fiction.* Waterloo, ON: Wilfred Laurier UP, 2007.

About the Editor

Carol L. Beran earned an MAT in English from the Johns Hopkins University and a PhD in English from the University of California, Berkeley, where she specialized in British literature's modern period, the novel, and Thomas Hardy. Meeting Robertson Davies excited her interest in Canadian literature, and several grants from the Canadian Embassy in Washington, DC, including a Senior Scholar Award, helped turn a hobby into a vocation. Beran's publications include a book on Margaret Atwood's *Life Before Man*, titled *Living Over the Abyss*, and journal essays and book chapters on works by such writers as Margaret Atwood, Robert Kroetsch, Margaret Laurence, Hugh MacLennan, Alice Munro, Michael Ondaatje, and Aritha van Herk. She serves as an associate editor of *The American Review of Canadian Studies* and on the editorial board of *Margaret Atwood Studies*. Active in Canadian Studies in the Western United States, she helped found the Western Canadian Studies Association and served as its first president. She is Professor of English and Chair of the English department at Saint Mary's College of California, where she slips Canadian texts into as many courses as possible and occasionally gets to teach her favorite course, A Literary Tour of Canada.

Contributors

Holly L. Collins is an Assistant Professor of French at Baylor University. Her main areas of research are twentieth- and twenty-first-century Francophone literatures, particularly migrant narratives, and nineteenth-century French literature, with a focus on Émile Zola and naturalism. Her article "Finding Their Wings," on Ying Chen's *L'Ingratitude* and Madame de Lafayette's *La Princesse de Clèves*, appeared in the literary publication *Romance Notes*. "The Semantic War: The Pen as Sword in the Battle Against Western Representations of Haiti in the Media," an article on Dany Laferrière's *Tout bouge autour de moi*, appears in the *International Journal of Francophone Studies* (16.1 & 2).

Janice Fiamengo is a Professor in the department of English at the University of Ottawa. She specializes in Canadian literature and has published numerous articles on Canadian women's writing. She is the author of *The Woman's Page: Journalism and Rhetoric in Early Canada* (2008) and is the editor of *Home Ground and Foreign Territory: Essays on Early Canadian Literature* (2014).

Shannon Hengen is Professor Emerita in the Department of English at Laurentian University in Sudbury, Ontario, Canada, where she taught North American literature, having created a pair of courses entitled Canadian Thought and Culture and American Thought and Culture. Her publications include monographs on the work of Margaret Atwood, indigenous Canadian theatre, and comedy: *Where Stories Meet: An Oral History of De-ba-jeh-mu-jig Theatre* (2007); *Comedy's Edge* (1999); *Margaret Atwood's Power: Mirrors, Reflections, and Images in Select Fiction and Poetry* (1993); *Stories from the Bush: The Woodland Plays of De-ba-jeh-mu-jig Theatre Group* (2009); *Performing Gender and Comedy: Theories, Texts, and Contexts* (1998); and *Approaches to Teaching Atwood's* The Handmaid's Tale *and Other Works* (1996).

Mary K. Kirtz is Professor Emerita of English and Canadian studies at the University of Akron and an affiliate scholar at Oberlin College. She is co-editor of *The Elections of 2000: Politics, Culture and Economics in*

North America and has published numerous articles on Canadian literature in journals and in essay collections, including *Canadian Ethnic Studies, The Great Plains Quarterly, MLA Approaches to Teaching Margaret Atwood's* The Handmaid's Tale *and Other Works, Canada Observed, Margaret Atwood's Textual Assassinations,* and *Margaret Atwood: Reflection and Reality.* Her article, "'Facts Become Art Through Love': Narrative Structure in Marian Engel's *Bear*," published in *The American Review of Canadian Studies,* won the Rufus Z. Smith Prize awarded by the Association of Canadian Studies in the United States.

Patricia Linton is Professor of English at the University of Alaska Anchorage and Senior Associate Dean for academics in the university's College of Arts and Sciences. She specializes in contemporary literature, particularly international fiction composed in English, and narrative theory. She has published in *Modern Fiction Studies, MELUS, Studies in American Indian Literatures,* and *American Review of Canadian Studies,* as well as in the critical collections *Multicultural Detective Fiction: Murder from the "Other" Side, Post-Colonial Literatures: Expanding the Canon,* and *Alien Identities.* As associate dean, she is responsible for curriculum and academic affairs.

Judith McCombs is a scholar and poet, educated at the University of Chicago, and a retired literature professor from the Center for Creative Arts College of Art in Detroit, Michigan. She has held National Endowment for the Humanities and Canadian Embassy Senior Fellowships and won Maryland State Council's 2009 Individual Artist Award for Poetry. Her scholarly books are *Critical Essays on Margaret Atwood* and the co-authored *Margaret Atwood: A Reference Guide.* Poetry books are *Sisters and Other Selves, Against Nature: Wilderness Poems,* and *The Habit of Fire: Poems Selected and New.* She has a baker's dozen of scholarly articles on subjects such as Atwood; Canadian literature; Munro; nature concepts; and women's writing in Canada, the United States, and Britain. These articles appear in journals and collections, including Bloom's *American Women Poets, Canadian Literature, MLA Approaches to Teaching Margaret Atwood's* The Handmaid's Tale *and Other Works, Margaret Atwood: Writing and Subjectivity,* and *Women's Studies.*

Rita Ross is a folklorist and anthropologist who has been studying the Acadians and their heroine Evangeline for many years. Her latest Evangeline paper, "Evangeline, Acadians, and Tourism Imaginaries" is forthcoming in the edited volume *Tourism Imaginaries: Place, Practice, Media*. In recent years, her work has increasingly considered the relationships between literature, folklore, popular culture, and the broader cultural contexts in which they are embedded. In addition to her work as Assistant Director at the Canadian Studies Program at UC Berkeley, she taught for a number of years at San Jose State University and at California State University Hayward (now Cal State East Bay) in the departments of Anthropology and Women's Studies, teaching a variety of courses in folklore, anthropology, language and culture, and gender and sexuality. She is a past president of the Western Canadian Studies Association.

Nora Foster Stovel teaches twentieth-century fiction, poetry and drama, and contemporary Canadian and women's fiction. She has published numerous articles on Jane Austen, D. H. Lawrence, Margaret Laurence, Margaret Drabble, and Carol Shields. She has published *Margaret Drabble: Symbolic Moralist*; two readers' guides—*Rachel's Children: Margaret Laurence's A Jest of God* and *Stacey's Choice: Margaret Laurence's The Fire-Dwellers*—for ECW's *Canadian Fiction Studies* series; and two volumes of *Margaret Laurence's Early Writings—Embryo Words* and *Colors of Speech*—for the Juvenilia Press. She has edited Margaret Laurence's *Long Drums and Cannons: Nigerian Dramatists and Novelists* and *Heart of a Stranger*. She was awarded a SSHRC grant and University of Alberta McCalla Research Professorship to compose *Divining Margaret Laurence: A Study of Her Complete Writings* (2008). Her forthcoming works, also supported by prestigious grants, include *"Sparkling Subversions": Carol Shields' Vision and Voice*, and *Women with Wings: The Romantic Ballerina*.

Charlotte Templin is Professor Emerita of English at the University of Indianapolis and has taught at the Ningbo Institute of Technology (a campus of Zhejiang University) in Ningbo, China. She is the author of *Feminism and the Politics of Literary Reputation* and the editor of *Conversations with Erica Jong*. She has written articles on comedy, women writers, and literary reputation, dealing with Erica Jong, Alix Kates Shulman, Marietta

Holley, Margaret Atwood, Carol Shields, and others. Her interviews with writers, including Jong, Shulman, Marge Piercy, Rosellen Brown, and Mary Oliver, have appeared in the *Missouri Review*, the *Indiana Review*, *Glimmer Train Stories*, and other publications. Her interest in comedy led her to publish an article on cartoons about Hillary Clinton as First Lady.

Aritha van Herk is the author of five novels, *Judith, The Tent Peg, No Fixed Address* (nominated for the Governor General's Award for fiction), *Places Far From Ellesmere* (a geografictione), and *Restlessness*. Her critical work is collected in *A Frozen Tongue* and *In Visible Ink*. Her popular and irreverent *Mavericks: An Incorrigible History of Alberta* frames the permanent exhibition on Alberta history at the Glenbow Museum in Calgary. Her latest works, *In This Place* and *Prairie Gothic* (with George Webber) develop the idea of geographical temperament as tonal accompaniment. She is Professor of English at the University of Calgary, Alberta, Canada.

Sharon R. Wilson is an Emerita Professor of English and Women's Studies at the University of Northern Colorado, where she taught twentieth-century English and American literature, postmodern fiction, magical realism, humanities, and women's studies. Publications include *Margaret Atwood's Fairy-Tale Sexual Politics* (UP of Mississippi and ECW 1993–94), *Myths and Fairy Tales in Contemporary Women's Fiction: Atwood to Morrison* (Palgrave 2008), and articles on Doris Lessing, Samuel Beckett, Jean Rhys, Iris Murdoch, *Citizen Kane*, and E. R. Eddison. She has edited *Approaches to Teaching Atwood's The Handmaid's Tale and Other Works* with Thomas Friedman and Shannon Hengen (MLA 1996); *Margaret Atwood: Textual Assassinations: Recent Poetry and Fiction* (Ohio SUP 2003*)*; and *Women's Utopian and Dystopian Fiction* (Cambridge Scholars 2013).

Index